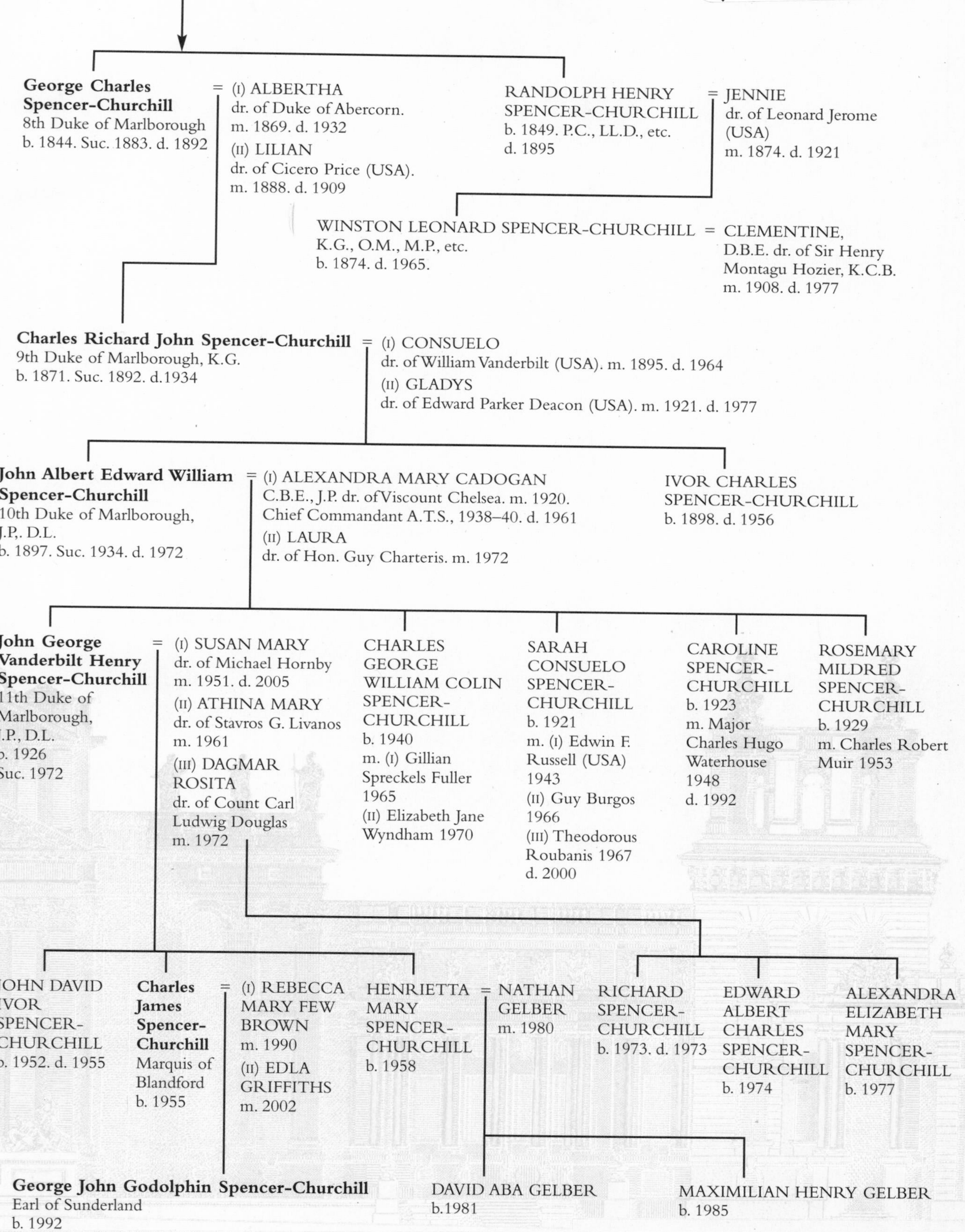

George Charles Spencer-Churchill
8th Duke of Marlborough
b. 1844. Suc. 1883. d. 1892
= (I) ALBERTHA
dr. of Duke of Abercorn.
m. 1869. d. 1932
(II) LILIAN
dr. of Cicero Price (USA).
m. 1888. d. 1909
RANDOLPH HENRY SPENCER-CHURCHILL
b. 1849. P.C., LL.D., etc.
d. 1895
= JENNIE
dr. of Leonard Jerome (USA)
m. 1874. d. 1921
WINSTON LEONARD SPENCER-CHURCHILL
K.G., O.M., M.P., etc.
b. 1874. d. 1965.
= CLEMENTINE,
D.B.E. dr. of Sir Henry Montagu Hozier, K.C.B.
m. 1908. d. 1977
Charles Richard John Spencer-Churchill
9th Duke of Marlborough, K.G.
b. 1871. Suc. 1892. d.1934
= (I) CONSUELO
dr. of William Vanderbilt (USA). m. 1895. d. 1964
(II) GLADYS
dr. of Edward Parker Deacon (USA). m. 1921. d. 1977
John Albert Edward William Spencer-Churchill
10th Duke of Marlborough,
J.P,. D.L.
b. 1897. Suc. 1934. d. 1972
= (I) ALEXANDRA MARY CADOGAN
C.B.E., J.P. dr. of Viscount Chelsea. m. 1920.
Chief Commandant A.T.S., 1938–40. d. 1961
(II) LAURA
dr. of Hon. Guy Charteris. m. 1972
IVOR CHARLES SPENCER-CHURCHILL
b. 1898. d. 1956
John George Vanderbilt Henry Spencer-Churchill
11th Duke of Marlborough,
J.P., D.L.
b. 1926
Suc. 1972
= (I) SUSAN MARY
dr. of Michael Hornby
m. 1951. d. 2005
(II) ATHINA MARY
dr. of Stavros G. Livanos
m. 1961
(III) DAGMAR ROSITA
dr. of Count Carl Ludwig Douglas
m. 1972
CHARLES GEORGE WILLIAM COLIN SPENCER-CHURCHILL
b. 1940
m. (I) Gillian Spreckels Fuller 1965
(II) Elizabeth Jane Wyndham 1970
SARAH CONSUELO SPENCER-CHURCHILL
b. 1921
m. (I) Edwin F. Russell (USA) 1943
(II) Guy Burgos 1966
(III) Theodorous Roubanis 1967
d. 2000
CAROLINE SPENCER-CHURCHILL
b. 1923
m. Major Charles Hugo Waterhouse 1948
d. 1992
ROSEMARY MILDRED SPENCER-CHURCHILL
b. 1929
m. Charles Robert Muir 1953
JOHN DAVID IVOR SPENCER-CHURCHILL
b. 1952. d. 1955
Charles James Spencer-Churchill
Marquis of Blandford
b. 1955
= (I) REBECCA MARY FEW BROWN
m. 1990
(II) EDLA GRIFFITHS
m. 2002
HENRIETTA MARY SPENCER-CHURCHILL
b. 1958
= NATHAN GELBER
m. 1980
RICHARD SPENCER-CHURCHILL
b. 1973. d. 1973
EDWARD ALBERT CHARLES SPENCER-CHURCHILL
b. 1974
ALEXANDRA ELIZABETH MARY SPENCER-CHURCHILL
b. 1977
George John Godolphin Spencer-Churchill
Earl of Sunderland
b. 1992
DAVID ABA GELBER
b.1981
MAXIMILIAN HENRY GELBER
b. 1985

BLENHEIM
AND THE
Churchill Family

BLENHEIM
PALACE

Best wishes
Henrietta Spencer-Churchill
Dec. 2005.

BLENHEIM AND THE *Churchill Family*

A PERSONAL PORTRAIT

HENRIETTA SPENCER-CHURCHILL
WITH
ALEXANDRA PARSONS

CICO BOOKS
London

This book is dedicated to my father, 'Sunny', and all future custodians of Blenheim.

RIGHT: *Pillared and pilastered, the great hall is today still home to the first Duke's battle standard.*
HALF-TITLE PAGE: *This detail of the Schellenberg tapestry, from the celebrated Victories series of tapestries at Blenheim, shows the first Duke of Marlborough triumphant in battle.*
FRONTISPIECE: *Blenheim's architect, John Vanbrugh, shows how to make an entrance; here Blenheim's clock tower is seen through the triumphal arch of the great east gate. In turn, the clock-tower gate gives onto the great court, the inner sanctum of Blenheim.*

First published in 2005 by
Cico Books Ltd
32 Great Sutton Street London EC1V 0NB

10 9 8 7 6 5 4 3 2 1

A CIP catalogue record for this book is available from the British Library

ISBN 1-904991-14-9

Editing: Alison Wormleighton
Design: Christine Wood
Special photography: Andreas von Einsiedel, Geoff Dann

Printed in China

Contents

Foreword by His Grace the Duke of Marlborough

I am very pleased to welcome this new book on Blenheim and my family. Written by my daughter Henrietta from a personal point, it includes a wealth of memories of events of recent years.

Many of these are my own vivid memories too. They are of happy, family times, but they remind me also of the problems we have had to face, and continue to face, in preserving for future generations a magnificent part of the nation's heritage that the palace, park and gardens at Blenheim represent.

The account is an ideal blend of the informative and the entertaining. It is beautifully illustrated, often with newly taken photographs or ones from the family albums and with perceptive use of original family documents.

In a very pleasant way the book charts a human and visual story, over three

Sir James Thornhill's painted ceiling over the great hall, showing Marlborough kneeling to Britannia, a plan of Blenheim in his hand.

hundred years. It begins with a particularly clear account of the personalities of John and Sarah, the first Duke and Duchess, of the relationship between them and their relationship with Queen Anne.

It brings out vividly how eleven generations of my family have, in their various ways, adapted to and contributed to a house designed not only as a family home but also as a monument of such significance that it is now identified as a World Heritage Site.

Henrietta has achieved an admirable balance in her response. It is warmly personal on the one hand and yet properly objective on the other. I feel the reader will find this combination absorbing.

Marlborough

Introduction

Writing and researching this book has definitely been an eye-opener. I thought I knew a fair amount about my family but soon realized that I still had a lot to learn. The experience has been both fascinating and enjoyable.

Much has been written about many of my ancestors, notably John Churchill, the first Duke of Marlborough, and Sir Winston Churchill, who were phenomenal individuals. However, as I have discovered, there were others who contributed not only to Blenheim but also to society (albeit occasionally in somewhat scandalous or unconventional ways).

I have always felt that the Churchill genes in respect of physical traits were incredibly dominant. Looking at portraits of my ancestors dating back eleven generations, the family resemblance is uncanny. As for character traits, it is surprising to see how certain strengths and weaknesses have persisted through the centuries. We are strong and determined, with a sense of justice. In particular, we are passionate about what we want to achieve or create, and persistent in making it happen, whether it is public speaking, painting, writing or creating homes and gardens. The strong will and stubbornness have landed some of us in trouble but these characteristics have also been responsible for our successes. Certainly these family traits were key factors in the creation of Blenheim three centuries ago.

Our family motto, Faithful But Unfortunate, has something of a double meaning—although some have interpreted it to mean they should be faithful to a cause, others have been more faithful to themselves, while the cause, in this case Blenheim, suffered as a result.

My ancestry and upbringing have certainly influenced my career. Even from a young age I think I was subconsciously drip-fed a love and understanding of architecture, art and antiques. I was also fortunate enough to travel a lot, a passion I still have today, so learning about different cultures and their history was also part of my education.

I suppose it was not until after I had started my interior design company that I really began to appreciate Blenheim fully. We never took our privileged upbringing for granted, but when I was a teenager I had other priorities in my life. Today, I am still learning, not only about the history of my family and Blenheim but also about interior design; every job brings new challenges and valuable experience.

As an adult, I do appreciate the importance of my heritage and am determined to do all I can to help preserve this great World Heritage site and home for many generations to come. Meanwhile, I hope you enjoy this book and the memories I have shared with you.

OPPOSITE: *The red drawing-room is dominated by Sargent's portrait of the ninth Duke, his wife, née Consuelo Vanderbilt, and their two sons.*

CHAPTER ONE

Memories of Blenheim

My brother James and I grew up at Lee Place, a beautiful Georgian house about five miles from Blenheim, which my parents bought when they married. My grandfather Bert, the tenth Duke of Marlborough, was ensconced at Blenheim all year round until he died in 1972. So while Blenheim wasn't exactly our home, it was nevertheless an intrinsic part of our everyday lives. We spent a great deal of time there and my father was actively involved in running the estate.

Looking at Blenheim now, at its monumental and stately proportions, I am impressed almost on a daily basis, but back then I don't remember ever being intimidated by the scale and grandeur of it all—it was just my grandparents' house, offering huge potential for fun and games as long as we behaved when we bumped into adults. Like any young children brought up in the countryside, our priorities were simple: family, friends, pets and outdoor life.

SCHOOLDAYS

My brother went to a preparatory boarding school in Shrivenham and I went to Headington, a day school in Oxford. James came home only for the odd weekend and for the holidays, so more often than not I would have school friends to stay with me at weekends. We would spend our time outdoors, riding ponies and making the most of what the countryside, and Blenheim, had to offer.

My cousins Rachel and Tracey Ward attended my school, so we shared the journey from Woodstock, where we met most mornings. We were taken to Oxford by my nanny, Audrey Highmore, or by their driver. On the way home Nanny and I often made a detour and drove through Woodstock, stopping off at the sweet shop by the entrance to Blenheim to get an ice cream and enjoy the scenic route through Blenheim to Ditchley Gate. That was how the landscape and vistas of Blenheim became woven into the fabric of my life. In those days, London and city life had no place on our agenda.

OPPOSITE: *The south, or garden, front of Blenheim Palace.*
BELOW: *My brother James and myself, photographed by Lord Snowdon.*

This is one of my favourite family portraits, as all the characters have a story to tell. The painting, by John Closterman, hangs in the great hall and depicts the first Duke, John Churchill, his feisty Duchess and their children. I am standing below the second Duchess, Henrietta, who succeeded to the title in 1722 and after whom I am named.

My nanny, Audrey, and her husband, Ray. Nanny has been with our family for over fifty years and Ray is my father's valet.

THE ONASSIS YEARS

In 1961 my father, John (Sunny), married Tina Livanos, who was previously married to Aristotle Onassis, so suddenly my brother and I had an older stepbrother, Alexander, and a stepsister, Christina. Initially we saw very little of them, as they were at school abroad, but Christina then came to live with us at Lee Place and she too went to Headington School. These were happy times for Christina. For the first time, she was having a relatively normal childhood—attending a local school, riding her horse Cobweb, and enjoying sport and pets as opposed to the high social life.

Christina, who was ten years older than I was, was like my big sister. I hero-worshipped her, and anything she did I wanted to copy or be involved with. She adored my father, calling him 'Sun Bun', although she was supposed to call him Uncle Sunny, while we called my stepmother Aunt Tina. Christina adored my nanny, who, unlike anyone else, treated her like one of us, disciplining and punishing her and thus earning her respect.

Christina was always encouraging James and me to be naughty, to have bad table manners and to play jokes on guests. Of course, we loved her challenges but we never got away with much. She used to love going to Blenheim, and I have fond memories of her leaning out of the car window, shouting at the paying public that this was her home. She had quite an obsessive character, often playing the same song over and over on her record player. One in particular I remember is 'Black Is Black, I Want My Baby Back', which to this day haunts me when I hear it. She was also addicted to Coca-Cola and Mars Bars. Luckily for both of us, we had a tuck shop at the end of the back drive at Lee Place where we could sneak off to satisfy our sugar cravings.

HOLIDAY JOBS

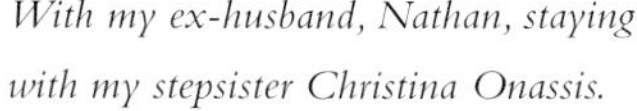

With my ex-husband, Nathan, staying with my stepsister Christina Onassis.

During the school holidays James and I were encouraged to spend some time working at Blenheim. This was normally in one of the gift shops, where we helped sell guidebooks and ice creams, but I often used to go to the kitchen garden and help Mr Page, the head gardener, to pick home-grown fruit and vegetables.

We didn't spend a lot of time in the house, as we were somewhat intimidated by our grandfather, Bert. When we *were* in the house, it was generally on the public side, either trying to scare the visitors by pretending to be ghosts (our favourite hiding place was on the gallery above the great hall) or exploring the endless roofs and towers, and the staircases leading to them.

In our teenage years, the lake played a large part in our summer life at Blenheim, and my father taught both my brother and me to water-ski on it. We had many a fun weekend entertaining our friends with barbecues and jet-skis, using the boathouse built by the eighth Duke and Duchess Lily as our base camp.

MOVING IN

When my grandfather died, in 1972, it was my father's turn to take over the reins at Blenheim. He had just married my stepmother, Rosita, and they became the eleventh Duke and Duchess of Marlborough, my brother took the title Marquis of Blandford, and the Marlborough heritage tumbled down another generation.

James and I were allowed to choose (within limitations) the bedrooms we would occupy. He opted for two small, low-ceilinged rooms, with small, north-facing porthole windows, between the main and second floors. I chose a light, south-facing, sunny room known as South Room One. I then had the daunting task of picking a fabric for the curtains and a wallpaper to match. I remember being taken to Colefax and Fowler in London by Rosita and selecting a pretty blue-and-pink floral-printed cotton fabric and a blue wallpaper with a small geometric print, with which the room was duly decorated. This was my first attempt at designing a room—I enjoyed it then and luckily I still do today.

ABOVE: *Formerly my brother's bedroom, this is part of a newly renovated guest suite in a small area between the main floors.*

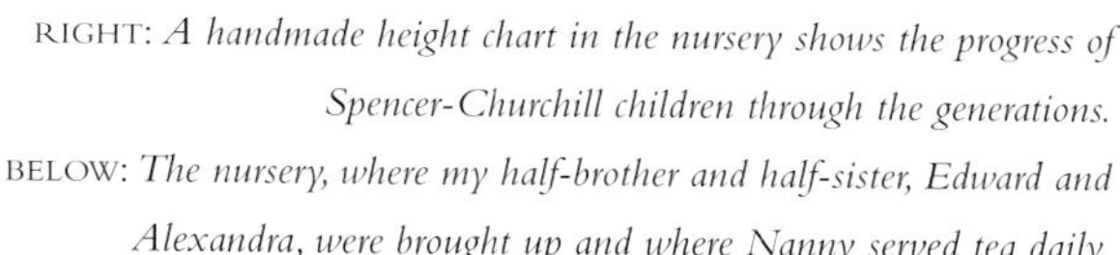

RIGHT: *A handmade height chart in the nursery shows the progress of Spencer-Churchill children through the generations.*

BELOW: *The nursery, where my half-brother and half-sister, Edward and Alexandra, were brought up and where Nanny served tea daily.*

My stepmother Rosita, my father, my brother James and myself, all ready to party. This was a triple celebration for my father's fiftieth birthday, James's coming-of-age and my coming-out.

DOMESTIC ARRANGEMENTS

When Blenheim was built, in the early 1700s, there was only one bathroom—for the Duchess. Many more have since been added, where possible, but some of the bathrooms are less than conveniently located. All the guest bedrooms are on the second floor, spanning the east and south wings. My father's bedroom is on the main floor, the *piano nobile*, in the east wing, in the areas that were used by the first Duke and Duchess.

The family areas at Blenheim are surprisingly comfortable and welcoming. My stepmother, Rosita, made quite a few changes when she moved in, and, with the addition of my half-brother and half-sister, Edward and Alexandra, the nursery was re-established and the house came alive again. Our nanny, who is now married to Ray, my father's valet, took charge of that area.

I feel it must have been a great pleasure for all who worked in the house to see it revitalized and being used as a family home again. Although the family continued to spend the summer months at Lee Place, Blenheim was now our home and very much part of our lives. But for me the two big disadvantages of being at Blenheim were the lack of privacy, in particular in the garden, and not having a family kitchen, as I love to cook.

FAMILY CELEBRATIONS

Blenheim has been the venue for many memorable family celebrations throughout its 300-year history. Today many of the functions are corporate, to help keep the finances viable, but Blenheim is still a magical venue for a great family party. A combined celebration for my father's fiftieth birthday, my brother's coming-of-age and my coming-out, for example, was as traditional a party as you could get, with the ladies dressed in ballgowns and tiaras and the men in white or black tie. But in all honesty, it was not an evening I look back on with fondness. Having lived abroad for eighteen months in Florence and Paris, I was not part of the London 'deb' scene and had no real desire to be so. A lot of the guests who attended the party were there because they were expected to be, so it didn't go down in my book as being the best of evenings.

The next big event of my life at Blenheim was my wedding in March 1980. I was married in the church at Woodstock and had the reception in the long library. The church was not big enough to hold our seven hundred guests, so around half were invited to the church and the remainder to the reception only. Despite the blustery and rainy weather, it was a wonderful occasion and I was honoured to have the opportunity to be married in such splendid surroundings.

My wedding group photograph taken in the bow window room in 1980. My half-brother and half-sisters, Edward and Alexandra Spencer-Churchill and Larissa Hardy, were page and bridesmaids.

My favourite rooms

The second state room, displaying the Bouchain tapestry third panel *(see pages 78–81).*

It is impossible to have favourite rooms at Blenheim as all of them are special and carry important historical reference and personal memories. The east wing, where we live as a family today, has a more informal feel, yet the state rooms offer an abundance of wonderful architecture and antiques. I have therefore selected rooms from both areas to feature here, as well as my favourite spots outdoors.

THE SALOON

BELOW: *The frescoes on the walls of the forty-foot-high saloon are by the French painter Louis Laguerre.*

Ever since I was a young girl, the saloon has conjured up happy memories of many family get-togethers. For as long as I can remember, the family has celebrated Christmas with dinner in the saloon. For me it began when my grandfather Bert was still alive. At that time there was a strict rule that children could attend only after they had started going to public school (around the age of twelve or thirteen) or, in a girl's case, once she had gone to boarding school. I remember feeling great resentment that my brother James was allowed to attend while I was left firmly in the nursery with Nanny, having possibly been allowed a brief appearance during the pre-dinner drinks. What made it harder to bear at the time was the fact that my first cousins and contemporaries, the Muirs and Waterhouses, were there. Although I was a couple of years younger than they were, we were like one big family, and Christmas was a time that we all met up and had tremendous fun.

On this special evening, my family has always observed two traditions which my father continues today. One is the tribute and toast he gives to the chef and the butler for producing a spectacular dinner, and the other is drinking brandy from a very oversized glass. One particular tradition that has mercifully not survived from my grandfather's time was the annual dare to see who would be brave enough to set my grandfather's paper hat from his Christmas cracker on fire! We all took turns trying and on one occasion he swiftly brushed it off his head, only for it to land in the giant brandy glass, which, needless to say, caused an even bigger upset.

BELOW: *The ceiling of the saloon is also by Laguerre, whose fee for this magnificent work of art, and the wall frescoes, was beaten down to £500 by Sarah, the first Duke's Duchess. The outer moulding is* trompe l'oeil *and made to look as if it is carved, but it is, in fact, flat.*

Looking back on this time, I suppose I didn't appreciate the stunning architecture of this room. But I did love how the vast open log fires (sadly now converted to gas) and the candlelight gave the room a mystic glow, bringing to life the figures depicted in Louis Laguerre's frescoes on the walls and ceiling.

At that time it was more the atmosphere of the celebration that made the saloon special to me, whereas now it is my awareness of the talent of those skilled craftsmen who, three hundred years ago, painstakingly created what the saloon is today.

OPPOSITE: *A view looking south-east showing the magnificent doorcase designed by Grinling Gibbons and carved in marble.*

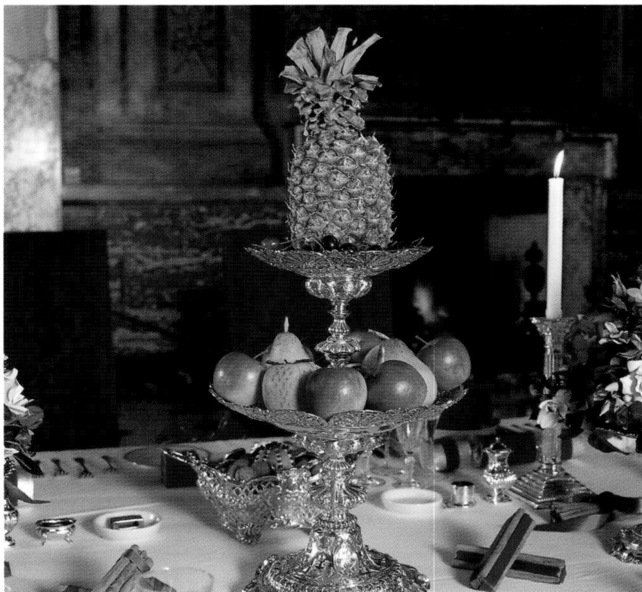

OPPOSITE AND LEFT: *The table is decorated for Christmas dinner and the room is mainly lit by candlelight, which gives an eerie atmosphere. You can almost feel the people depicted in the murals coming to life.*

BELOW: *The family dinner service and silver are stored in the pantry and brought out for special occasions.*

THE CHRISTMAS TABLE

The Christmas table is always beautifully and imaginatively decorated, and in spite of the huge proportions of the room, the atmosphere is warm and inviting. The layout of Blenheim is not at all practical in terms of cooking and eating. The kitchen is on the floor below the saloon, and there is a long walk from the pantry, where the food is sent from the kitchen, to the saloon. That the food is still hot when it is finally wheeled in is no mean tribute to the chef.

THE SMOKING ROOM

The smoking room is our family sitting room, a room where we all gather before or after lunch to have a drink or cup of coffee, and a place to read the papers or watch television. In spite of the vast proportions compared with most rooms in the palace, it is warm and inviting.

My favourite painting at Blenheim, Stubbs's *Tiger*, hangs proudly in here. Everyone is captivated by this painting, in which the tiger's eyes follow you as you move about the room. Other paintings are by John Wootton, the eighteenth-century equestrian and landscape painter, and in terms of content are in reality more suitable for a country house than Stubbs's *Tiger*. One wall is hung with a vast tapestry, the scale of which is perfect, as you would need at least ten large paintings to fill the same space; it also helps improves the acoustics.

The walls of the smoking room are covered in a coral-coloured fabric added by my stepmother after my grandfather died. There is a huge, deep sofa in a green chenille fabric, large enough for five people to sit comfortably and for a small child to get quite lost in.

My earliest memory of this room is of my grandfather sitting in his green leather chair, smoking a cigar, with his boxer, Ben, firmly at his feet. The chair is still there in the same leather. This year we were due to re-cover it, but I think nostalgia got the better of my father and he decided to leave it for another year.

This well-worn leather chair was my late grandfather's favourite and its shabby chic is an essential element of the country house look. I am seated with Bounty, my Border terrier/Jack Russell cross.

Although the smoking room can now also be viewed by the paying public, along with some of the private apartments, it remains very homely and personal. The tables are covered with a mass of family photographs, books, and plants from the estate greenhouses. Some of the chairs are threadbare and the chintz slipcovers are in need of replacement, but in my view these make it all the more comfortable and welcoming.

We do not carry out a lot of renovation at Blenheim, and I feel that this adds to the character of the place. Apart from the expense, we don't want to wipe out the previous generations' history and style. Much of the budget is spent on essential renovation of the infrastructure, keeping the roof in good repair (all three acres of it) and rewiring, which is not only necessary to keep the house up to legal standards but essential to reduce the risk of fire. The big challenge is to carry out these works without affecting the architectural fabric of the house, much of which is, of course, listed and of huge importance to the nation.

Serving as our family sitting room, the smoking room is the cosiest of all the rooms, full of family photos, books and a television. We congregate here for drinks, tea, to read the papers or to play games. The tapestry hanging behind the sofa is part of the Alexander series, showing episodes from the life of Alexander the Great. The set was specially commissioned by the first Duke.

MY FATHER'S DRESSING ROOM

The main bedroom is on the *piano nobile,* the raised main floor, and leads off what is now the dining room. It forms part of the *enfilade* of rooms typical of many grand country houses. Off this is my father's dressing room, which is small compared with all the other rooms on that floor but which in my view is a perfect space for a gentleman.

Decorated in a Regency style that is one of my favourites, it has a tobacco-coloured Suedel fabric on the walls above the painted dado, and curtains in a *café-au-lait* linen.

The furniture consists of a suite of elegant Empire pieces. The focal point is the daybed upholstered in duck-egg-blue linen bordered with a decorative braid. There is a pair of French armchairs made by Georges Jacob and still carrying the original canvas, which has survived because the chairs are rarely used. In spite of the somewhat threadbare carpet, the worn parts of which are largely disguised by a decorative rug, the room has a supremely elegant feel and a style unlike any other room in the house.

My father's dressing room is a beautiful, light room that is sunny in the mornings and has views over the Italian garden. Decorated in an elegant yet masculine way, it is personalized by my father's favourite pictures and photographs.

THE CHAPEL

Although not strictly categorized as a room, the chapel is attached to the house and is certainly part of it. It is entered either from the upper level of the west colonnade leading from the long library or from the ground-floor level beneath. The space is light and airy, with the altar, unusually, on the west side. I love the elegant architecture—you feel more like you are walking into a grand hall than into a chapel.

Described as 'very plain' by the first Duchess, it is dominated by the huge tomb designed by William Kent and constructed by Michael Rysbrack as a monument to the first Duke and Duchess and their two sons. The base depicts the surrender of Marshal Tallard after the battle of Blenheim. When I was a child I always thought it strange that the first Duke was wearing a theatrical Roman costume while Sarah was in a refined dress.

Though consecrated in 1731, the chapel was not completed until two years later, which was some time after the first Duke's death in 1722. He was first buried in Westminster Abbey, and it was not until 1744, when Sarah died, that his body was brought back to Blenheim to rest alongside hers. Until the demise of the tenth Duke in 1972, former family members were buried in the chapel tomb, but the tenth Duke had stated that he did not wish to be buried there, and so he is buried in the churchyard at Bladon with his wife, Mary.

BELOW: *A view looking west from the top of the steps, showing the striking tomb of the first Duke and Duchess designed by William Kent and executed by Michael Rysbrack.*

My one sadness about the chapel is that it is rarely used by the family today except on Christmas Eve, when we have a service for the family and estate workers. Unfortunately, I am rarely able to attend, as, by tradition, I cook dinner that night, so that the staff may have an evening off before the hectic days to follow. My great-grandmother Consuelo recalled a daily ritual of morning prayers attended by the family and estate workers. Although totally impractical to install today, a regular Sunday service would certainly be a good way to bring life back into this somewhat neglected shrine.

OPPOSITE: *The view looking east showing the small organ and wooden pews installed in Victorian times and still used today for the occasional family service. The simplicity of the pews allows the architecture to shine forth.*

O SING VNTO THE LORD

LEFT: *The vantage point from which these views of the roofs are taken is the highest point over the great hall.*
BELOW: *Looking west over the water terraces and the lake and up the hill beyond to High Lodge, formerly a royal hunting lodge for the kings of England.*

THE ROOFS

To appreciate the scale and complexities involved in the building of Blenheim, there is no better vantage point than the rooftops. There are numerous ways of getting to the different parts, whether it is to one of the four towers or to the central roof over the great hall and saloon, but whichever way you go, there is always a dark stone spiral staircase to negotiate.

As children we loved to take our friends up one of the staircases that lead off the great hall and are inconspicuous behind the large leather hall-porter's chairs. Three-quarters of the way up, you can mistakenly open a door you think may lead to another floor or room but which, in fact, perilously leads to the stone ledge around the great hall, giving access to the windows above. Up a few more turns and you arrive at a small, locked door, which leads onto the parapet

surrounding the main leaded, pitched roof topped with two gilded balls. From here the views are breathtaking and you gaze in wonderment, trying to imagine just how this magnificent structure was assembled with no mechanical aid. You can also truly appreciate the scale of some of the structures from here—for example, atop each of the four towers is a finial (designed and executed by Grinling Gibbons) 30 feet tall.

Even today, after innumerable visits, the roofs are among my favourite places to go. It is here that you can truly admire all those geniuses involved in Blenheim, from John Vanbrugh, Nicholas Hawksmoor and Grinling Gibbons to Henry Wise, Capability Brown and Achille Duchêne, each of whom made a huge contribution to the palace or garden in his own time.

View over the east colonnade and north courtyard, across Capability Brown's magical lake, towards the town of Woodstock.

THE ITALIAN GARDEN

This delightful spot enjoys a sheltered position between the east wing, where the private apartments are sited, and the orangery. The focal point is the Mermaid fountain, set in the middle of patterned beds delineated with dwarf box hedges. The garden is a delight all year round, but its finest season is when the orange blossom is out and a wonderful scented rose perfumes the south-east corner.

The French landscape gardener Achille Duchêne designed this garden for my great-grandfather, the ninth Duke. I particularly like the way Duchêne worked: he was typical of the Arts and Crafts movement of the time in that he took an old tradition and overlaid it with a fine attention to planting and construction detail. For his inspiration, he looked both backwards and forwards, which for me is as good a design philosophy as any. Duchêne gave up on grand gardens soon after finishing this project. In 1935 he published *Les Jardins de l'Avenir* (Gardens of the Future), in which he accurately predicted that gardens would become smaller and more functional.

OPPOSITE: *The focal point of the Italian garden is the Mermaid fountain (1892), by the American sculptor Waldo Story.*
BELOW: *Looking east over the Italian garden, created by my great-grandfather and the French landscape gardener Achille Duchêne.*

ohn Duke of Marlborough

CHAPTER TWO

A Grateful Nation

England in the middle of the seventeenth century, with the Civil War raging, was a time to watch your back, even within families. My illustrious ancestor John Churchill was born in 1650, the eldest surviving son of Winston and Elizabeth Churchill. Winston was a modest landowner in England's West Country, a Tory Member of Parliament and a staunch Royalist, supporting the autocratic King Charles I, while Elizabeth, née Drake, hailed from a line of Puritan Parliamentarians opposed to the King. As a result, the Churchill family fortunes lurched from famine to feast and back again. John Churchill's descendant and twentieth-century biographer, Winston Churchill, wrote:

'[This] might well have aroused in his mind two prevailing impressions... first a hatred of poverty and dependence, and secondly, the need of hiding thoughts and feelings from those to whom their expression would be repugnant. To have one set of opinions for one part of the family, and to use a different language for the other, may have been inculcated from John's earliest years...

ABOVE: *The first Duke's armorial bearings. The double-headed eagle was the crest of the Holy Roman Empire, of which the Duke had been made a Prince following his victory at the battle of Blenheim. The St George's Cross was awarded to his father, Sir Winston Churchill, by Charles II.*

OPPOSITE: *The Closterman portrait of John, Duke of Marlborough, hangs in the green writing room at Blenheim. When he was ageing and weakened by a stroke, the Duke stood in front of this portrait, which had been painted in his prime, and pondered: 'This once was a man.'*

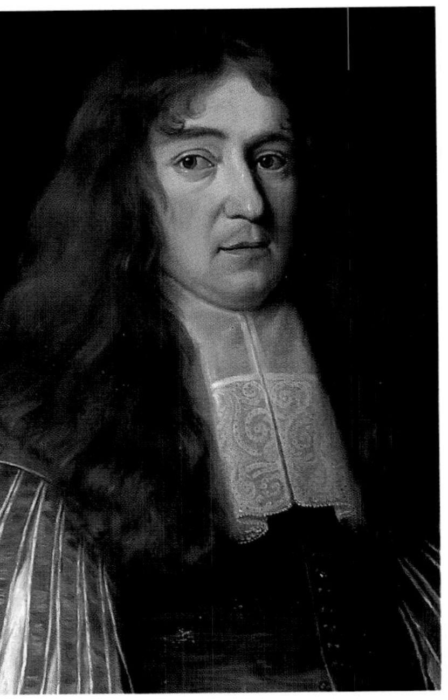

ABOVE: *John Churchill's father, Winston, was a loyal Royalist whose fortunes waxed and waned during the English Civil War.*

ABOVE: *Arabella, John's sister, became the favoured mistress of the Duke of York, later King James II. She was as determined as her brother to escape the boom-and-bust conditions of her childhood.*
OPPOSITE: *The Spencer-Churchill family tree showing the line of descent from the first Duke of Marlborough.*

To these was added a third, the importance of having friends and connections on both sides of a public quarrel... Certainly the whole life of John Churchill bore the imprint of his youth.'

John's father, Winston, had a volatile career—he tellingly chose as his motto (still used by his descendants) *Fiel Pero Desdichado*, Faithful But Unfortunate. His legacy was not financial, for he was to die in debt, but it was the making of his children. Following the end of the English Civil War and the restoration of the monarchy, Charles II found places at court for Winston's daughter, Arabella, and his handsome, strategic thinker of a son, John, to reward their father for his loyalty to the Crown in the Civil War.

AT THE COURT OF CHARLES II

John's education was piecemeal. He probably had tutors when his father could afford them, and at the age of thirteen was enrolled as a scholar at St Paul's School in London. However, he showed no interest in books, and his spelling throughout his life remained execrable. Aged about sixteen, John was appointed as a page to the King's brother James, Duke of York, the future James II. John's sister, Arabella, had already become a maid of honour to James's wife.

James was a complex character—dark, humourless and masochistic—but with a relentless sexual appetite. The multitude of women he took to his bed were so plain that Charles II remarked they must have been imposed upon him as a penance by his priests. Arabella Churchill, young, tall and pale-complexioned, was not as plain as most, and it was only a matter of time before James seduced her. Unlike the other women at court, Arabella was neither flirtatious nor impulsive; she was a Churchill and she had a master plan.

Arabella became the Duke of York's favoured mistress and was well provided for. The Duke set her up in a house in St James's Square, London, where she created a warm, domestic environment and gave birth to his children, four of whom survived. The two sons were to become formidable soldiers, which must say something for the power of the Churchill genes. The Duke and Arabella's affair lasted for over ten years, until she was replaced in his affections by yet another maid of honour. Arabella eventually made a comfortable and happy marriage to 'honest Colonel Godfrey', producing two surviving children.

With his charming manners and his handsome looks, John Churchill had no trouble fitting in with the pleasure principle that characterized the court of Charles II. Many of his days were spent watching military drills and parades with the Duke of York, which fired his desire to become a soldier. As for his nights, there was much on offer—in particular the King's mistress Barbara Villiers, Duchess of Cleveland, who was, according to an observer of the times, '*the lewdest as well as the fairest of King Charles's concubines*'. There is a recorded incident in which, in the best farcical tradition of Restoration comedy, a jealous courtier

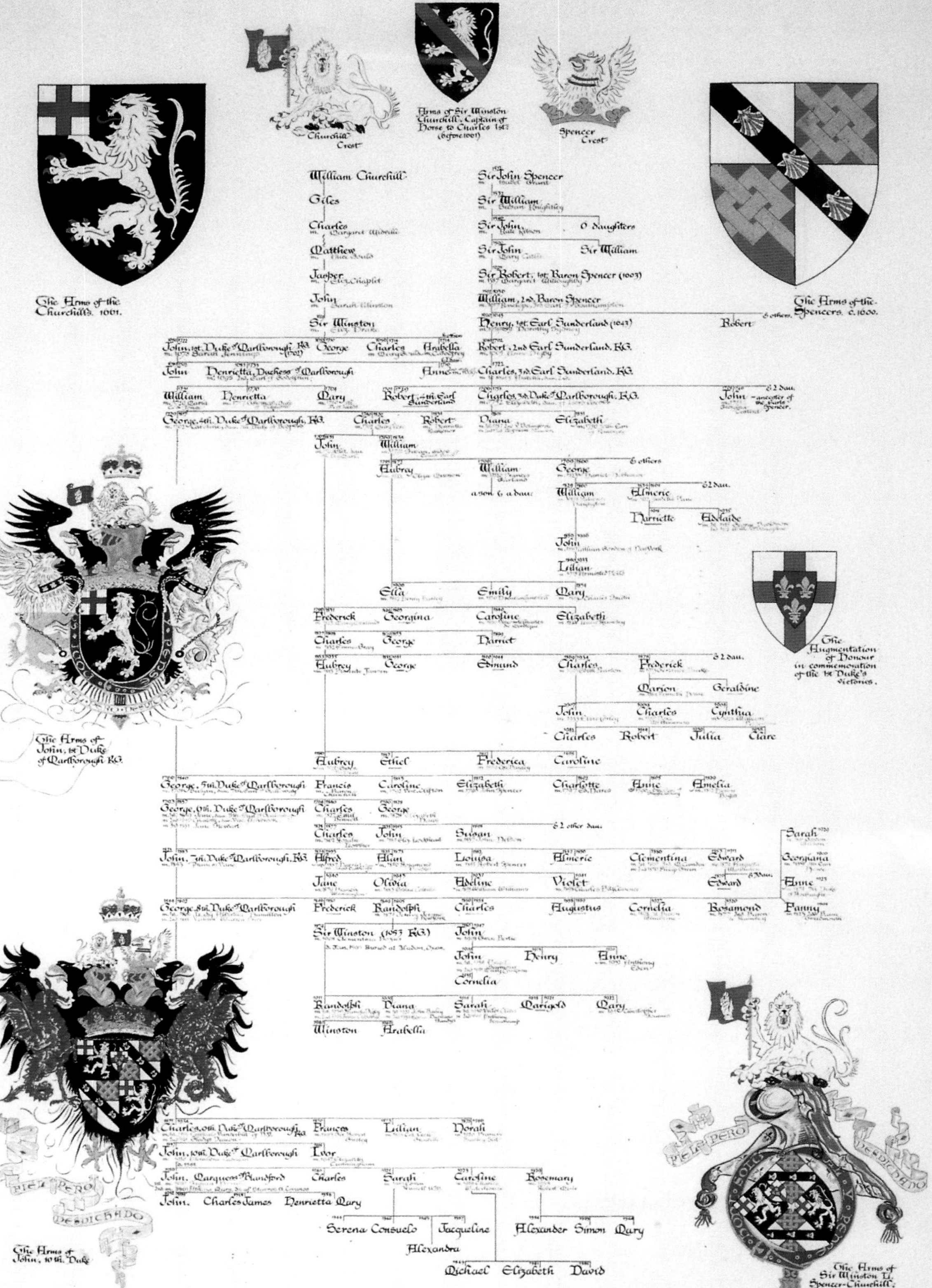

The Spencer-Churchills

P.G.P. Keyes,
Invt et delt. 1953

RIGHT: *John wrote frequent and passionate love letters to Sarah, many of which survive in the Blenheim archives.*

encouraged the King to call on Barbara when he knew Churchill would be in her bed. In one account Churchill leapt out of bed and through the window; in another he hid in a cupboard, was discovered by the King but was forgiven with the words: *'You are a rascal, but I forgive you because you do it to get your bread.'*

And get bread he did. It is rumoured that Barbara gave her impoverished lover (and father of her third daughter) a large sum, with which he prudently bought an annuity of £500.

Churchill cut an impressive figure at court. His military and tactical abilities, together with his sister's lover's patronage, ensured his speedy rise through the ranks. He was only twenty-three when he played a courageous part in the siege of Maastricht, and was singled out for congratulations by no less a glorious being than the Sun King, France's King Louis XIV, who referred to him as a *'young Adonis in scarlet and gold'*. Back at court, Barbara was waiting with open arms to welcome her young Adonis home, but John Churchill had been sidetracked, by the fifteen-year-old Sarah Jennings.

BELOW: *Detail from a romantic painting by Sir Godfrey Kneller showing the beautiful Sarah playing cards.*

SARAH—A FORCE OF NATURE

Sarah was born in 1660 into a well-established Royalist family. Her father, Richard Jennings, was a Tory Member of Parliament. Her childhood was comfortable, but her father died when Sarah was eight years old. Mrs Jennings—something of a virago by all accounts—brought her four good-looking daughters to court, occupying rooms in St James's Palace. Sarah, an attractive thirteen-year-old with cherry lips, flashing blue eyes and golden hair, was appointed maid of honour to James's second wife, Mary of Modena, and attendant to her stepdaughter, the young Princess Anne.

Mrs Jennings, horrified by the behaviour she saw at the court of King Charles II, tried to have Sarah removed, but the spirited Sarah was having none of it. Turning the tables on her meddlesome mother, Sarah had her dismissed.

'She is a mad woman,' wrote Sarah to a friend. *'She would provoke a saint.'* Her mother had cause to be concerned—all around her, maids of honour were being dishonoured and ladies-in-waiting were falling pregnant—and the diarist Samuel Pepys described the court as *'nothing but bawdry... from top to bottom'*. However, it was an environment in which Sarah thrived, holding onto her position and her virginity by sheer force of personality.

John Churchill was entranced by this beautiful, wilful teenager. Sarah resisted the advances of the handsome young man—she didn't want to be just another of his conquests, inevitably to be discarded. She wanted commitment, and wrote to him:

> *'If it were true that you have the passion for me which you say you have, you would find out some way to make yourself happy—it is in your power. Therefore press me no more to see you, since it is what I cannot in honour approve of and, if I have done too much, be so just as to consider who was the cause of it.'*

Barbara Villiers, the King's mistress and mother of five of his children, was Sarah's rival for the heart of John Churchill, and the mother of his first child.

She played him on a line like a fish: *''Tis to no purpose to imagine that I will be made ridiculous in the world, when it is in your power to make me otherwise,'* she insisted. John was twenty-six, Sarah sixteen. He was hopelessly in love but he had not the means to make an offer of marriage. Barbara and their daughter were still at court making trouble, and his parents were busily negotiating on his behalf a marriage with Catherine Sedley, a woman of taste, intelligence and wealth. It was a match that, given his circumstances, made all kinds of sense. But on this occasion—perhaps for the only time in his life—his heart prevailed over his head. The letters that passed between them at this time show John to be the tortured romantic and Sarah the pragmatist. She was adamant that she was not to be *'made ridiculous in the world'*, a fear that was to inform her behaviour throughout her life.

> *'If your happiness can depend upon the esteem and love I have for you, you ought to be the happiest thing breathing for I have never anybody loved to that height I love you, I love you so well that your happiness I prefer much above my own.'*

A loving sentiment from one of John's many letters to Sarah

They married in the winter of 1677–78. It would appear that the Duke and Duchess of York made some financial provisions for the couple they had learned to trust and depend upon. John had an income from his post and from his vigorously earned annuity, and Sarah probably had about the same level of income from her father's estate. It wasn't much to live on, especially in court circles, so it was fortunate they were both by nature very careful with money. A reputation for meanness was to follow them all their lives: it was said that Sarah never dotted her 'i's' in order to save ink.

A MUTUAL PASSION

John and Sarah were also fortunate to be very much in love at a time when love matches at court were extremely rare. Their mutual passion sustained everything they did and it lasted until the end. It is said that Sarah wrote to a friend that on one occasion when John returned from a campaign, he 'pleasured her' before removing his boots. Years later, when going off to war, he wrote to her:

> *'It is impossible to express with what a heavy heart I parted with you when I was at the waterside. I could have given my life to come back... I did for a great while have a perspective glass looking upon the cliffs in hopes I might have had one sight of you.'*

She wrote to him:

> *'Wherever you are, whilst I have life, my soul shall follow you, my ever dear Lord Marlborough, and wherever I am I should only kill the time wishing for night that I may sleep and hope the next day to hear from you.'*

Sarah's force of character was remarked upon by all who knew her. She would take on anyone and anything, and she always passionately believed she was right, whereas Marlborough, the great soldier, was altogether more understanding and conciliatory. It is evident from her portraits that Sarah had a formidable presence. She has a broad, confident brow, a determined set to her jaw and commanding eyes that look down on all who gaze at her.

This is the most significant painting of the first Duke and Duchess and their children, painted in 1693 by John Closterman.

'A love never known by man'

ABOVE: *Sarah Churchill, later Duchess of Marlborough.*
RIGHT: *Princess Anne, later Queen Anne.*

Princess Mary and her younger sister Princess Anne—each of whom later became Queen of England—were the daughters of James, Duke of York (the future James II), by his Protestant marriage to his first wife, Anne Hyde. She had died when the girls were very young. The motherless sisters were bought up at Richmond Palace surrounded by female companions and, despite their father's attempts to stop them from reading fiction, a ready supply of sentimental French romances. Both girls had passionate relationships with women. Mary, from the age of twelve, conducted a loaded correspondence with twenty-year-old Frances Apsley: *'I love you with more zeal than any lover can, I love you with a love that was never known by man,'* she gushed. Perhaps it was just as well that the sexual orientation of her husband, William of Orange (whom she married when she was fifteen), is rumoured to have been predominately homosexual.

Anne, while still a child, had settled her affections on a new arrival at court, Sarah Jennings. In her early teens, Sarah was five years her senior. Anne valued Sarah's lively temper and her plain speaking, and they remained close friends and confidantes for more than thirty-five years, long after Anne had become Queen.

Looking back on the relationship, Sarah wrote:

> *'Kings and princes for the most part imagine that they have a dignity peculiar to their birth and station, which ought to raise them above all connexion of friendship with an inferior...The Princess had a different taste.*

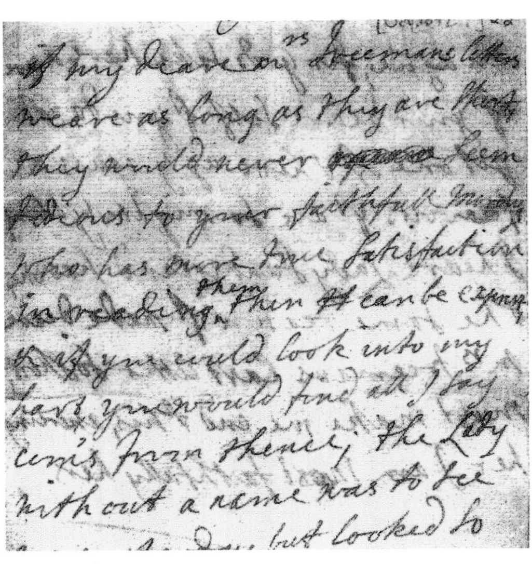

if my deare Mrs Freemans letters
weare as long as thy are short
they would never seem
tedious to your faithfull Morley
who has more true satisfaction
in reading them then can be exprest
& if you could look into my
hart you would find all I say
comes from thence; the Lady
without a name was to see
but looked so

RIGHT: *This letter, dating probably from October 1692 and incorporating Anne's and Sarah's pet names (Mrs Morley and Mrs Freeman), reveals that Anne's attachment to Sarah continued unabated: 'If my dear Mrs Freeman's letters were as long as they are short, they would never seem tedious to your faithful Morley who has more true satisfaction in reading them than can be expressed...'*
BL, Blenheim, 61415

RIGHT: *Anne wrote remarkably frankly to Sarah. Although the women used 'feigned' names and the letters were always unsigned, Anne did not hesitate to commit her love to written records: 'So kind a letter as I received yesterday deserves more thanks than I shall ever be able to pay... no tongue nor pen can ever express how happy those few lines has made me; I was ashamed to say so little to you last night which I hope you will excuse since it was not my fault, for having taken the waters I durst not write presently after dinner and all the rest of the day I had not a moment's time but just the one that I write in; this may... sound like an excuse but I assure you 'tis none for though I don't naturally love writing yet to dear Mrs Freeman I could write for ever it being next to hearing from you one of the greatest satisfactions I have in your absence, I am all impatience for Thursday till when farewell; and let my dear dear Lady Marlborough be assured I am so fully persuaded of her kindness there is no room left for doubts if I would never so faine; and if I shall never cease to love her with all the real passion imaginable as long as I have a moment's breath.'*
BL, Blenheim, 61414

LEFT: *Anne was a vigorous letter- and note-writer in private matters, and expected equal devotion to correspondence from Sarah, as this letter, probably from 1686, reveals: 'I have been so unfortunate again today as not to hear from my dear Lady Churchill which has put a thousand melancholy thoughts into my head, I am very unwilling to think it is unkindness has hindered you from writing and yet know not how to believe you are sick because I desired if you were if you would let me know it some way or other, but after having been so kind as to leave off play to write to me I can't imagine what has been the occasion of your missing writing two days together except your Lord's coming home from the camp. If this be the reason I am satisfied and 'tis the only glimpse of comfort that I have for if I should hear nothing tomorrow morning neither from you nor of you I shall conclude with reason that I am quite forgot and never trouble you anymore with my dull letters.'*
BL, Blenheim, 61414

A friend was what she most coveted and... was fond even of that equality which she thought belonged to it. It was this turn of mind which made her propose to me that... we might in our letters write ourselves by feigned names such as would import nothing of distinction between us.'

With the perspective of hindsight, Sarah observed that for Anne:

'every moment of absence she counted a sort of tedious lifeless state. To see [Sarah] was a constant joy, and to part with her for never so short a time a constant uneasiness... She used to say she desired to possess her wholly and could hardly bear that she should ever escape this confinement into any other company.'

Sarah described her own reactions, again in the third person:

'She had too great a sense of her favour not to submit to all such inconveniences to oblige one she saw loved her to excess... But though there was this passionate love on the one side and, as I verily believe, the sincerest friendship on the other, yet their tempers were not more different than their principles and notions on many occasions appeared to be.'

Portrait by Charles Jervas of Sarah Churchill as a young woman, when she was a close friend of Princess Anne.

TACT AND DIPLOMACY

John and Sarah Churchill initially divided their time between court and John's parents' home in Dorset. John's inherent diplomatic and tactical skills were stretched in every direction. On the home front there was peace to be kept between Sarah and his mother, while at court James, as heir to the throne and later (1685–88) as King, was a further complication. He was obstinate and charmless and, even worse, had upset the establishment by converting to Catholicism.

John had learned to handle his monarch well, never exactly disagreeing and never overtly agreeing with him. He timed a shift of allegiance to James's Protestant elder daughter, Mary, and her Dutch husband, William of Orange, so well that on James's downfall in 1688, John and Sarah's transition to the court of William and Mary was seamless. William granted John Churchill an earldom—John chose the title Marlborough after a cousin who had died without issue.

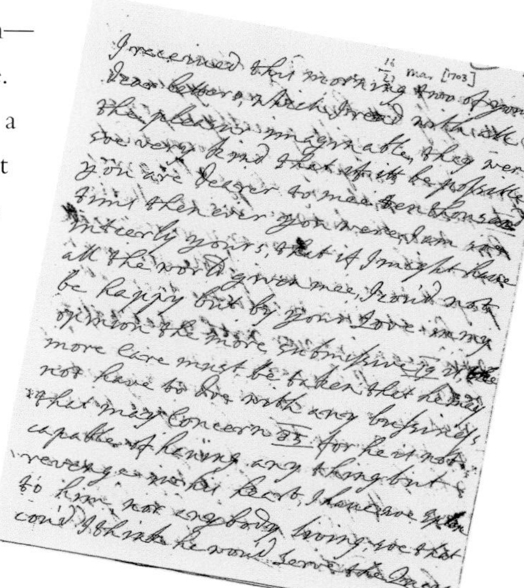

One could argue that Marlborough's defection was motivated purely by a desire to be on the winning side, but there is another, equally valid view, that he had only his country's interests at heart—that England under James II was taking the wrong turn. In any event, Marlborough must have agonized over his decision to betray the man who had given him every opportunity in life, and he probably didn't want to be reminded of it. There is not one portrait, not even an engraving, of James II in all of Blenheim.

Sarah's relationship with Princess Anne was a key factor in the Marlboroughs' rise to the top. Ever since their early teenage years, the plain, stolid, generous Princess had loved the vibrant, dazzling Sarah with a passion. The passion not only lasted for years but was, if anything, intensified by Anne's marriage to the dull but well-meaning Prince George of Denmark. Sarah was made lady of the bedchamber, a post that required her, in her own words, *'to employ all her wit and all her vivacity, and almost all her time, to divert and entertain and serve the Princess'*

William and Mary were not the easiest monarchs to serve. William was convinced that no English commander could do better than a Dutch one, which meant that Marlborough was left waiting in the wings as the autocratic Louis XIV consolidated power in Europe. As for Sarah, she found herself the focus of a bitter jealousy that raged between Queen Mary and her sister, Princess Anne. These were testing times, but when Queen Anne finally acceded to the throne after the death of William in 1702, the Marlboroughs' position seemed unassailable.

John's letters to Sarah were deeply affectionate and domestic: 'whilst I have life I am faithfully yours'. He mentions that 'I have taken your physic three days together so that I hope it has cured me of my headache'.

BL, Blenheim, 61427

HOME AND ABROAD

John's and Sarah's various posts at court and in the military earned them enough money to set up a comfortable home for their growing family at Holywell, near St Albans. They took great joy in rebuilding the house to suit them, in laying out the garden and planting fruit trees. In his letters home from the battlefields of Europe, John often wrote of his plans for the place, and he sent home crates of china and tapestries, pictures and furniture to decorate the haven he held so dear.

The family was well provided for. Their daughters were growing up and getting married, and Princess Anne was characteristically generous with wedding settlements for them.

Anne suffered the loss of all her children but one, yet the cruellest blow was the loss of her last surviving son. Sarah and John's remaining son and heir, John, was struck down by smallpox in 1703. Anne wrote to Sarah: *'It would have been a great satisfaction to your poor unfortunate faithful Morley, if you would have given me leave to come to St Albans, for the unfortunate should come to the unfortunate.'* Devastated by grief, Sarah lashed out in anguish at those closest to her while Marlborough even considered hanging up his commander's baton and retiring: *'I have lost what is so dear to me, it is fit for me to retire and not toil and labour for I know not who.'* Luckily for England, and for the fortunes of our family, both John and Sarah rallied to face John's finest hour.

Holywell House, near St Albans, was John and Sarah's first family home—they put a lot of care and thought into their living arrangements. Home was important to both of them.

THE BEGINNING OF A GOLDEN AGE

The accession of Queen Anne in 1702 marked the beginning of a golden age in the decorative arts and architecture. Britain was now a confident nation with a recognizably English monarch (William had spoken no English). At her right hand, as commander-in-chief of the British and Dutch forces, stood a brave, handsome and clever soldier with England's best interests at heart.

The understanding between the Queen and the Marlboroughs was complete. Queen Anne heaped lucrative posts and honours on her favourites and their children. She granted Sarah a lease for life on Windsor Lodge simply because Sarah had ridden past it one day and remarked how pleasant it would be to live there. And she granted John both a marquessate (of Blandford) and the dukedom of Marlborough. The Queen wrote to Sarah:

> *'I know my dear Mrs Freeman does not care for anything of that kind nor am I satisfied with it, because it does not enough express the value I have for Mr Freeman [their code name for Marlborough], nor nothing ever can show how passionately I am yours, my dear Mrs Freeman.'*

In fact, Sarah wasn't all that thrilled about the honour. She saw it as a fuss too far and an obligation to become embroiled in much useless, and expensive, grandeur. She wrote at once to her husband to tell him to refuse it, but he'd learned not to take too much notice of Sarah's demands when they didn't suit him. A dukedom was important to him—it would raise his standing with the European princes, and besides, he felt he'd earned it.

When Marlborough set off to battle in 1704, he wrote to Sarah assuring her of his love—*'Whatever becomes of me, whatever happens to me... my heart is entirely yours'*—and reassuring her of his victory—*'Let them send what they will, I have great hopes God will bless this undertaking.'* He rested in a country house with magnificent views of the Rhine but couldn't help adding that he *'would be much better pleased with the prospect of St Albans'*.

The battle of Blenheim, or Blindheim, in Bavaria in 1704 was a magnificent victory, and a source of great national pride. In February 1705 Queen Anne granted the Duke the royal manor and honour of Woodstock in Oxfordshire as her gift, and a grateful nation was to build for him there the magnificent palace that is Blenheim. Sadly, no terms, no conditions, no budget, nothing, was put in writing regarding the construction of the palace that was to be named after the great battle—which was unfortunate, because the close understanding between the Marlboroughs and their monarch would eventually unravel.

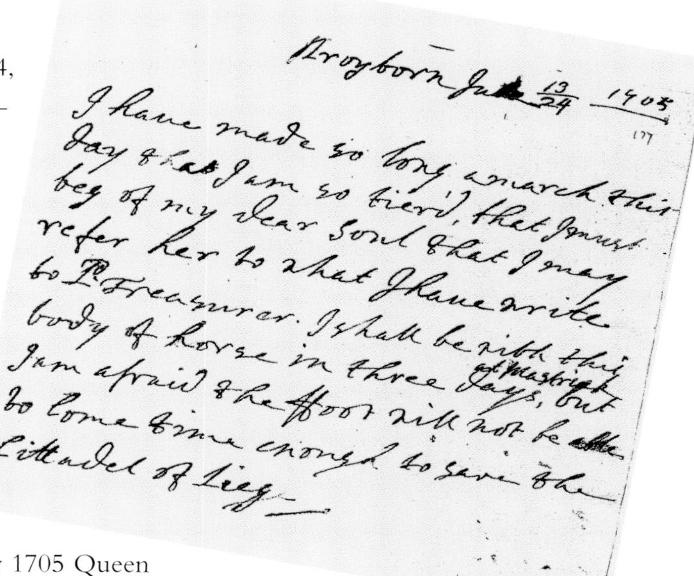

Kroyborn July 13/24 1705

I have made so long a march this day that I am so tierd, that I must beg of my dear Soul that I may refer her to what I have write to Ld Treasurer. I shall be with this body of horse in three days at Mastricht, but I am afraid the ffoot will not be able to come time enough to save the Cittadel of Liege

Dating from June 1705 and carried by horsemen from the army camp of his offensive in the Spanish Netherlands, this note was sent by Captain-General Lord Marlborough, commander-in-chief of the Allied armies, to his wife: 'I have made so long a march this day that I am so tired, that I must beg of my dear soul that I may refer her to what I have written to [the] Lord Treasurer. I shall be with this body of horse in three days at Maastricht, but I am afraid the foot will not be able to come [in] time enough to save the citadel of Liège.'
BL, Blenheim, 61428

A glorious victory

The battle of Blenheim in 1704 was a decisive victory in the war against the French and Bavarians. This so-called War of the Spanish Succession had been precipitated by the death of the Spanish King. European powers had agreed not to fight over the childless King's estate, but to divide it up peacefully. However, Louis XIV of France had torn up the agreement, helped himself to what is now Belgium, put his grandson on the throne of Spain and declared that the exiled son of James II was King of England. It was a provocation impossible to ignore.

Because Louis XIV had already taken what he wanted, he only needed to fight defensively. For a while the situation was at stalemate. Then one of the Bavarians changed sides, allowing the French to go on the offensive and march on Vienna—the linchpin of the Alliance. Marlborough, now commander-in-chief of the British and Dutch forces, determined to confront the enemy. In alliance with Prince Eugène of Savoy, his Austrian opposite number, he would cut off the Franco-Bavarian forces before they got to Vienna.

Detail from a map of Blenheim battlefield, author/artist unknown. BL, Blenheim, 61343 F

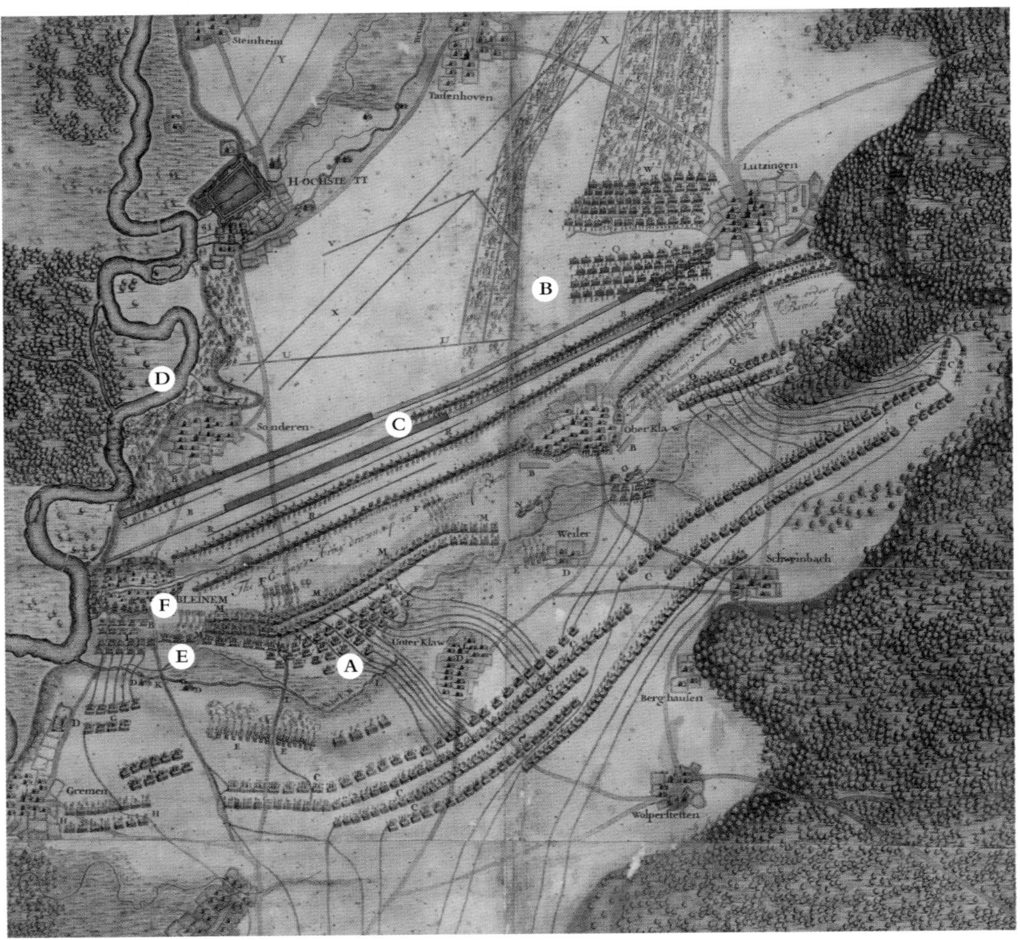

English troops **A**
Bavarian troops **B**
French troops **C**
River Danube **D**
River Nebel **E**
Village of Blenheim **F**

The battle of Blenheim itself was really only half the battle. Marlborough first had to march his army nearly three hundred miles, and provide for their supply, while not advertising their presence or their intentions. Unusually for the times, he took care of his men, ensuring that they were well fed, well rested and well shod.

The march itself was a strategic triumph. Sir Winston Churchill wrote of this historic feat:

> *'The annals of the British Army contain no more heroic episode than this march from the North Sea to the Danube. The strategy which conceived, the secrecy and skill which performed, and the superb victory which crowned the enterprise have always ranked among the finest examples of the art of war.'*

ABOVE: *Another detail of the map of Blenheim battlefield shown opposite. This remarkable document shows, in graphic detail, the topography of the battlefield, troop positions and troop movements.*
BL, Blenheim, 61343 F

The superior Franco-Bavarian forces were lined up in a hurriedly entrenched defensive position—their strong right flank protected by the Danube and the rising ground of the village of Blenheim, their left flank on the foothills north of the Danube, their front protected by the river Nebel. Marlborough planted 'deserters' along the way to give the French the false information that the British forces were in retreat, so that once the armies were within range, the French would not go on the attack.

Marlborough took them by surprise by subverting all the rules of conventional warfare and attacking hard and fast at Blenheim, the strongest point in the whole French line. It was a tactic characteristic of a man who combined caution with extreme daring.

British brigades pressed forward through merciless fire, losing a third of their men, but inflicting even more severe losses on the enemy. Meanwhile a second British thrust to the centre and Austrian attacks to the right were serving to thin out the central core of the French army.

When Marlborough drew his sword to lead the final attack, the French centre disintegrated. The English and Austrian troops rounded on Blenheim, where twenty-seven French battalions were by now penned in. Outflanked and outmanoeuvred, they finally laid down their arms.

BELOW: *The first Duke's staff of office, and a detail of the medallion at one end, with Queen Anne on one side and Prince Eugène on the other.*

VLM
HOOGHSTET
INGOLSTAT

The famous tapestry (see pages 52–3 and 78–81) of the battle of Blenheim shows the action in progress.

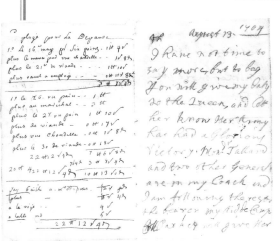

Shortly after capturing the enemy leader, the Duke of Marlborough famously scribbled a note to his wife on the back of his tavern bill. Known as the Blenheim Dispatch, it begins:

> *'I have not time to say more but to beg you will give my duty to the Queen, and let her know her army has had a glorious victory.'*

The final toll of killed and wounded was 34,000 on the French side and 13,000 on that of the Alliance. Austria was saved, Bavaria conquered, and the grandiose dreams of Louis XIV, for a united Europe under France, in ruins.

The defeat at Blenheim changed the dynamics of warfare in Europe. Until that day, warfare had consisted of a measured pursuit of sieges, marches and set-piece battles that were often inconclusive. Marlborough had ripped up the rule book and shocked Louis XIV—French monarchs had been used to interfering whenever they wished in the internal and external affairs of Great Britain. Louis gave orders that in future the best troops should be used against the English. Blenheim marked a line in the sand—the beginning of the final phase of the Anglo-French struggle that would end only with the battle of Waterloo more than a century later.

At the age of fifty-four, Marlborough was not a young man when he enjoyed his first major victory in battle, but he was to have many more great victories against the French, right up to the age of sixty.

TOP AND OPPOSITE: *A Quit Rent Standard at Blenheim. A new Quit Rent Standard is sent to the sovereign every year on the anniversary of the battle of Blenheim, as 'quit rent' for the royal manor of Woodstock, the site of Blenheim Palace.* ABOVE: *The Blenheim Dispatch—the note from John to Sarah scribbled on a tavern bill informing her of the victory at the battle of Blenheim. The original is in the British Library. Seeing it and holding it, some three hundred years after it was written, was an amazing experience.*

THE BLENHEIM TAPESTRY

Of all the works of art housed at Blenheim, the eighteenth-century tapestries celebrating the first Duke's victories in war are the most stunning, in both scale and workmanship. The Blenheim tapestry – jewel in the crown of the 'Victories' series of tapestries (see pages 78–81)—shows, in incredibly accurate historical detail, key moments in the battle. Not only is it beautifully composed as a whole, but you can follow the story of the entire day of the battle.

The main focus of the canvas shows Marlborough, victorious in his eye-catching red uniform, seated on his famous white charger, accepting Louis XIV's surrender from a blue-coated, pale-faced Marshal Tallard.

Behind the Marshal's shoulder are the the events that led up to the momentous victory. The English cavalry charges across a battlefield thick with flames and smoke towards the French lines—all very authentic, as the French troops had set fire to local watermills in an unsuccessful attempt to trap the valiant cavalrymen. On the far left horizon you can see the steeples and roofs of the tiny village of Blindheim, or Blenheim, after which the battle was named. To the front, an English grenadier guard is surrounded by the trophies of war.

TOP LEFT: *Despite the political significance and fame of the battle of Blenheim, the cartouche at the top of the tapestry names the battle 'Hoogstet', which is how it was known internationally. The English used 'Blenheim' to distinguish the battle from the battle of Hochstadt in the previous year.*

TOP RIGHT: *Despite the fact that Marlborough did not use a battle artist, the military details are extremely accurate. Here gun assistants, or matrosses, are attending to the brass and iron guns. Marlborough's attention to gun positioning was unusual but brought him great success.*

RIGHT: *The village of Blindheim, or Blenheim, in Bavaria. Amid the church and thatched cottages, French troops can be seen struggling to move; the village was barricaded with carts, tree trunks and hedges.*

BELOW: *The centre of the tapestry shows, in exquisite detail, Marlborough (on the right) about to accept the surrender of Marshal Tallard, who marks his defeat by doffing his hat to the English General.*

AN AFFAIR THAT ENDED BADLY

The dynamics of court changed gradually once Anne became Queen. While William III was King, Anne and Sarah were united in their detestation of the 'Dutch abortion', as they called him. Once he had died, they had no one to scratch but each other. At this time, two seeds were sown that were eventually to destroy Sarah and Anne's cosy relationship. The first was the presence in court of Abigail Hill, a pretty, witty and charming young cousin of Sarah's; the second was politics.

Sarah had no time for the Church, which to her was *'a spell to enchant weak minds'*. Nor did she admire the Tory party, which stood for passive obedience and the divine right of kings; Sarah was a rational Whig. Marlborough, though more tactful, was no great believer in the divine right of kings either, nor was he a fan of the Tory desire to sue for peace at such a critical time in the war.

Queen Anne sympathized with the Tories, and Sarah took it upon herself to lambast the Queen, bombard her with her liberal views and fight Marlborough's political battles at home while he was racking up military triumphs abroad. After months of such battering, Anne wrote: *'I have the same opinion of Whig and Tory as I ever had. I know both their principles very well, and when I know myself to be in the right, nothing can make me alter mine.'* Sarah should have heard the warning bells, but she ignored them. Priding herself on her plain speaking, she continued to bully the Queen, who took to addressing her as *'dear unkind friend'*. The final straw was when Sarah reminded the Queen of her connivance in the downfall of her own father, James II. The insult was never forgotten, and the more malleable Abigail moved to the position of lady of the bedchamber.

This painting by Sir Godfrey Kneller, depicting Queen Anne magnanimously handing over the plans of Blenheim to the victorious Duke of Marlborough, stems from a time when John and Sarah could do nothing wrong. Only a short time later, they could do nothing right. Such is life at the top.

Anne's passion for Sarah had been overwhelming and suffocating. Sarah, with a husband she adored and a family, could not fully requite it—and yet, like the proverbial dog in the manger, she couldn't bear anyone to take her place.

Outraged, she didn't let up. She continued to berate the Queen and torment her with the scurrilous ballads and gossip doing the rounds about the nature of the Queen's relationship with Abigail. Anne demanded the return of her love letters; Sarah refused to reply, intimating blackmail. Marlborough intervened, persuading Sarah to apologize, but it was too late—the

Queen was totally estranged. Embittered and adamant that she was the one who was in charge, she commanded Marlborough to promote Abigail's brother to the rank of colonel—Marlborough refused.

In 1711, the Queen dismissed Marlborough and Sarah from all their posts. She gave Sarah two days to remove her possessions from St James's Palace. Petulantly, Sarah stripped the rooms bare, even taking the locks from the doors. The two women never spoke again. The day after Marlborough's dismissal, twelve new Tory peers were created (Abigail's brother being one of them), giving the government a majority to push through the peace treaty that Marlborough felt was so wrong. Accusations flew in the press—that he had misappropriated public funds, that he had embroiled Britain in unnecessary battles for his own self-aggrandizement, that the gifts and endowments he'd received were out of all proportion to his efforts—tiny granules of truth blown out of all proportion by spite and envy.

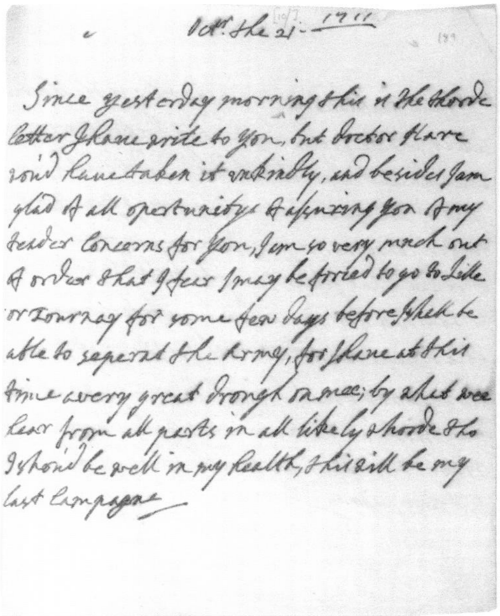
Oct. the 21 – 1711

Since yesterday morning this is the third letter I have write to you, but Doctor Hare would have taken it unkindly, and besides I am glad of all opertunity of assuring you of my tender concerns for you, I am so very much out of order that I fear I may be forced to go to Lille or Tournay for some few days before I shall be able to seperat the Army, for I have at this time a very great drought on mee; by what wee hear from all parts in all likely hoode tho I should be well in my health, this will be my last Campagne

Despite their troubles at court, Marlborough was still devoted to Sarah. In this letter from the 1711 French campaign he wrote: 'Since yesterday morning this is the third letter I have written to you... I am glad of all opportunity of assuring you of my tender concerns for you, I am so very much out of order that I fear I may be forced to go to Lille or Tournay for some few days...' He ended the letter: 'Though I should be well in my health, this will be my last campaign.'

BL, Blenheim, 61431 (762)

IN AND OUT OF EXILE

Tired and ill, Marlborough set off with a small retinue for the Continent, where he was better appreciated than at home. Sarah came out to join him. It was the first time she had been abroad and she saw everything with fresh eyes and wonderment:

> *'All the places one passes through in these parts have an air very different from London. The most considerable people I have seen have but just enough to live, and the ordinary people, I believe, are half starved. But they are all so good and so civil that I could not help wishing (if it were possible to separate the honest from the guilty) that they had the riches and liberties that our wise citizens and countrymen have thrown away, or at best put in great danger, and that they were punished as they ought to be by an arbitrary prince and war.'*

However interesting the scenery and the change of air, affairs at home rankled:

> *'When I was a great favourite, I was railed at and flattered from morning to night, neither of which was agreeable to me, and where there were but few women that would not have poisoned me for the happiness they thought I enjoyed, I kept the worst company of anybody upon earth.'*

During this time of exile, Marlbourgh kept a low profile, while Sarah fired off letters in all directions, unable to believe she couldn't change their situation by sheer will power. In Frankfurt she witnessed a march past (a formal march of troops past a saluting point) and wrote:

> *'To see so many brave men marching was a very fine sight, but it gave me melancholy reflections and made me weep: I was so much animated that I wished I had been a man that I might have ventured my life a thousand times in the glorious cause of liberty.'*

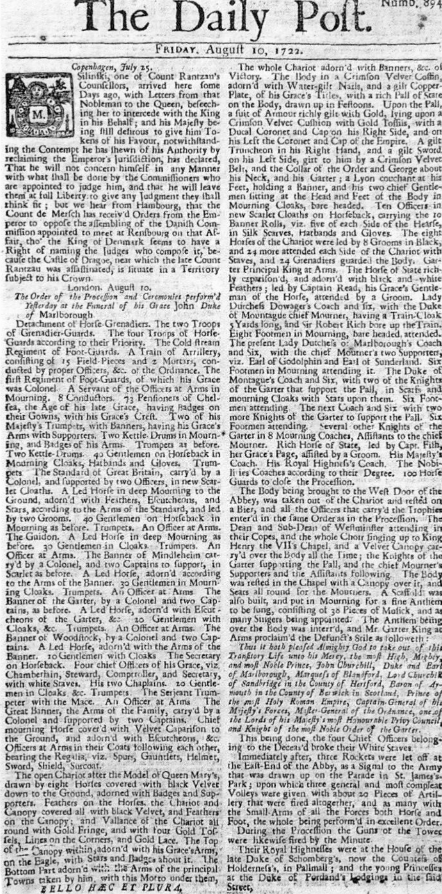

The Daily Poſt.

Numb. 894

FRIDAY, Auguſt 10, 1722.

Copenhagen, July 25.

M. Silinſki, one of Count Rantzau's Counſellors, arrived here ſome Days ago, with Letters from that Nobleman to the Queen, beſeeching her to intercede with the King in his Behalf; and his Majeſty being ſtill deſirous to give him Tokens of his Favour, notwithſtanding the Contempt he has ſhewn of his Authority by reclaiming the Emperor's Juriſdiction, has declared, That he will not concern himſelf in any Manner with what ſhall be done by the Commiſſioners who are appointed to judge him, and that he will leave them at full Liberty to give any Judgment they ſhall think fit; but we hear from Hambourg, that the Count de Merſch has receiv'd Orders from the Emperor to oppoſe the aſſembling of the Daniſh Commiſſion appointed to meet at Renſbourg on that Affair, tho' the King of Denmark ſeems to have a Right of naming the Judges who compoſe it, becauſe the Caſtle of Dragoe, near which the late Count Rantzau was aſſaſſinated, is ſituate in a Territory ſubject to his Crown.

London, Auguſt 10.

The Order of the Proceſſion and Ceremonies perform'd Yeſterday at the Funeral of his Grace John *Duke of* Marlborough.

Detachment of Horſe-Grenadiers. The two Troops of Grenadier-Guards. The four Troops of Horſe-Guards according to their Priority. The Cold ſtream Regiment of Foot-Guards. A Train of Artillery, conſiſting of 15 Field-Pieces and 2 Mortars, conducted by proper Officers, &c. of the Ordnance. The firſt Regiment of Foot-Guards, of which his Grace was Colonel. A Servant of the Officers at Arms in Mourning. 8 Conductors. 73 Penſioners of Chelſea, the Age of his late Grace, having Badges on their Gowns, with his Grace's Creſt. Two of his Majeſty's Trumpets, with Banners, having his Grace's Arms with Supporters. Two Kettle-Drums in Mourning, and Badges of his Arms. Trumpets as before. Two Kettle-Drums. 40 Gentlemen on Horſeback in Mourning Cloaks, Hatbands and Gloves. Trumpets. The Standard of Great Britain, carry'd by a Colonel, and ſupported by two Officers, in new Scarlet Cloaths. A Led Horſe in deep Mourning to the Ground, adorn'd with Feathers, Eſcutcheons, and Stars, according to the Arms of the Standard, and led by two Grooms. 40 Gentlemen on Horſeback in Mourning as before. Trumpets. An Officer at Arms. The Guidon. A Led Horſe in deep Mourning as before. 30 Gentlemen in Cloaks. Trumpets. An Officer at Arms. The Banner of Mindleheim carry'd by a Colonel, and two Captains to ſupport, in Scarlet as before. A Led Horſe, adorn'd according to the Arms of the Banner. 30 Gentlemen in Mourning Cloaks. Trumpets. An Officer at Arms. The Banner of the Garter, by a Colonel and two Captains, as before. A Led Horſe, adorn'd with Eſcutcheons of the Garter, &c. 20 Gentlemen with Cloaks, &c. Trumpets. An Officer at Arms. The Banner of Woodſtock, by a Colonel and two Captains. A Led Horſe, adorn'd with the Arms of the Banner. 20 Gentlemen with Cloaks. The Secretary on Horſeback. Four chief Officers of his Grace, viz. Chamberlain, Steward, Comptroller, and Secretary, with white Staves. His two Chaplains. 20 Gentlemen in Cloaks &c. Trumpets. The Serjeant Trumpeter with the Mace. An Officer at Arms. The Great Banner, the Arms of the Family, carry'd by a Colonel and ſupported by two Captains. Chief mourning Horſe cover'd with Velvet Capariſon to the Ground, and adorn'd with Eſcutcheons, &c. Officers at Arms in their Coats following each other, bearing the Regalia, viz. Spurs, Gauntlets, Helmet, Sword, Shield, Surcoat.

The open Chariot after the Model of Queen Mary's, drawn by eight Horſes covered with black Velvet down to the Ground, adorned with Badges and Supporters. Feathers on the Horſes, the Chariot and Canopy covered all with black Velvet, and Feathers on the Canopy; and Vallance of the Chariot all round with Gold Fringe, and with four Gold Toſſels, Lines on the Corners, and Gold Lace. The Top of the Canopy within, adorn'd with his Grace's Arms, on the Eagle, with Stars and Badges about it. The Bottom Part adorn'd with the Arms of the principal Towns taken by him, with this Motto under them, *BELLO HÆC ET PLURA.*

The whole Chariot adorn'd with Banners, &c. of Victory. The Body in a Crimſon Velvet Coffin, adorn'd with Water-gilt Nails, and a gilt Copper-Plate, of his Grace's Titles, with a rich Pall of State on the Body, drawn up in Feſtoons. Upon the Pall, a ſuit of Armour richly gilt with Gold, lying upon a Crimſon Velvet Cuſhion with Gold Toſſils, with a Ducal Coronet and Cap on his Right Side, and on his Left the Coronet and Cap of the Empire. A gilt Truncheon in his Right Hand, and a gilt Sword on his Left Side, girt to him by a Crimſon Velvet Belt, and the Collar of the Order and George about his Neck, and his Garter; a Lyon couchant at his Feet, holding a Banner, and his two chief Gentlemen ſitting at the Head and Feet of the Body in Mourning Cloaks, bare headed. Ten Officers in new Scarlet Cloaths on Horſeback, carrying the 10 Banner Rolls, viz. five of each Side of the Hearſe, in Silk Scarves, Hatbands and Gloves. The eight Horſes of the Chariot were led by 8 Grooms in Black, and 24 more attended each Side of the Chariot with Staves, and 24 Grenadiers guarded the Body. Garter Principal King at Arms. The Horſe of State richly capariſon'd, and adorn'd with black and white Feathers; led by Captain Read, his Grace's Gentleman of the Horſe, attended by a Groom. Lady Dutcheſs Dowager's Coach and ſix, with the Duke of Mountague chief Mourner, having a Train-Cloak 5 Yards long, and Sir Robert Rich bore up the Train. Eight Footmen in Mourning, bare headed, attended. The preſent Lady Dutcheſs of Marlborough's Coach and Six, with the chief Mourner's two Supporters, viz. Earl of Godolphin and Earl of Sunderland. Six Footmen in Mourning attending it. The Duke of Montague's Coach and Six, with two of the Knights of the Garter that ſupport the Pall, in Scarfs and mourning Cloaks with Stars upon them. Six Footmen attending. The next Coach and Six with two more Knights of the Garter to ſupport the Pall. Six Footmen attending. Several other Knights of the Garter in 8 Mourning Coaches, Aſſiſtants to the chief Mourner. Rich Horſe of State, led by Capt. Fiſh, her Grace's Page, aſſiſted by a Groom. His Majeſty's Coach. His Royal Highneſs's Coach. The Nobilities Coaches according to their Degree. 100 Horſe Guards to cloſe the Proceſſion.

The Body being brought to the Weſt Door of the Abbey, was taken out of the Chariot and reſted on a Bier, and all the Officers that carry'd the Trophies enter'd in the ſame Order as in the Proceſſion. The Dean and Sub-Dean of Weſtminſter attending in their Copes, and the whole Choir ſinging up to King Henry the VII's Chapel, and a Velvet Canopy carry'd over the Body all the Time; the Knights of the Garter ſupporting the Pall, and the chief Mourner's Supporters and the Aſſiſtants following. The Body was reſted in the Chapel with a Canopy over it, and Seats all round for the Mourners. A Scaffold was alſo built, and put in Mourning for a fine Anthem to be ſung, conſiſting of 30 Pieces of Muſick, and as many Singers being appointed. The Anthem being over the Body was interr'd, and Mr. Garter King at Arms proclaim'd the Defunct's Stile as followeth:

Thus it hath pleaſed Almighty God to take out of this Tranſitory Life unto his Mercy, the moſt High, Mighty, and moſt Noble Prince, John Churchill, Duke and Earl of Marlborough, Marqueſs of Blandford, Lord Churchill of Sandbridge in the County of Hertford, Baron of Aymouth in the County of Berwick in Scotland, Prince of the moſt Holy Roman Empire, Captain-General of his Majeſty's Forces, Maſter-General of the Ordnance, one of the Lords of his Majeſty's moſt Honourable Privy Council, and Knight of the moſt Noble Order of the Garter.

This being done, the four Chief Officers belonging to the Deceas'd broke their White Staves.

Immediately after, three Rockets were let off at the Eaſt-End of the Abby, as a Signal to the Army that was drawn up on the Parade in St. James's-Park; upon which three general and moſt compleat Volleys were given with about 20 Pieces of Artillery that were fired altogether, and as many with the Small-Arms of all the Forces both Horſe and Foot, the whole being perform'd in excellent Order.

During the Proceſſion the Guns of the Tower were likewiſe fired by the Minute.

Their Royal Highneſſes were at the Houſe of the late Duke of Schomberg's, now the Counteſs of Holderneſs's, in Pallmall; and the young Princeſſes at the Duke of Portland's Lodgings in the ſaid Street,

ABOVE: *A contemporary press cutting reporting the Duke's funeral in August 1722.*

To *'have been a man'*, in the days when men basically ruled the world, was a wish Sarah made more than once.

By this time, Queen Anne was bloated with gout and dying, her last days made a misery by the political wranglings of Tories and Whigs. Marlborough wound his way back home through Europe, strategically making overtures to both the Hanoverian court (in the event of the expected Protestant succession of the House of Hanover) and the exiled Catholic son of James II, just in case things swung the other way. He wisely kept his dealings a secret from Sarah, who could so easily have blown his cover. On their return to England, the Marlboroughs received a welcome more rapturous than in the days of the Duke's victories. When the Hanoverian Elector, George, arrived in England in the summer of 1714 to take up the English throne, Marlborough was the first to greet him. Although no longer fit for active duty, the Duke was reappointed to all his posts and reinstated at the King's right hand. King George greeted him (in French, as the new King spoke no English): *'My Lord Duke, I hope your troubles are now all over.'*

THE BEGINNING OF THE END

The strain of holding everything together was beginning to tell. Marlborough suffered a stroke in 1716 and never really recovered. His aim in life was for peace and quiet now to enjoy Sarah and Blenheim, the building of which had begun eleven long years ago. But a life of quiet retirement was not what Sarah had in mind. You couldn't keep her down. She continued to push and pull and stir things up with her daughters and her

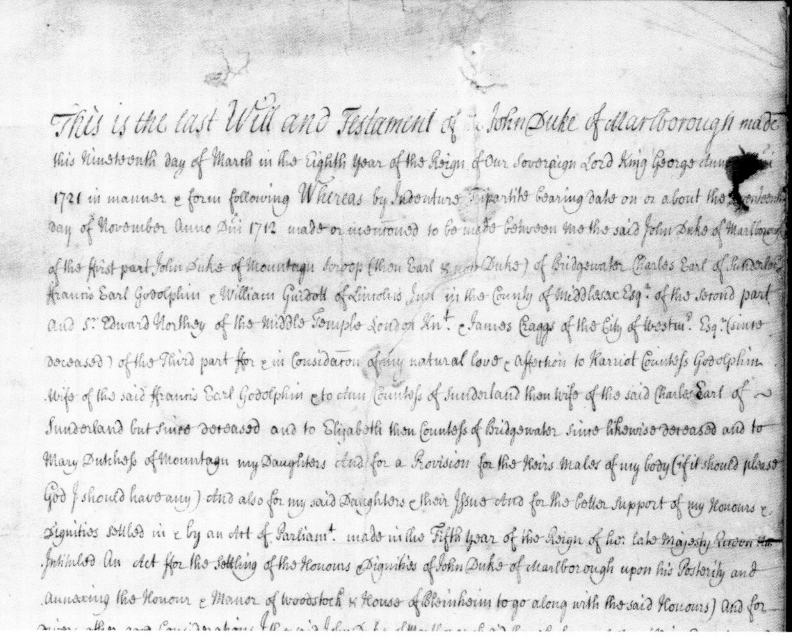

This is the last Will and Testament of [illegible] John Duke of Marlborough made this Nineteenth day of March in the Eighth Year of the Reign of Our Sovereign Lord King George Anno [illegible] 1721 in manner & form following Whereas by Indenture Tripartite bearing date on or about the [illegible] day of November Anno Dni 1712 made or mentioned to be made between me the said John Duke of Marlborough of the first part John Duke of Mountagu Scroop (then Earl & now Duke) of Bridgewater Charles Earl of Sunderland Francis Earl Godolphin & William Guidott of Lincolns Inn in the County of Middlesex Esqr. of the second part And Sr. Edward Northey of the Middle Temple London Knt. & James Craggs of the City of Westmr. Esqr. (since deceased) of the Third part for & in Consideraon of my natural love & affection to Harriot Countess Godolphin wife of the said Francis Earl Godolphin & to Ann Countess of Sunderland then wife of the said Charles Earl of Sunderland but since deceased and to Elizabeth then Countess of Bridgewater since likewise deceased and to Mary Dutchess of Mountagu my Daughters And for a Provision for the Heirs Males of my body (if it should please God I should have any) And also for my said Daughters & their Issue And for the better support of my Honours & Dignities settled in & by an Act of Parliamt. made in the Fifth year of her late Majesty Queen [illegible] Intituled An Act for the settling of the Honours & Dignities of John Duke of Marlborough upon his Posterity and annexing the Honour & Manor of Woodstock & House of Blenheim to go along with the said Honours) And for [illegible]

RIGHT: *The Duke's will is long and detailed, but his major concern was addressed in a paragraph underlined in his own hand, which reads: 'My intention being declared therein that the lands to be purchased should continue and remain to all issue of my body… to go along with my Honour and Dukedom of Marlborough.' In other words, he wanted to hand his estate, intact, down through the generations.*

This Day is publish'd,
BRITAIN'S HERO: A Poem on the Death of
His Grace, JOHN, Duke of MARLBOROUGH.
Marlborough's *Exploits appear divinely bright,*
And proudly shine in their own Native Light:
Rais'd of themselves, their Genuine Charms they boast,
And those who Paint 'em truest, Praise 'em most. Add. Camp.
Printed for H. Cole, at Rowe's Head without Temple-Bar, and Sold by J. Peele, at Locke's Head in Pater-Noster-Row. Price 6 d.

ABOVE: *This contemporary press cutting from the* Daily Post *laments the Duke's death with an elegy.*

sons-in-law, and she also made mischief at court. At first Sarah was the best of friends with Princess Caroline, the wife of the Prince of Wales (later George II). However, Caroline was well educated, well read and a match for Sarah's wit. Though initially enchanted by the lively, forthright Duchess, she certainly wasn't going to stand for being bullied or provoked by her. Sarah found herself wrong-footed and thereafter took every opportunity to mock the future Queen.

Marlborough rose above it all, never taking sides, as was his way. He spent his last years quietly occupied with the ongoing works at Blenheim. He was to spend only two summers there before he died in Sarah's arms at Windsor Lodge in 1722. In his will, Marlborough provided generously for his family, left trusts and settlements for the completion of Blenheim and expressed a wish to be buried *'in my chapel in Blenheim House'*.

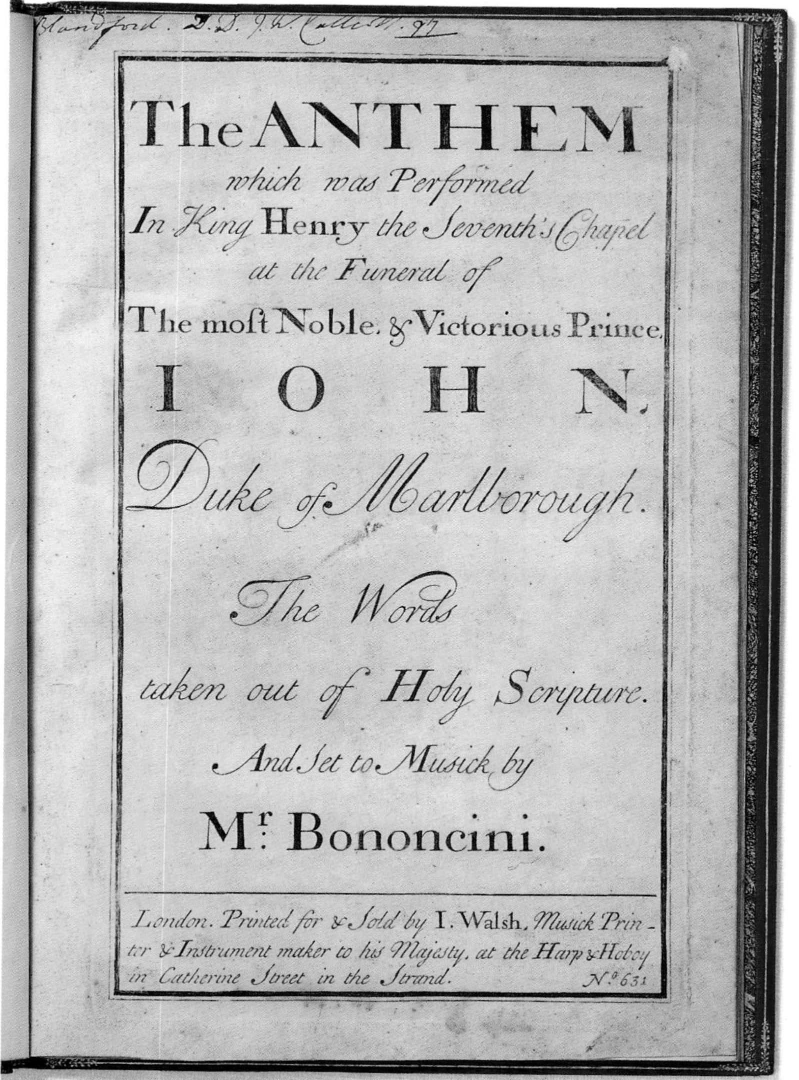

Blandford. D.D. J.W. Collett. 97

The ANTHEM
which was Performed
In King Henry the Seventh's Chapel
at the Funeral of
The most Noble, & Victorious Prince,
IOHN.
Duke of Marlborough.
The Words
taken out of Holy Scripture.
And set to Musick by
Mr. Bononcini.

London. Printed for & Sold by I. Walsh, Musick Printer & Instrument maker to his Majesty, at the Harp & Hoboy in Catherine Street in the Strand. No. 631

LEFT AND BELOW: *The frontispiece and cover of a memorial anthem composed for the funeral of John, Duke of Marlborough.*

CHAPTER THREE

Building Blenheim

The magnificent estate granted to the first Duke of Marlborough in 1705 by Queen Anne contained the crumbling remains of the royal manor of Woodstock, a royal residence that was in its heyday in the twelfth and thirteenth centuries. The first monarch to inhabit the manor was Henry I (King of England 1100–1135). In the grounds, Henry II (King of England 1154–89) built a romantic bower around a natural well for his mistress, Rosamond Clifford. Legend has it that his jealous wife, Queen Eleanor, found her way to this secret bower, stripped poor Rosamond naked, roasted her over a fire and then bled her to death in a hot bath. The truth is more prosaic—Rosamond died of natural causes in a convent—but Rosamond's Well, with its never-failing spring, survives as the oldest structure at Blenheim. The manor was embellished by succeeding monarchs, but eventually abandoned to nature and the gentle, marshy meanderings of the river Glyme.

Queen Anne was so close to both John and Sarah at the time of this gift, and so great was the national feeling of gratitude to Marlborough, that expectations ran high. Louis XIV had built Versailles to demonstrate France's self-confidence, and now Queen Anne and her commander-in-chief were set to commission something equally splendid. No one could have foreseen that the palace would be decades in the making and fraught with problems.

*In the great hall, the ceiling painted by Sir James Thornhill in 1716 shows the Duke presenting his plan for the battle of Blenheim. Found among the Blenheim papers is a letter of explanation of this ceiling: 'Britannia sitting on a globe giving the laurel to a HERO that is introduced by a bountiful GENIUS who presides over him... Underneath are figures piling up trophies of colours, drums, trumpets, etc, taken from the enemies of Britannia... At the end of the oval is Clio the Muse of HISTORY, writing in her book these words: "*Anno Memorabile *1704" being the year in which that glorious battle of Blenheim was fought.'*

A NEW BATTLEFIELD

Sarah was against the building of Blenheim from the beginning; it offended her frugal nature. But this proved to be a battle of wills with her husband, and one she was set to lose. Their current living arrangements suited Sarah well, including as they did her family home at Holywell, near St Albans, and a house in Windsor Park—where she was ideally positioned to continue exerting her influence over the Queen and the privy purse. Sarah was opposed to the choice of architect (she would have preferred Sir Christopher Wren) but was again overruled by the Duke, who picked John Vanbrugh, a fellow member of the Kit-Cat Club (a convivial haunt of prominent Whigs).

Sir John Vanbrugh

The architect of Blenheim, Sir John Vanbrugh (1664–1726), remains an enigma. Although he was a soldier and a successful playwright before becoming an architect, little is known about his private life. He left few clues: he was not a prolific draughtsman, and his plays revealed little about himself or his family life.

THE MAKINGS OF A RENAISSANCE MAN

During his army career Vanbrugh was accused of spying and imprisoned in the Bastille, where it is assumed he had the time to dream and to hone his creative ability as a writer. Before that, in 1681–82, he had been employed by a relative in the wine trade in London and he had also worked for the East India Company based at Surat, an important trading centre north of Bombay.

Portrait of the architect of Blenheim, Sir John Vanbrugh, attributed to Thomas Murray, circa 1718.

By 1698, his Restoration-style comedies *The Relapse* and *The Provok'd Wife* had been successful enough to make him eligible for membership of the Kit-Cat Club, the London political and literary club for Whig grandees. Here he was to meet his future architectural clients the Earl of Carlisle and the Duke of Marlborough. Undoubtedly, theatre work gave Vanbrugh a dramatic sense of the flamboyant. Despite having had no architectural training, he was self-assured, daring and high-spirited, with both vision and a flair for the heroic.

DEFYING THE PURISTS

Vanbrugh's career as an architect began in 1699 with the commission for Castle Howard in Yorkshire, built for the Earl of Carlisle. From the outset, Vanbrugh, who worked closely with Nicholas Hawksmoor (see pages 82–3), was determined to be individual in his style. Much to the disdain of the purists who backed the Palladian style, he chose to break with classical tradition in various ways. For example, he positioned his houses to allow the main rooms to benefit from sunlight. He also happily used different orders (styles of column) on different sides of a house. (Blenheim has Corinthian columns supporting the rising pediment at the entrance, and colonnades of Doric columns connecting the pavilions to the main building.)

Vanbrugh's work is described as baroque, but it is actually difficult to put a precise label on his style. His work shows some European baroque influence, probably gained during his time in France, but it was also often referred to as neo-medieval. He did tend to include eighteenth-century Gothic elements but never included true Gothic traits. Instead, he used his own expression of the medieval style, leaning more towards the romantic and childhood interpretations of castles and describing his work as having a 'castle air'. Surprisingly, his time in the Orient seems to have had no influence on his architecture.

Vanbrugh's design priorities were 'state, beauty and convenience', but convenience came a very poor third, and comfort wasn't even an issue. In fact, the concept of living comfortably is a relatively recent notion. It wouldn't be until much later that home-owners in Britain would take pleasure in combining beauty and comfort.

RESTING PLACES AND REPUTATIONS

At some point during his early career, Vanbrugh developed an interest in churches, and in cemeteries in particular. He wanted cemeteries to be landscaped gardens rather than morbid burial places, and although few of his designs were actually put into practice, they did prove his skills as a landscape architect. Indeed, his fascination with the subject led to his designing a mausoleum at Castle Howard and a vault at Blenheim, so that his illustrious clients could rest eternally in a place worthy of their status.

Although Vanbrugh was knighted in 1714, it was not until some time after his death that he began to be considered in a favourable light—during his lifetime his work was criticized for being heavy, clumsy and eccentric, as this contemporary description of Blenheim illustrates:

> *'Its beauties and absurdities are so blended, that while you are expatiating upon one, you are checked by the intervening ideas of the other... Who can admire the largeness and magnificence of the house and not deplore the absence of beauty and taste from this place?'*

> *Under this stone, Reader, survey*
> *Dead Sir John Vanbrugh's house of clay.*
> *Lie heavy on him, Earth! For he*
> *Laid many heavy loads on thee!*
>
> Epitaph on Sir John Vanbrugh's Grave by Abel Evans

Later architects and artists were to be more complimentary about Vanbrugh's distinctive architecture. The Adam brothers offered some understanding and praise for his works, and Sir John Soane praised his versatility. Artists such as Joshua Reynolds accepted that much of Vanbrugh's unique style and imagination must be put down to the fact that he was a *'poet as well as an architect'*.

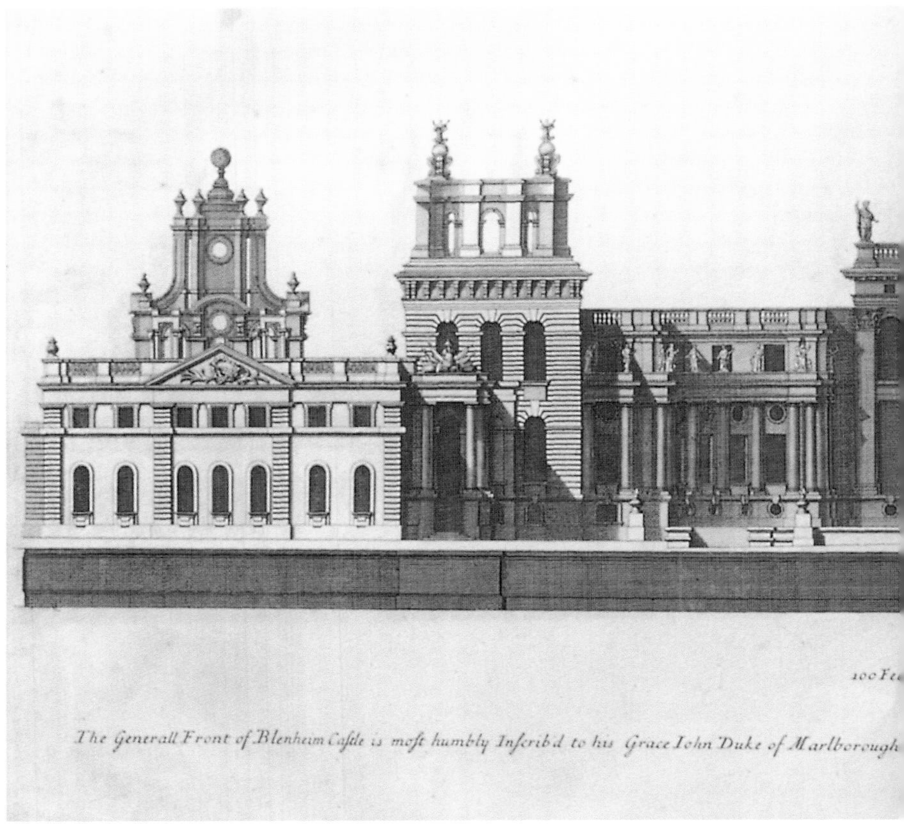

100 Fee
The Generall Front of Blenheim Castle is most humbly Inscrib'd to his Grace John Duke of Marlborough

ABOVE RIGHT: *Engraving showing Vanbrugh's design for the north front of Blenheim. The engraving, along with those shown overleaf, is from* Vitruvius Britannicus. *This design book, which contains many of Britain's great houses, was put together by Colen Campbell, a Scottish architect and publisher, and was published in the early eighteenth century. In its complete form, it comprises five volumes with 375 engraved plates.*

RIGHT: *The north front and great court of the palace in an early eighteenth-century engraving.*

Extends 490
the Holy Empire Capt Generall of all his Majesty's forces and Knight of the most Noble Order of the Garter &c.
Design'd by Sr John Vanbrugh Kt
ion General du Chateau de Blenheim

BELOW: *Engraving from* Vitruvius Britannicus *showing the east front of Blenheim Palace.*

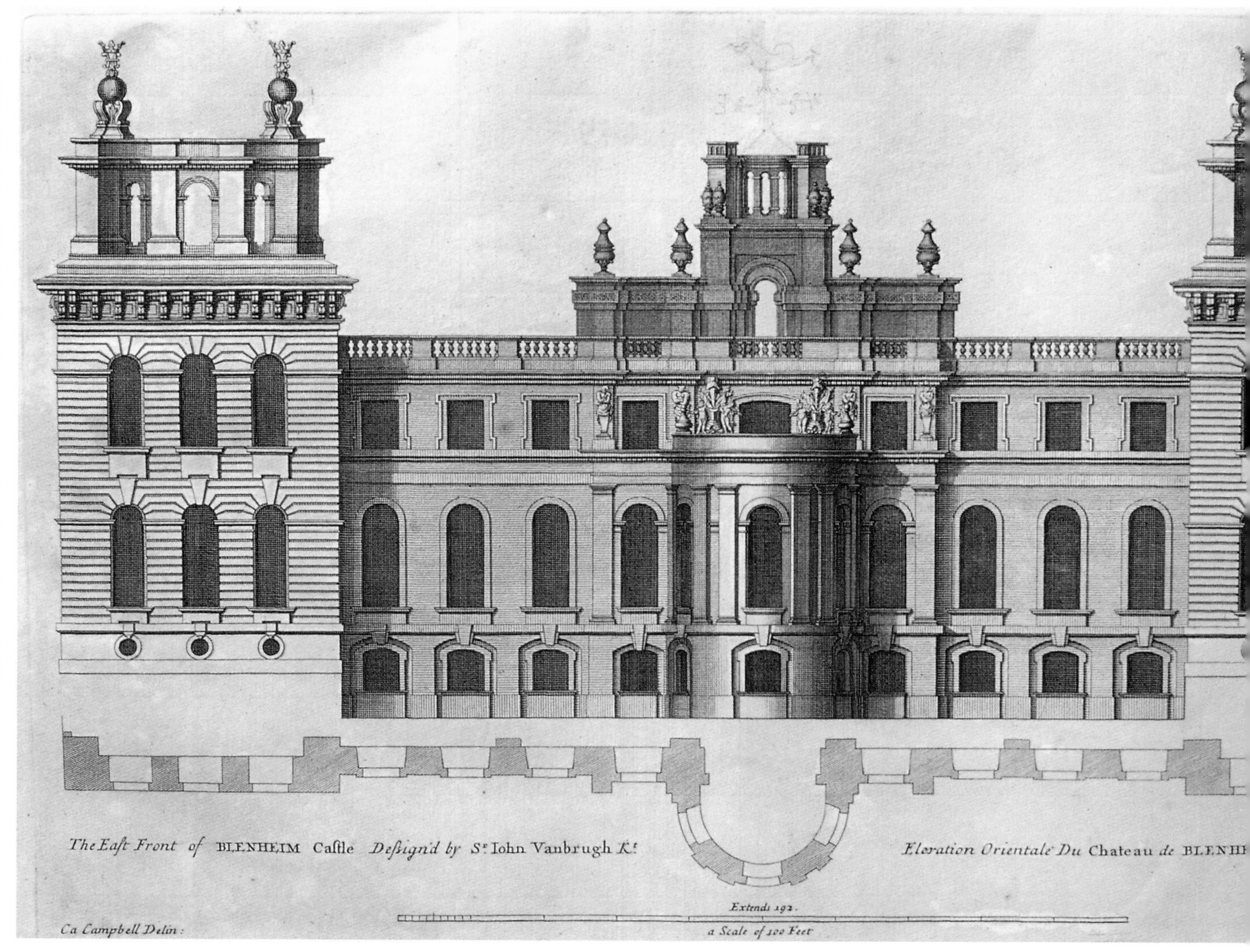

The East Front of BLENHEIM Castle Desiign'd by Sr Iohn Vanbrugh Kt
Elevation Orientale Du Chateau de BLENH
Extends 192.
Ca Campbell Delin:
a Scale of 100 Feet

RIGHT: *A painting of Vanbrugh's grand bridge over the river before the lake existed.*

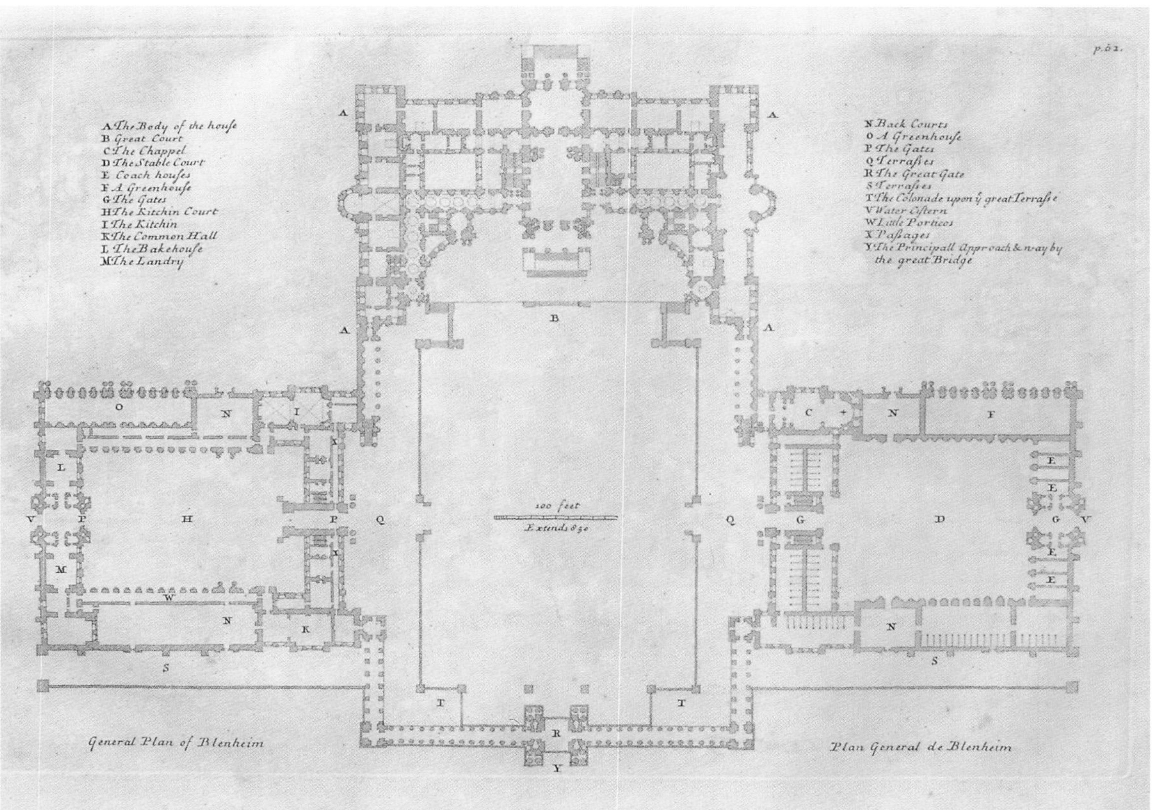

BELOW: *Engraving from* Vitruvius Britannicus *showing the layout of Blenheim's ground floor.*

OVERLEAF: *Vanbrugh's grand bridge as seen today, spanning the lake created by Capability Brown in the 1760s.*

The dish-vaulted ceiling in a 'room' inside the grand bridge.

A TESTAMENT TO GLORIOUS DEEDS

Vanbrugh and the Duke shared a vision of a habitation with *'something of a castle air'* about it. The palace, to be called Blenheim at the Queen's insistence, was to be not so much a home for the Churchill family as a grand testimonial to military glory—a national monument to the all-vanquishing Duke, his gracious monarch and his glorious armies.

It was not a vision shared by Sarah. She hated the whole idea of such a grandiose and uncomfortable home. She deplored *'all grandeur and architecture'*, and wrote of Vanbrugh in her characteristically forthright way: *'I never had spoken to him. But as soon as I knew him and saw the madness of the whole design, I opposed it all that was possible for me to do.'* And oppose she did. Sarah was never going to stand by and let Blenheim Palace happen. She was destined to interfere with just about every aspect of the design and construction.

Vanbrugh surveyed the site and made a bold, typically theatrical choice in siting the new, seven-acre palace on a raised plateau at the southern end of the park, with its main approach over a deep, marshy valley that Vanbrugh saw in his mind's eye as an ornamental lake crossed by *'the finest bridge in Europe'*. He had a model built for Queen Anne so that she could see exactly what was planned. Although no documents were drawn up relating to the ongoing financing of the building, clerks of works were appointed, Vanbrugh was made surveyor, and work began. Assisting Vanbrugh was the architect Nicholas Hawksmoor (see pages 82–3).

Vanbrugh's original plan for the grand bridge, which Sarah opposed because she found it too ostentatious.

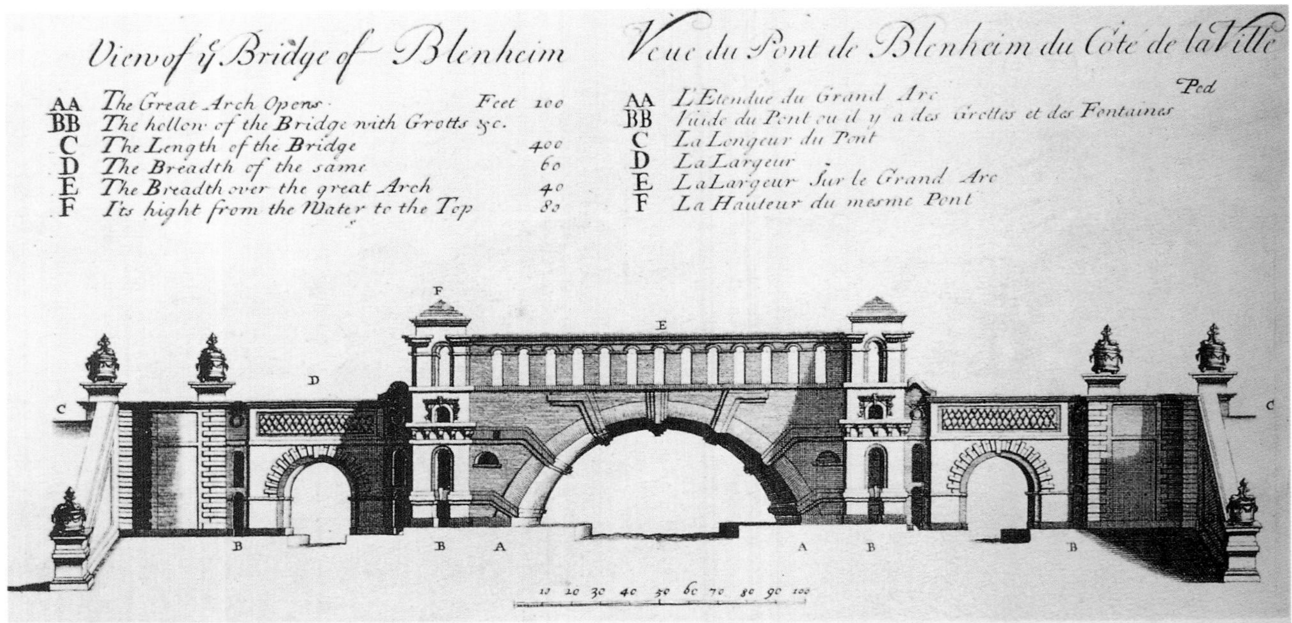

43. Grand Bridge: Vanbrugh's original elevation, showing the proposed towers and arcading. (*Vitruvius Britannicus*, Vol. I, 1717).

MORRIS DANCING AND CONFLICTING VISIONS

The foundation stone was laid on June 18, 1705, to the accompaniment, in the words of an eyewitness, of morris dancing, cake, claret *'for the gentry and the better sort'* and eight barrels of ale *'for the common people'*. The plans were for a proud and ambitious house, unique in Britain. John Churchill, still the man from uncertain beginnings among the minor gentry, wanted that house with a passion. No sooner had work started than he wanted it completed, and he wanted the gardens finished at the same time.

Vanbrugh, too, wanted everything to proceed together. By August 1705 there were some 1,500 workmen on site. *'The garden wall was set a-going the same day as the house,'* he reassured the Duke, promising that *'the whole gardens will be formed and planted in a year from their beginning.'* Vanbrugh's haste was in part to do with his strained relationship with Sarah. During the Duke's long absences abroad from 1705 to 1711, when he was negotiating vital treaties and alliances and heroically defeating the French in battles such as Tirlemont, Ramillies, Oudenarde, Malplaquet and Bouchain, Sarah was left to oversee the works.

Despite differences with the Duchess, Vanbrugh kept up correspondence with the Marlboroughs. The beginning of a letter from July 1709 shows the more practical aspects of building a palace: 'When my Lord Duke was at Blenheim last winter… I showed him a general plan of the whole building I proposed, in which appeared two back courts, one for the out offices necessary to the house, and the other to the stables.' The letter continues with plans for the servants' quarters and 'a large drying yard with space for fowl', all to be 'regular, decent, and clean'.
BL, Blenheim, 61353

In Marlborough's absence, Sarah found fault with everything. She was convinced all architects were mad and that they wanted to build only what pleased them. I can sympathize with Sarah's position. The site of the main house was nothing but mud and scaffolding. The local quarries were exhausted, which meant lengthy delays in transporting stone over considerable distances. There were winter frosts to contend with and severe troubles with the budget even at this early stage. On top of that, Vanbrugh was coming up with further grandiose schemes for a massive orangery, a vast bridge and any number of garden grottoes, temples and lakes. Vanbrugh wanted to build a conservatory in the stable court, but Sarah was scathing in her dismissal of a building to house *'foolish plants'*. Vanbrugh patiently explained that the building was needed for architectural balance and that it would become *'a room of pleasure'* with books, statuary and pictures. For both architect and client it was to be an uphill struggle.

At a time when she was losing her influence over Queen Anne, Sarah was getting letters in every post from Marlborough, craving information on the grand house that was or was not taking shape. A year after work started, he urged her to *'do all you can that the house at Woodstock may be carried up as much as possible that I might have the prospect of living in it'*. The next year he was asking:

> *'If possible, I should wish that you might… taste the fruit of every tree, so that what is not good might be changed. On this matter you must advise with Mr Wise [the garden designer], as also what plan may be proper for the ice-house: for that should be built this summer so that it might have time to dry.'*

Not surprisingly, it was all about to come unstuck.

'A large sum for a house'

Blenheim Palace was to be the nation's gift to the Duke, with an understanding (never recorded) that the nation would pay for it. Warrants appointing the architect and the controllers of works (responsible for payment for materials, craftsmen and workers) were drawn up in Marlborough's name, not the Crown's.

The Duke had in mind a house costing £40,000. When Sir Christopher Wren, surveyor-general of royal works, visited the site in July 1705, he estimated the cost at £100,000, excluding the park, service courts and northern approach over the bridge. As the work dragged on, beset by delays over finding suitable stone and compounded by Sarah's querying every decision, Vanbrugh's own estimates for finishing the work varied from £54,000 to £287,000. *'A large sum for a house, but a poor reward for the services that occasioned building it,'* he complained.

By 1710 the money supply had dried up and Sarah ordered a stop to all works until the Crown agreed to meet the costs. Crown money came in reluctant dribs and drabs and finally all commitment to the project was severed on June 1, 1712, Sarah and John having been dismissed from the Queen's service the previous year. Shortly afterwards, the Duke and Duchess found it expedient to go into self-imposed exile.

At this stage the Crown had paid out £240,000 and was still facing a pile of unpaid bills. Many of the workers were left destitute and starving. One worker successfully sued the Duke, and others were persuaded to take action against the

One of the lowest estimates created by Vanbrugh for submission to the Duchess, this meticulous account for 'finishing' Blenheim includes the lavish Portland carving required in the hall, as well as £500 to put locks, bolts and hinges on the palace doors and £147 and 10 shillings for paving the garden.
BL, Blenheim, 61354

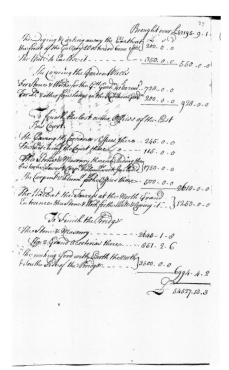

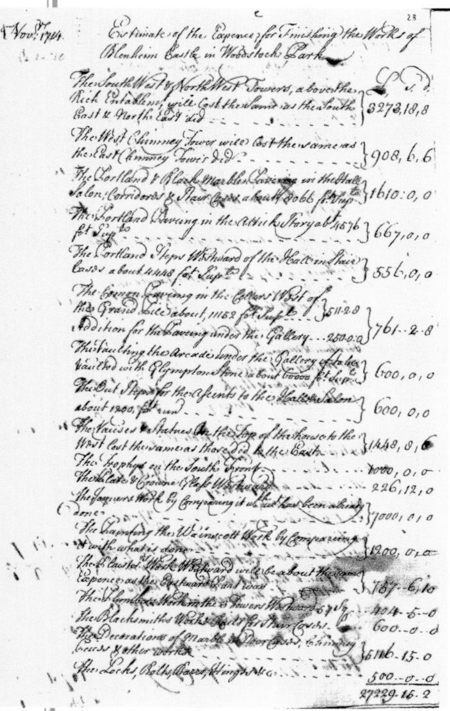

Estimate of the Expence for Finishing the Works of Blenheim Castle in Woodstock Park

The South West & North West Towers, above the Rich Entablem.t will Cost the same as the South East & North East did ... 3273,18,8

The West Chimney Tower will Cost the same as the East Chimney Tower did ... 908, 6, 6

The Portland & Black Marble Carving in the Hall, Salon, Corridores & Stair Cases [illegible] ... 1610:0,0

The Portland Carving in the Attick Story [illegible] ... 667,0,0

The Portland Steps [illegible] of the Hall [illegible] ... 556,0,0

[illegible] ... 761-2-8

[illegible] ... 600,0,0

[illegible] ... 600,0,0

[illegible] ... 1448,0,6

[illegible] ... 1000,0,0

[illegible] ... 226,12,0

[illegible] ... 1000,0,0

[illegible] ... 1000,0,0

[illegible] ... 787-6,10

The Blacksmiths Works [illegible] ... 404-5-0

[illegible] ... 600-0-0

The Decorations of Marble [illegible] ... 6116-15-0

The Locks, Bolts [illegible] ... 500-0-0

27229-16-2

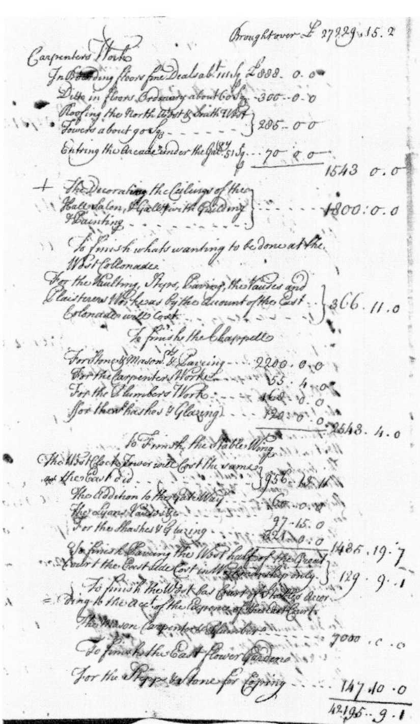

Brought over £ 27229.15.2

Carpenters Work

[illegible] ... 888. 0.0

[illegible] ... 300-0-0

[illegible] ... 285-0-0

[illegible] ... 70-0-0

1543 0.0

[illegible] ... 1800:0.0

To finish what's wanting to be done at the West Collonade [illegible] ... 366 11.0

To finish the Chappell [illegible] ... 2448. 4.0

To Finish the [illegible] ... 956 [illegible]

... 97-15.0

1486.19.7

... 129.9.1

... 7000.0.0

To finish the [illegible] Garden

For the [illegible] ... 147 10.0

4295.9.1

Crown. The magnificent gift from a grateful nation stood abandoned and unfinished, while bad feelings festered.

With the accession of the new King, George I, in 1714, the Marlboroughs were reinstated into royal favour, and work on the abandoned site recommenced in 1716. *'All [the rooms] without doors,'* complained Sarah, poking around the scaffolding, *'a chaos that turns one's brains to think of it and it will cost an immense sum to complete.'* The Crown was persuaded to pay one-third of the outstanding bills. However, leading craftsmen of the day, who were still owed large sums of money, were now told not to expect any back wages and to reduce their rates, so rather than lose face, they left their foremen to finish the jobs they had started. Grinling Gibbons completed only one of the four marble doorcases in the saloon. Vanbrugh himself finally walked off the job in a rage, never to return, worn down by Sarah's railings over costs and design.

'It was as a monument, not as a dwelling that he so earnestly desired it... As the Pharaohs built their pyramids, so he sought a physical monument which would certainly stand, if only as a ruin, for thousands of years. About his achievements Marlborough preserved a complete silence, offering neither explanations nor excuses for any of his deeds. His answer was to be this great house.'

Sir Winston Churchill

Marlborough spent £60,000 of his own money to complete his palace. After his death in 1722, Sarah turned her energies towards a new mission, extending the monument to her beloved John and spending a further £25,000. Many hundreds of thousands of pounds have been spent on it since.

BELOW: *Vanbrugh's note of Thornhill's decorating task measures Blenheim's beauty by the yard. The ceiling, ornaments and mouldings were each paid for at 25 shillings a yard, with extra pence for the odd foot or two.* BL, Blenheim, 61354

December 1716

To Mr James Thornhill

for Work done by him in Painting the Great Hall at Blenheim Castle in Woodstock Park for the Service of his Grace the Duke of Marlborough.

For 460 Yards 2 foot of the Historicall and Ornamental parts of the Ceiling, Mouldings and Covering at 25 shillings per yard £ 575.5.–

yds ft

For 321 : 4 more painted with Trophys and other ornaments, on the Peers between and under Windows there, above the Grand Cornice at 25s p Yd 402.15.0

978.–.–

The abovementioned work was measured and cast up by

Tilleman Bobart

John Desbrough

Allowed

The above mentioned price, of five and twenty shillings pr Yard, Figures & Ornaments, one with another is what the Duke of Marlborough directed me to agree with Mr Thornhill for.

J Vanbrugh

Feb: the 19th 1716/7

Hodges, I desire you to pay this bill to Mr Thornhill for paynting the Hall at Woodstock being nine hundred and seventy eight pounds & take an acquittance upon this paper in full

S: Marlborough

S: Marlborough

Feb: 19th 1716/7

Rec'd of his Grace the Duke of Marlborough the full contents of this Bill & all accounts by the hands of Mr Hodges [illegible]

James Thornhill

978–0–0

LEFT: *As work resumed, Sarah gave instructions to pay bills. This is her instruction to pay Sir James Thornhill £978 for painting the hall.*

BELOW LEFT: *His receipt for the bill, paid the same day, is still to be found in the palace accounts.* BL, Blenheim, 61354

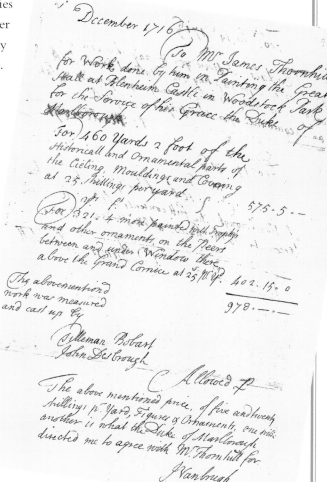

All the Building on this Plan Encompass'd with a black Line was brought up to it's heighth and Cover'd in before the work Stopp'd in 1710. And as much finishing as is now inscrib'd unless a very little ordinary Deal Wainscot in the Attick floor not worth mentioning.

Every thing was wanting but glazing and window-linings

p no Floor not

q Chimney piece.

nothing done but glazing.

nothing done but one Door Case. 'tis to be finish'd with Marble

y Painting & gilding no floor nor so much as Ceiled.

N the same as M.

no floor

finish'd all but Chimney piece

r.

t a Passage no paving

t not Pav'd

all but Chimney

water Closet not done.

C piece

x

all to do but u glazing.

Painting

z Upper windows and Paving to do

wants only Chimney pieces M And some additions.

f no Floors

k k k k no pavement.

e no Chimney Piece.

g g

16

no Chimney piece.

h no Chimney piece or floor.

this was pav'd so far.

Chimney d Piece wanting.

no Chimney c piece.

Chimney piece

a No floors wainscot

the great Stairs to ... also the other next the ...

10 20 30 40 50

10

*Commissioned by the first Duchess, this 1716 floorplan of the works not completed (*BL, Blenheim, 61355*) shows how sadly unfinished Blenheim was when building stopped. Even the roof was only part-built, as the top caption explains: 'All the building in this plan encompassed with a black line was brought up to its height and covered in before the work stopped in 1710.' Only the marked-off area of the palace (to the left of the plan) had protection from the elements. With each room assessed, the plan reveals that by 1716 the great hall (z) had 'upper windows and paving to do', while the saloon (y) fares worse: 'Nothing done but one doorcase. 'Tis to be finished with marble. Painting and gilding/no floor not so much as coiled.' The north corridor east (k) has 'no pavement', while quite a few of the rooms lacked chimney pieces. Many rooms, including the suite that functions as Blenheim's exhibition hall today, are simply labelled 'Nothing'. Upside-down at the base of the plan, a scrawled note adds: 'Three or four towers built in this house after the Queen stopped it in 1712, and then there was not one of the staircases finished in the whole house.'*

ABOVE: *Marlborough House, designed by Sir Christopher Wren for the Duchess of Marlborough and built while Blenheim was still under construction.*

NEW DEVELOPMENTS

In 1707 Vanbrugh had second thoughts and drastically altered the scale of the facades, raising the main block by a third in height and changing the whole south elevation from austere Doric to triumphant Corinthian. Queen Anne does not appear to have been informed of this change, but it must have been done with the Duke's approval. The change caused more delays and expense. Marlborough desperately wanted some part of the house to be habitable, and pressurized the architect to put the roof on and complete the east wing, but Vanbrugh was more occupied with his bridge, into which he put what seem to be rooms, though none of them could be called habitable. When Sarah came down to inspect the works, Vanbrugh rigged up a temporary ceiling and door in her bedroom in the palace, to give the impression that more had been done, but Sarah wasn't deceived.

Furious about the whole enterprise, she turned her attention to building a London town house. Her first stipulation was that Vanbrugh should have nothing to do with it. Instead, she chose Sir Christopher Wren as her architect, demanding

RIGHT: *The famous equestrian painting of Charles I by Van Dyck was one of many art treasures the Duke purchased and sent home while he was involved in military campaigns on the Continent.*

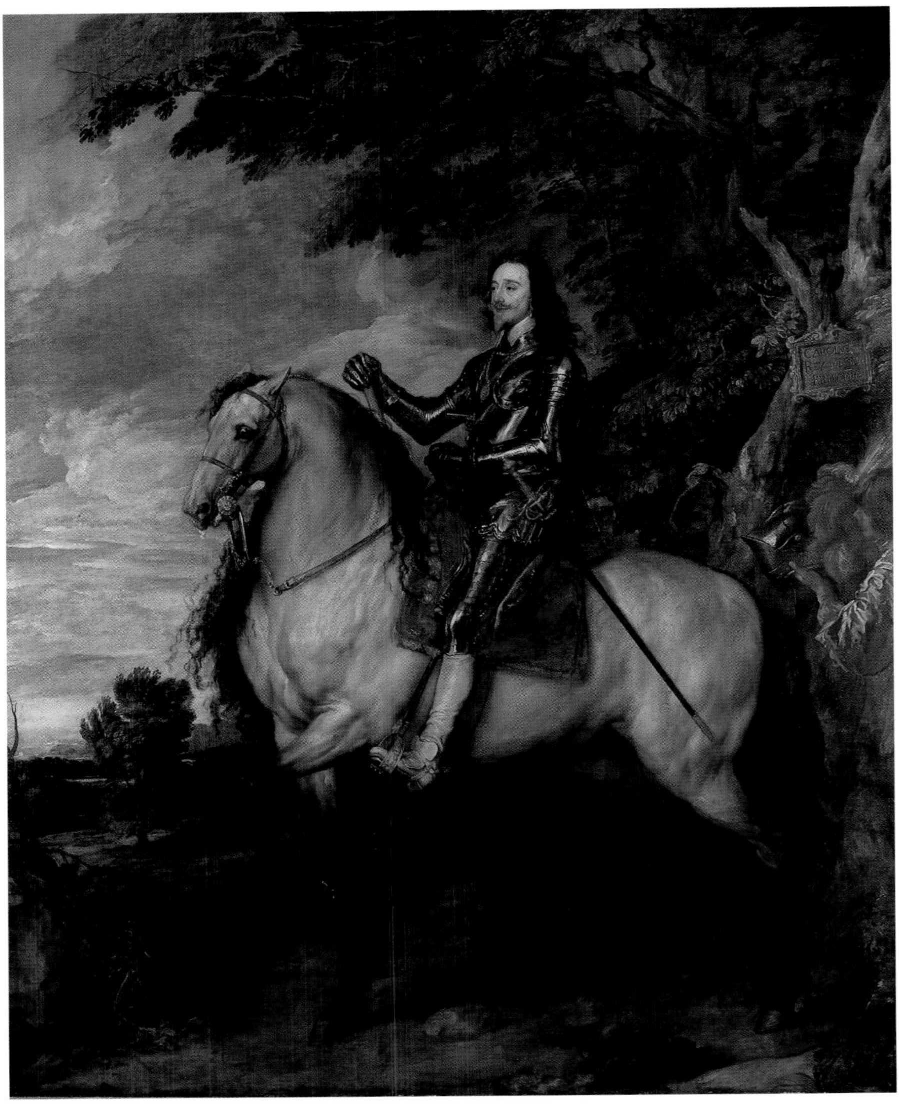

a *'strong, plain and convenient house'* that must *'not have the least resemblance of anything in that called Blenheim which I had never liked'*. Having poached the craftsmen for Marlborough House from Blenheim (thereby adding to the delays at the latter), Sarah proceeded to overspend her £30,000 budget by nearly a hundred per cent. She argued over every bill, sacked the elderly and bewildered Sir Christopher and finished Marlborough House herself in 1711, just at the time she and the Duke were sacked from the Queen's service and ousted from St James's Palace.

Bronze of the first Duke of Marlborough, on display in the third state room. Facing it in the same room is a very similar bronze of the Duke's old adversary, Louis XIV.

'I COULD WISH YOU HAD A PLACE FOR THEM'

Meanwhile, during his travels all over Europe, the Duke was collecting furnishings and art treasures for his roofless palace. He was offered a very fine set of hangings, but where could he put them? In a letter to Sarah, he said he was *'so fond of some pictures I shall bring with me that I could wish you had a place for them till the gallery at Woodstock be finished'*. Marlborough didn't baulk at spending money to beautify his palace. He bought Van Dyck's equestrian portrait of Charles I and commissioned six sets of Flemish tapestries, including the Victory series (see pages 50–53 and 78–81) depicting scenes from his battles. He bought gems and silver and silks and could not resist an immense, 30-ton marble bust of his old opponent Louis XIV, the creator of Versailles. Placed on the roof of the south front, the bust to this day looks out on a landscape created to honour the Duke of Marlborough.

A CHANGE OF GOVERNMENT

In 1710 the Tories came to power and the Crown stopped paying for Blenheim. The Marlboroughs could not admit financial responsibility, or they might have been held accountable for all the past debts. Sarah ordered work to be stopped, the unpaid workmen threatened to riot and tempers rose all round. *'I think she has given orders she'll repent of,'* wrote Vanbrugh petulantly, *'but be it as she thinks fit. If she orders the house to be pulled down, I desire you'll comply with her.'*

Sarah weighed in with an I-told-you-so:

> *'Every friend of mind knows that I was always against building at such an expense… I always thought it too great a sum even for the Queen to pay… I never liked any building so much for the show and vanity of it as for its usefulness and convenience and therefore I was always against the whole design of Blenheim as too big and unwieldy.'*

Allowing the partially completed palace to fall into ruin would have been a waste of the nation's money, and so a sum was granted to cover the house to protect it from damage until such time as a solution could be found. By 1711, when the Marlboroughs went into exile, the house, though unfinished, was safe. Vanbrugh moved into the restored Woodstock Manor and, free from Sarah's interference, lived in some comfort, tinkering with Blenheim's exterior and outbuildings.

The furnishings and works of art

A memorial bronze in the state apartments.

Marlborough fought his way across Europe securing political deals and military victories but always with an eye out for artworks, furniture and fabrics to keep his dream of Blenheim alive. *'I expect every day to hear of three looking-glasses I have bought in Paris,'* he writes to Sarah from a distant battlefield. And then: *'I desire you will let me know what use you can make of this velvet… only one hundred and nineteen pounds.'* While on diplomatic and military missions, he ordered crimson damask bed-hangings edged in gold thread and acquired collections of medals, coins and bronzes. He bought French and Italian gilded furniture—English furniture was considered second-rate—and shipped back elaborate gifts from grateful princes along with paintings by Rubens, Raphael, Titian and Van Dyck. He commissioned portraits of his own family, by Closterman and others, in the grand manner.

Fortunately the first Duke and all his successors commissioned family portraits, and so we still have good records of each one at various stages of their lives. What struck me as a child, and still does today, is how strong the family resemblance is. Certain features like the eyes are very distinctive and I can the see the similarities between my father and the first Duke, and even myself and the second Duchess, Henrietta (see pages 96–7).

While much of the architecture at Blenheim remains as Vanbrugh and Hawksmoor designed and built it, the furniture and room layouts have changed with the times. The furniture is not laid out as it would have been, but you can still get a sense of the amount of thought and expense that went into commissioning each unique piece. As a designer, I find it fascinating to look back at some of the old photographs and study the different layouts. For example, in photos in which the saloon was furnished as a living room, the sofas and chairs look quite lost and out of proportion against the great height of the ceiling, and would be completely inappropriate for today's lifestyle.

A lot of the rooms, especially those on the public side, have not been redecorated for many years. However, this is just as well, because not only would the cost be exorbitant but, in my view, some signs of wear and tear add a sense of real life to a house.

An Account of the Furniture belonging to the Executors of the late Duke of Marlborough at Blenheim Hous in 1740

A List of the Tapestry Hangings that are at Blenheim.
In the Dutchess of Marlborough's Bed Chamber a very fine Suit, I don't know the Story
In the Bow Window Room Tapestry Hangings of Alexanders Battles
In the Dukes Dressing Room a Suit of Alexanders Battles
In the Dukes Bed Chamber Tapestry Hangings Alexanders Battles
In the Grand Bed Chamber Tapestry Hangings of Battles
In the Great Room beyond that, Tapestry Hangings of Battles —
In the Appartment next the Salon West two very fine Suits of Tapestry Hangings of Battles and Seiges.
Eight Suits of the fine Hangings on that Floor all as fresh as New.

A List of the Pictures.
In the long Closet.
A Madonna of Raphael very fine which Cost Six hundred Pistoles
One of the same Size over the Chimney very fine
Lesser Pictures of different Sizes One hundred and twenty Six all of Great Masters and Gold Frames. There is a Printed Book which tells who are the Masters that Painted all these Pictures.
In the Dutchess of Marlboroughs Bed Chamber over the Doors two Madonnas one of Reubens and the other of Van Dyke over the Chimney the Duke of Marlboroughs Picture at length done by Sr Godfrey Kneller. I am in some doubt whether I did pay for that myself.
In the Room just before that Bed Chamber.
A Madonna over the Chimney with our Saviour and Joseph — done by Rubens
Pictures in the Bow Window Room.
Over the Chimney and three Doors four, two of them Rubens one the Woman taken in Adultry the other a Lady in a Ruff
In the Duke of Marlboroughs Dressing Room.
One of Rubens of the Holy Family Lord Strafford with his Secretary & two Ladys both Vandykes

LEFT: *'An account of the furniture belonging to the executors of the late Duke of Marlborough at Blenheim House in 1740.' Sarah's inventory of the household contents offers contrasts that epitomize the upper-class way of life. As the account progresses, a Raphael Madonna she lists as 'very fine' shares the records with 'eleven round towels'.* BL, Blenheim, 61473

OPPOSITE: *Raphael's* Ansidei Madonna, *pictured here, could be the Raphael Madonna that Sarah was referring to in her inventory. It was later sold by the eighth Duke.*

SALVE MATER CHRISTI

Tapestries at Blenheim

Among the best of the art treasures at the palace today, Blenheim's tapestry collection was commissioned by John, first Duke of Marlborough, who ordered at least six sets of hangings from the studios of master-weavers in Brussels and around Flanders. They are known as the Art of War set, the Alexander set, the Teniers Peasants set, the Pleasures of the Gods set, the Virtues set and the Victories set.

While many of the tapestries are still on show at Blenheim today, the Victories tapestries, featured here, are the most prized. Along with the Virtues set, the Victories tapestries were specially designed for John Churchill to commemorate his best-known achievements in battle during the War of the Spanish Succession. The set consists of eleven panels, which depict and are named after Allied 'steps forward' in the war: Blenheim, Ramillies (now missing, its fate unknown), Oudenarde, Bouchain (three panels), Donauworth, Lille, Wynendael, Malplaquet and Lines of Brabant.

The most important Victories tapestry commemorates the great battle of Blenheim (see pages 50–53). With the Ramillies tapestry now missing, the Oudenarde panel is the next most important. Malplaquet is also valued; although it was considered a great victory, the Alliance suffered huge losses of 24,000 men, both sides claimed victory and Marlborough's star waned after this battle.

BELOW: *The Oudenarde tapestry from the Victory set.* OPPOSITE: *The Malplaquet tapestry, also from the Victory set at Blenheim.*

MONTES HANNONIÆ

THE VICTORIES TAPESTRIES

The Bouchain III tapestry panel from the Victories set. Mistakes were inevitably made when the tapestries were woven; for example, the galloping dog pictured below has horse's hooves.

The unique 'Victories' series was commissioned by the Duke of Marlborough in the winter of 1708–09. The designs were created in the de Hondt studio, a Flemish father-and-son team. To catch the details and flavour of the battlefield, the designers were sent portraits of the generals, maps of the battlefield and eyewitness reports. Based on these, they produced a life-sized oil painting, known as a cartoon, for the weavers to work from.

The cartoon went to the workshop of Judocus de Vos and his team of weavers in Brussels, which was one of the centres of Europe's tapestry trade. The cartoon

was sliced into sections and used as a guide by the weavers, who would lay a section under their loom and painstakingly recreate each brushstroke in wool and silk. Master weavers, or 'faceworkers', created the faces, hands and bodies of the most important soldiers. Also using the finest thread, other skilled weavers filled in realistic-looking trees and villages, while others were allotted sky and clouds. Not surprisingly, the large panels in this series took about eight months each to weave.

Seen in their true home at Blenheim, the Victories not only celebrate the Duke's military prowess, but have stayed with us through the centuries to illuminate the craftsmanship and detail for which the tapestries are famed.

Nicholas Hawksmoor

With his thorough professional training under Sir Christopher Wren, Nicholas Hawksmoor (1661–1736) was the perfect collaborator for Vanbrugh, the brilliant amateur. Hawksmoor was closely involved in the building of Blenheim right from the planning stage. Although he made important contributions to most aspects of the design and construction, including details like cornices, doorcases and ceilings, he was responsible in particular for the decoration of the gallery (now the long library) and for the Woodstock gate.

Bust of Nicholas Hawksmoor, after a bust attributed to the sculptor Sir Henry Cheere.

ALWAYS THE BRIDESMAID

Having been an assistant to both Wren and Vanbrugh (working with the latter at Castle Howard in Yorkshire), Hawksmoor was well placed to be recognized in his own right. More often than not, however, he was known as a talented assistant, and so was unable to create his own architectural identity. It is not until you delve into his portfolio that you can understand his unique skills.

Hawksmoor's first job under Wren was in 1683 for Winchester Palace, which was followed by work in London at Whitehall, the Chelsea Hospital and Kensington Palace. During the 1690s he started work again under Wren on rebuilding many of the City of London churches including St Paul's. But it was to be no easy ride. As the new Palladians, influenced by neo-classical architect Palladio's work, became ensconced in the architectural establishment, he found it increasingly difficult to get his designs taken seriously.

A QUIRKY INDIVIDUALISM

Like Vanbrugh, Hawksmoor was an enigma, his style falling between two very different periods of architecture: rather emotional English baroque and cool, calm Palladianism. Although he is labelled an English baroque architect, there is no question that his work was at times unpredictable and unique. He was certainly influenced by the works of Inigo Jones and Palladio and by his own researches into classical architecture, but he refused to use them conventionally. He would add his own quirky interpretations, which is most noticeable in his church steeples.

A learned man and a capable mathematician and geometrician, Hawksmoor built up a vast library covering subjects ranging from botany, medicine and law to science and engineering. It was owing to his skills in engineering that many of the complex designs initiated by Wren and Vanbrugh actually were built and remained standing.

Hawksmoor's conventional side and his mastery of the vocabulary of classical architecture are revealed in his residential projects. His understanding of space and room layouts was superb, and his eye for detail allowed him to incorporate the latest trends in design. However, the only country house for which he was the sole architect was Easton Neston in Northamptonshire.

PRESTIGIOUS COMMISSIONS

Later in his life, Hawksmoor's time and skills were largely focused on his highly original designs for six new London churches and his work for the universities of Cambridge and Oxford. However, only a few of his many first-class designs for expanding and rebuilding colleges were executed, most of them having been considered too grand for a mere college. His best-known university commissions were the north quadrangle of All Souls College and the Clarendon building, both at Oxford.

Hawksmoor's last and most prestigious work is to be found at Westminster Abbey, where he designed the west towers, new stalls in Henry VII's chapel, and the choir screen. When he died in 1736, Hawksmoor left a great legacy of works which today are valued by all who see them. We are fortunate to have many fine examples of his work at Blenheim.

BELOW LEFT: *The original drawing, possibly by Hawksmoor, for a sundial.* BELOW: *Another sketch believed to be by Hawksmoor. I found both this sketch and the one on the left in the muniments room while researching this book.*

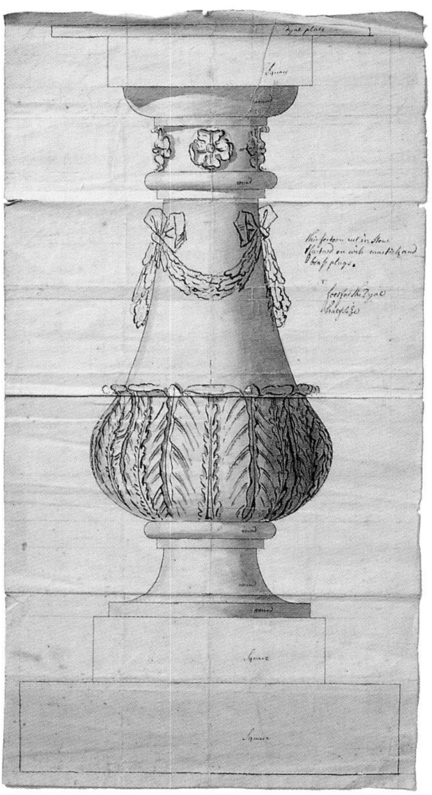

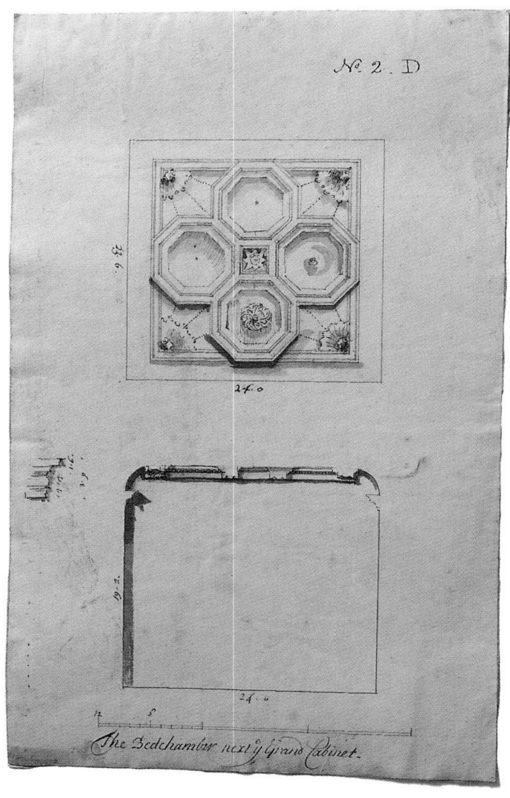

Grinling Gibbons

ABOVE: *Grinling Gibbons, the master craftsman who was responsible for most of the stone carving at Blenheim between 1705 and 1712.*

BELOW: *One of Gibbons's stone sculptures at Blenheim, depicting the British lion savaging the cockerel of France.*

When Sir John Vanbrugh was commissioned to be Blenheim's architect, he wanted to use none but the finest craftsmen of the day. This, of course, was to include Grinling Gibbons (1648–1721), the leading English baroque sculptor and woodcarver. At the time, Gibbons was busy working on the royal palaces, but somehow Vanbrugh and Nicholas Hawksmoor contrived to bring his unbeatable skills to Blenheim.

Born in Rotterdam, where his English parents were living, Gibbons had come to England in 1667 and worked in York with the carpenter John Etty. After a few years he went to London and continued in the carpentry business, working as a ship carver, and it was here that his talents were first recognized. He was appointed to the position of master carver in wood to the Crown by Charles II, remaining in it until the reign of George I. During this time he carried out works at Windsor Castle as well as Kensington Palace and Hampton Court Palace.

Gibbons was renowned for his delicate and naturalistic carved panels and garlands in limewood or oak, which were used to enrich cornices, architraves, pediments, overmantels and picture frames. However, he worked at least as much in marble, stone and bronze, and at Hampton Court Palace he was responsible for stone carvings on the exterior. This is probably what led to his working closely with Sir Christopher Wren on St Paul's Cathedral and Trinity College, Cambridge.

Some of Gibbons's finest work was executed at Petworth House, where his woodcarvings are used to enrich fixed picture frames with a ducal coronet above each and encasing Kneller portraits, between which are elaborate garlands of fruits, birds, musical instruments and foliage.

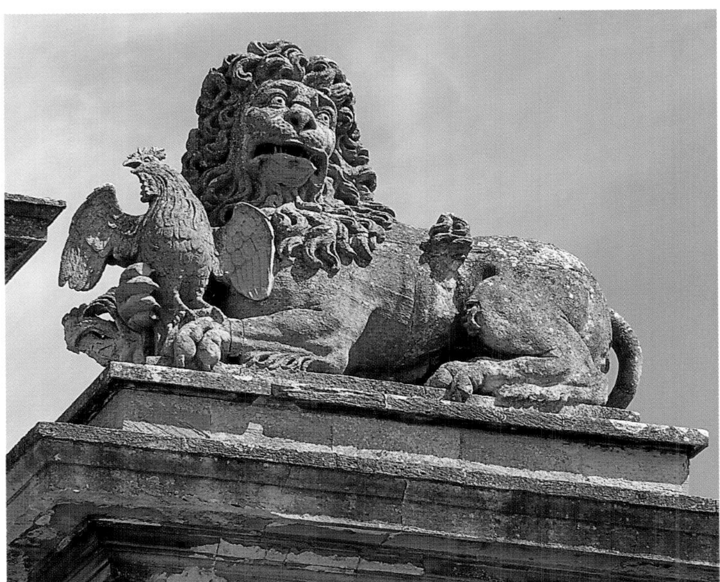

NOTHING BUT THE FINEST

At Blenheim, where Gibbons worked until 1712, he was responsible for most of the stone carving and more than twenty statues. On the exterior, Gibbons, with the help of apprentices, carried out some of his finest stone carvings. These start at the main gates of Hensington, where his '*basins of flower piers*', originally in the first Duchess's flower garden, now form an impressive entrance. Particularly fine and intriguing are his carvings of four British lions, each savaging a French cockerel. Overlooking the great court, they were commissioned by the first Duke to represent his victory over the French. Above the east and chapel colonnades sit the Duke's trophies—complete with stone cannons and cannonballs, drums, armour, standards and pikes. On the top of the four square towers sit four carved finials, each depicting a fleur-de-lys being crushed by a ducal coronet. Here, too, the symbolism is obvious.

Inside the house, Gibbons's work continues in the great hall, where he carved the Corinthian columns and deep cornice as well as Queen Anne's coat of arms, which sits proudly as a keystone over the main arch spanning the minstrels' gallery. In the saloon, Gibbons designed the statuesque arched doorcases in marble; he was able to complete the carving of only one of these before work was halted. The other three were executed later to his design.

Other, more modest interior carvings include the fine carved wood Corinthian columns in the bow window room, now used as the family dining room. He carved the marble fire surround there, and also the one in the Duke and Duchess's bedroom next door.

Records state that Gibbons was paid just over £4,000 for his entire works in stone, marble and wood, but as there is little evidence of any drawings for his commissions, history does not relate how many of the works were his own designs and how many were influenced by Vanbrugh and Hawksmoor.

Another stone lion by Gibbons sits atop the clock tower.

Henry Wise

The veteran landscape gardener responsible for the design and planning of the original gardens at Blenheim was Henry Wise (1653–1738). Royal Gardener to both Queen Anne and King George I, Wise designed in the elaborate formal style made fashionable by the French garden designer Le Nôtre at Versailles. So that the Blenheim gardens would be finished at the same time as the palace, Wise began laying these out as soon as the construction of the building was begun.

Born in Oxfordshire, Wise started his horticulture career under George London and in 1688 became his partner in the Brompton Park nurseries in London. He became deputy ranger of Hyde Park and superintendent of the royal gardens at Hampton Court and at Kensington Gardens following the accession of William III. In the 1690s he and London designed and planted the maze at Hampton Court. After Queen Anne had succeeded to the throne in 1702, he continued to be employed by the royal household. He had the task of replanting the Windsor Castle gardens after a storm in 1703.

He was employed at Blenheim along with Charles Bridgeman and Stephen Switzer, and it was Wise who created a canal from the river Glyme beneath Vanbrugh's grand bridge, before Capability Brown devised the lake. Wise's great parterre and military garden were also altered by Brown, but his walled kitchen garden, where he was able to use his expertise as a fruit gardener, survived the changes.

As well as landscaping Blenheim and the royal palaces, Wise designed gardens for the Chelsea Hospital in London, and elsewhere in the country at Longleat, Chatsworth, Melbourne Hall and Castle Howard.

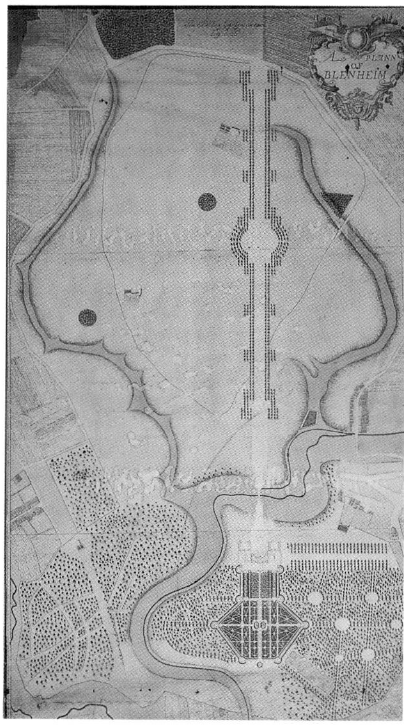

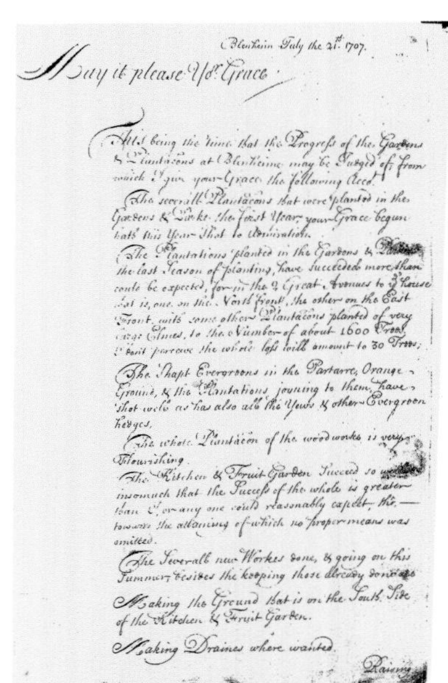

Blenheim July the 21st 1707.

May it please Yr. Grace

This being the time that the Progress of the Gardens & Plantacons at Blenheime may be Judged of; from which I give your Grace the following Acct.

The severall Plantacons that were planted in the Gardens & Parke the first Year your Grace begun hath this Year Shot to Admiration.

The Plantations planted in the Gardens & [illegible] the last Season of planting, have succeeded more than could be expected, for in the 2 Great Avenues to ye House that is, one on the North front, the other on the East Front, with some other Plantacons planted of very large Elmes, to the Number of about 1600 Trees, I dont perceive the whole loss will amount to 30 Trees;

The Shapt Evergreens in the Partarre, Orange Ground, & the Plantations joyning to them, have shot well as has also all the Yews & other Evergreen hedges.

The whole Plantacon of the woodworks is very flourishing.

The Kitchen & Fruit Garden Succeed so well insomuch that the Success of the whole is greater than I or any one could reasonably expect, the towards the attaining of which no proper means was omitted.

The Severall new Workes done, & going on this Summer besides the keeping those already done are

Making the Ground that is on the South Side of the Kitchen & Fruit Garden.

Making Draines where wanted.

Raising

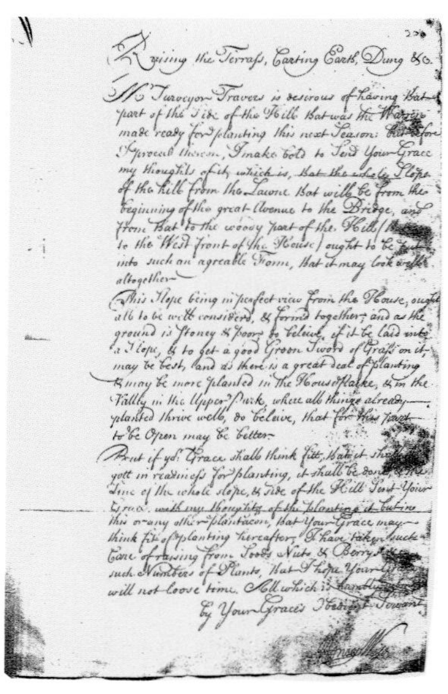

Raising the Terrass, Carting Earth, Dung &c.

Mr Surveyor Travers is desirous of having that part of the Side of the Hill that was the Warren made ready for planting this next Season: but before I proceed thereon, I make bold to Send Your Grace my thoughts of it, which is, that the whole Slope of the hill from the Lawne that will be from the beginning of the great Avenue to the Bridge, and from that to the woody part of the Hill ([illegible] to the West front of the House) ought to be put into such an agreable Form, that it may look well altogether

This Slope being in perfect view from the House, ought all to be well considerd, & formd together; and as the ground is Stoney & poor I do beleive, if it be laid into a Slope, & to get a good Green Sword of Grass on it, may be best, and as there is a great deal of planting & may be more planted in the House Parke, & in the Vally in the Upper Park, where all things already planted thrive well, do beleive, that for this part to be Open may be better

But if yr. Grace shall think fitt, that it should be gott in readiness for planting, it shall be done, & the Line of the whole slope, & side of the Hill Sent Your Grace with my thoughts of the planting it but in this or any other plantacon, that Your Grace may think fit of planting hereafter, I have taken such Care of raising from Seeds Nuts & Berry [illegible] such Numbers of Plants, that I hope Your Grace will not loose time. All which is humbly [illegible]

by Your Grace's Obedient Servant

[illegible]

TOP: *Portrait of Henry Wise by Godfrey Kneller.*

ABOVE: *Detail of a plan by Wise showing his ideas for the north side of the park.*

RIGHT: *Written to the Duke in July 1707, Wise's cheerful account of the progress of the gardens in summer reports that several plantations have 'shot to admiration'. Wise estimates that 1,600 trees were by then established and thriving in the palace's grand north and east avenues.*

BL, Blenheim, 61353

OPPOSITE: *The north front of the palace today.*

BUSINESS AS USUAL

After the Marlboroughs' reinstatement under George I, the Duke's first priority was to negotiate more Crown money for Blenheim and to persuade the King to grant Vanbrugh a knighthood, in hopes of healing old wounds and speeding up the building works. Vanbrugh felt confident enough of his position with the Duke to tease Sarah about her *bête noire*, the bridge:

> *'Even that frightful bridge will at last be kindlier looked upon... and I will venture my whole prophetic skill that... I shall have the satisfaction to see your Grace fonder of it than of any part whatsoever of the house, garden or park.'*

Vanbrugh's confidence was short-lived. The Duke had his first stroke in 1716 and Sarah took charge completely. If she'd been holding back about her opinion of Vanbrugh for the sake of the Duke, now she let rip, drawing up a thirty-page list of grievances. Vanbrugh, weary of the battle, replied with dignity:

> *'These papers, Madam, are so full of far-fetched laboured accusations, mistaken facts, wrong inferences, groundless jealousies and strained constructions that I should put a very great affront upon your understanding if I supposed it possible you could mean anything in earnest by them, but to put a stop to my troubling you any more. You have your end, Madam, for I will never trouble you more.'*

UPON THE DUKE OF MARLBOROUGH'S HOUSE AT WOODSTOCK

See, sir, here's the grand approach,
This way is for his Grace's coach:
There lies the bridge, and here's the clock,
Observe the lion and the cock,
The spacious court, the colonnade,
And mark how wide the hall is made!
The chimneys are so well design'd,
They never smoke in any wind.
This gallery's contrived for walking,
The windows to retire and talk in;
The council chamber for debate,
And all the rest are rooms of state.
'Thanks, sir,' cried I, ''tis very fine,
But where d'ye sleep, or where d'ye dine?
I find, by all you have been telling,
That 'tis a house, but not a dwelling.'

ABEL EVANS (ONCE ATTRIBUTED TO POPE)

SARAH TAKES OVER

With Vanbrugh, Hawksmoor and all the top craftsmen gone, Sarah set about managing the project her way. She sued more than four hundred people, Vanbrugh included, for plotting to *'load the Duke of Marlborough with the payment of the debts due on account of the building'* and for *'charging excessive and unreasonable rates'*. That done, Sarah appointed James Moore, a talented cabinetmaker, as her clerk of works. There was still much to be done. The exterior was more or less finished, but the inside was a mess. There were rooms without floors or ceilings, and the stone for the front steps had not been delivered. No part of the palace was habitable. Sarah set to with a will, moving heaven and earth to get their apartments in the east wing completed and furnished so that the Duke could finally realize his dream and move in. She oversaw every detail:

> *'I shall want a vast number of feather beds and quilts. I wish you would take this opportunity to know the prices of all such things as will be wanted in that wild unmerciful house. I would have some of the feather beds swansdown, all good and sweet feathers, even for the servants.'*

The Duke, though a shadow of his former self, had enjoyed two summers at Blenheim before his death in 1722. He was much amused by the theatrical performances that Sarah arranged for him starring his grandchildren bedecked in brocades intended for curtaining. He was perhaps less amused by the unfinished state of the palace.

For all Sarah's battles with Vanbrugh, Blenheim Palace remained far closer to the architect's original vision than to Sarah's wishes. It was neither plain nor convenient. Nor was it finished or anywhere near on budget.

July 1712 — Due to Several Workmen and Artificers for Worke performed by them at the Building of Blenheim as ℘ Contract Agreement or incidental Bills may appear.

	£	s	d
To Edward Strong Mason	6339	8	11
To Bartholomew Peisley Mason	1269	1	11
To John Townsend Mason	640	2	3
To Thomas Churchil and Richard Stacy Bricklay.rs	44	9	3
To Mathew Banckes and John Barton Carpenters	1886	6	10
To Henry Wise Gardner	873		8
To Charles Hale plummer	1872	6	2
To John Scriven plummer	187	6	1
To Tho: Davies Glazier	688	6	3
To Isaac Ellis Glazier	39	13	1
To Charles Scriven Glazier	24		
To Tho: Tarbox Glazier	47	10	8
To Charles Hopson Joyner	272	11	7
To John Smallwell Joyner	264	3	2
To Rob.t Barker Joyner	173	11	1
To Grinling Gibbons Carver	1117	18	4
To John Reynolds for Marble	81	1	4
To William Holland for Marble	49	4	6
To Josiah Key Smith	134	14	8
To Tho: Warren Smith	20	10	10
To Jos. Jolly paviour	48	4	6
To John Stockley for Drainage	6	11	8

£16080: 3. 9

To several persons for Materials and Carriage &c sold & delivered at Blenheim for the said Workes as ℘ Contract Agreem.ts Bills, or particulars may appear.

	£	s	d
To Edw.d Strong and Partner for Burford stone	3629	4	9
To John Sutton and partner for raising & Scapling Cornbury stone	1080	2	9
To Henry Banckes for Guyting stone & Carriage	519	7	4
To S.r Tho: Wheate for Glympton stone and Carriage	536	13	
To Edw.d Strong for Portland stone and part of Carriage	990	6	4

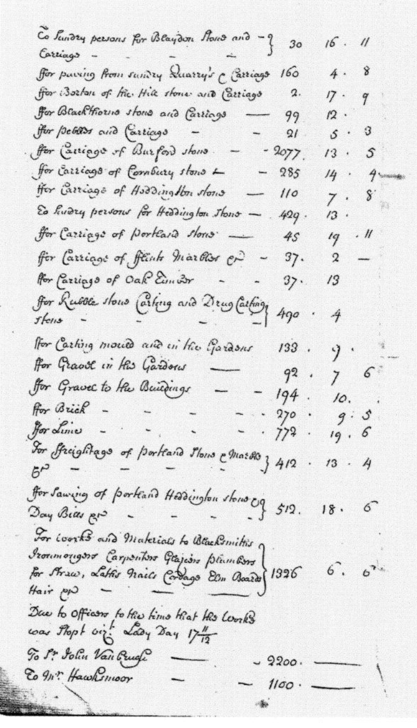

	£	s	d
To Sundry persons for Blaydon Stone and Carriage	30	16	11
For paving from sundry Quarry's & Carriage	160	4	8
For Borton of the Hill stone and Carriage	2	17	9
For Blackthorne stone and Carriage	99	12	
For pebbles and Carriage	21	5	3
For Carriage of Burford stone	2077	13	5
For Carriage of Cornbury stone	285	14	4
For Carriage of Headington stone	110	7	8
To Sundry persons for Headington stone	429	13	
For Carriage of Portland stone	45	19	11
For Carriage of Flints Marble &c	37	2	
For Carriage of Oak Timber	37	13	
For Rubble stone Carting and Drug Carting stone	490	4	
For Carting mould and in the Gardens	133	9	
For Gravel in the Gardens	92	7	6
For Gravel to the Buildings	194	10	
For Brick	270	9	5
For Lime	772	19	6
For Freightage of Portland Stone & Marble &c	412	13	4
For Sawing of Portland Headington stone & Day Bills &c	512	18	6
For Works and Materials to Blacksmiths Ironmongers Carpenters Glaziers plumbers for Straw, Laths Nails Cordage Elm Boards Hair &c	1326	6	6

Due to Officers to the time that the Works was Stopt viz.t Lady Day 17 11/12

	£	s	d
To S.r John Vanbrugh	2200		
To M.r Hawksmoor	1100		

	£	s	d
To M.r Joynes	400		
To M.r Bobart	500		
	34581	5	7

Sarah kept a careful record of the amount owing to the palace craftsmen and their teams. This 1712 account includes £1,117 to Gibbons, £2,200 to Vanbrugh and £1,100 to Hawksmoor. The list is headed by masons and, naturally, a series of plumbers, just one of whom was paid £1,872.
BL, Blenheim, 61354

RIGHT: *Thornhill's invoices for the painted ceiling are queried by the Duchess as 'not worth half a crown a yard'.* BL, Blenheim, 61354.

BELOW: *The battle to finish decorating the saloon, gallery and hall was characterized by vigorous haggling. Here, Sarah grumbles that the cost of ceiling painting and trophies 'came to a higher price than anything of that bigness was ever given for Rubens or Titian'.* BL, Blenheim, 61354

was paid for at Sr John's rate tho there was no article sign'd, but I remember that He drew ye Duke of Marlb in to like it by describing ye Historical painting as the finest thing that could be imagined and said Mr. Thornhill would not do it at that price for any body else, but the credit of it would advance him extreamly in ye Kings works not mentioning any thing of painting Trophies not worth half a crown a yard with ye Historical paint which as He order'd it came to a higher price than any thing of that bigness was ever given for Rubens or Titian

Mr. Thornhill's Bill to his Grace the Duke of Marlborough & his acquittance

Sr John put the figures to this bill as Mr Bobart told me to excuse the extravagance of the price, that he did not know what I was to pay for that not worth half a crown a yard, & I know they are Sr Johns figures & Mr Bobart writ the bill of measurement not distinguishing what sort of painting it was. This painting was

BELOW: *Taking issue with one of Vanbrugh's estimates, this letter notes that the Duchess has been quoted £1,800 for painting, gilding and decorating the gallery, saloon and hall in total—but that £978 has been paid to Thornhill for the hall alone (see page 71) while the other two rooms still need to be finished; and that the gallery 'is of a vast length'.* BL, Blenheim, 61354

Memm.

In one of Sr John Vanbrugh's estimates for finishing Blenheim in either his own or Joynes's hand writing He puts down 1800. for painting gilding and decorations of ye Gallery Salon & Hall at Blenheim and after that in Feb: 1716/7 signs thornhills account for nine hundred and seventy eight pounds for ye Hall only, The Gallery is of a vast length, the Salon of ye same dimensions the Hall one way the Ceiling of which has been painted & ye four sides of ye room down to ye wainscot since for 500 this must needs be a vast deal more work than only ye oval in ye Hall at Top & all ye critics say ye work his better done.

QUEEN ANNE

CHAPTER FOUR

After Marlborough

Sarah, Duchess of Marlborough, never understood the Duke's passion for Blenheim. For her the whole enterprise was a massive waste of effort, time and money, but it was Marlborough's Versailles and nothing was too good for his monument of a house. Surprisingly for a man so notoriously careful with his money, he never begrudged the sums he lavished upon the building or the furnishings. The historian A L Rowse described Marlborough's commitment to the palace as *'the absolute determination to make his place in history, as absolute as anything in Louis XIV'*.

In the Duke's lifetime Sarah barely tolerated this determination and complained about it constantly, but after his death she put her own views aside, picking up, I think, on this desire to make a mark and leave a legacy. She became determined that her Duke should have his monument, and immediately threw her considerable energies into completing the palace. In his will, as well as leaving her £15,000 per year, Marlborough House (for her lifetime) and Holywell House, he left Blenheim to Sarah for her lifetime. He also left her £10,000 per year for five years, with which to complete the building works. Vanbrugh was typically unimpressed: *'He has given his widow £10,000 a year to spoil Blenheim her own way,'* he sniped to a colleague. And finish it she did, scrimping here and saving there, for an outlay of £25,315.

Sarah re-employed Nicholas Hawksmoor to design an interior for the existing shell of the gallery (now the long library), which he did magnificently, and to produce the innovative and impressive ceilings in the green drawing room, red drawing room and green writing room. For the park and gardens Hawksmoor produced designs for monuments and archways, but of all his designs only the Woodstock gate was ever built. The Latin inscription on this triumphal arch reads:

> *'This gate was built the year after the death of the most illustrious John Duke of Marlborough by order of Sarah his most beloved wife to whom he left the sole directory of the many things that remained unfinished.'*

Just in case anyone had any doubts.

This imposing marble doorcase in the long library was designed by Nicholas Hawksmoor and commissioned by Sarah after she fell out with Vanbrugh. It sits opposite the bow window and, when the double doors are open, forms an impressive frame for the view down to the great hall.

Design tips from the first Duchess

Sarah held strong opinions about design. For example, writing about a marble chimneypiece she was contemplating for her Wimbledon home, she said:

> *'There is a good deal of carving upon it, which is not at all to my taste... I am determined to have no one thing carved in the finishing of my house at Wimbledon, my taste having always been to have things plain and clean from a piece of wainscot to a lady's face.'*

Her favourite home, Marlborough House, had an elegant simplicity that she loved, especially the handsome staircase with its '*large half paces*'. She was all for splendour, but she liked her splendour strong and plain, not gussied up or gilded. She liked to see rich red hangings set off with plain white walls. She approved of long pier glasses between windows to reflect light, and disapproved of large beds in small bedrooms. She didn't like over-elaborate, top-heavy furnishings or drapery that disguised or drew attention away from architectural features such as windows, cornices and doorcases. Nor did she like fancy frames on paintings. She wrote of a house she had visited:

> *'[They had] pictures of horses and dogs and some old sort of Dutch pictures as I took them to be, with vast heavy carved frames almost as large as the cornice on the outside of a house, all gilt. I dare say they cost a great deal of money, and are worth a great deal more to those that like such things than the pictures that are in them.'*

Sarah's favourite room at Blenheim was the bow window room on the private side, now used as a dining room, and you can see why. It has very elegant, soaring lines and lovely tall windows with pier glasses between them. By day the sunlight bounces around the room, and it looks magnificent at night, twinkling with reflections of candlelight. In my opinion, this room epitomizes her taste.

Although we do not have a record of how it was decorated in her day, I think she would have approved of how it is today. The walls are panelled and painted in three tones of a creamy yellow that emphasizes the panels without being loud. The curtains, now somewhat threadbare and stained, are in an elegant damask with swagged pelmets grand enough to suit the tall windows without being so ornate as to detract from the splendid view over the Italian garden. Set between the windows, beneath the pier glasses, is a pair of beautiful gilt console tables.

Because all the rooms at Blenheim are of a much larger scale than most average rooms, great care has had to be taken in selecting the furniture and furnishings. The challenge is to make the rooms feel inviting and lived in without detracting from the superb architecture. This is largely achieved through the scale of the furniture and artefacts and the use of colour.

A view of the bow window room on the private side of the palace. Part of the suite used by the first Duke and Duchess, it is a room that Sarah particularly liked.

Careful housekeeping

By 1740, Sarah was eighty years old and suffering from gout, but her mind was sharp. She sat in her bed and wrote out a twenty-page household inventory for Blenheim. Bearing in mind that she had been living in her other homes since the Duke's death and hadn't even set foot in the palace for four years, it was a remarkable feat of memory. She held every possession in her mind's eye, from the Van Dyck painting of Charles I to the number of damask napkins (809).

RIGHT AND BELOW: *A collection of copper and antique cooking utensils still used today. Some of the copper pans have the letter 'M' for Marlborough.*

An Account of the Linnen at Blenheim.
Damask and Diaper Napkins Sixty seven Dozen and five
Table Cloths of the best Sort Ninety three
Stewards Table Cloths Twenty
Fine Sheets Eighteen pair
Servants Sheets Forty five pair
Three Dozen of Damask Towells marked N 6
Round and Square pillow beers forty
Two Holland Bolster Cases
Eleven Round Towells
Four Dimity Blankets
Linnen for the Kitchen House Maids Butler & Housekeeper the particulars not worth putting down
The China both usefull and not usefull not much but is all the Dutchess of Marlboroughs
All the Glasses for the Desert and Pantry are the Trusts.
All the things in the Kitchen and Offices are Compleat and to be sure I must have bought a great many of them in Eighteen Years But as many of those things are Ordinary & would Swell this Account to a vast bigness and as I am determined not to take any of them away I don't think it necessary to do more than mention them but there are several Marble Tubs in the Garden (I don't know how many) which some of the Orange Trees are put in that I sent from the Lodge at Windsor and are Mine.
The Reason that I distinguish what is mine at Blenheim is because the House is now Compleat and to take them away would lessen the Beauty of it which I have no mind to do For perhaps I may alter my Mind and leave the things at my death that are indisputably my own.
I think it proper to insert here the Gold plate which the Electress of Hanover made present of to me with a Suit of Hangings part of which are in the following Account Claimed by me as my own, The Electress having Writ to me that she sent

19

LEFT: *Apart from listing 'Damask and diaper napkins sixty seven dozen and five', Sarah includes in her inventory the servants' linen, 'the particulars not worth putting down', and points out: 'But, as many of those things are ordinary I would swell this account to a vast bigness and as I am determined not to take any of them away I don't think it necessary to do more than mention them but there are several marble tubs in the garden (I don't know how many) which some of the orange trees are put in that I sent from the Lodge at Windsor and are mine.'*

OPPOSITE: *Showing the ducal crown and the letter 'B' for Blenheim, these copper saucepans are housed in the antiquated yet functional kitchen.*

Love for love

Henrietta—Sarah and John's oldest daughter to survive infancy, who was born in 1681—inherited the title in her own right on the death of her father in 1722. Childhood letters to her *'Dear Angell Mama'* reveal a clever, lively child desperate for approval and attention. This was probably hard to come by from a largely absent papa and a mama too preoccupied with her own plots and plans to make much of a success of motherhood. At the age of eighteen, Henrietta married the son of Marlborough's greatest ally at court, Godolphin, and the couple duly produced an heir to the dukedom. Named William after the King, he was nicknamed Willigo.

Godolphin was unambitious, would be called laid-back today, and spent a lot of time with his horses. Henrietta, on the other hand, wanted brilliance and wit, good company and a bit of flattery and attention. She found what she wanted in the poet and playwright William Congreve, and by his side she moved and sparkled in London's literary circles. These inevitably included one of Sarah's

A portrait of Henrietta by the studio of Godfrey Kneller. It was painted after her marriage but before she had become the second Duchess of Marlborough. Henrietta had a stormy relationship with her mother, which deteriorated to such a degree that by 1722, when she became Duchess, their only communication was through vitriolic notes. One witheringly short covering note to Sarah, accompanying a letter sent to Henrietta in error, read: 'Madam, I am very sorry for the accident of this letter coming to me because of giving your Grace the uneasiness of hearing from me, but indeed I took it to be for myself, as your Grace may be sure, and am Madam, your Grace's most obedient daughter. Marlborough.'

most detested human beings, the playwright and architect Vanbrugh. As far as Sarah was concerned, you were either with her or against her, and a daughter cavorting with *'low poets'* was not to be endured.

Henrietta had cause to be angry with her mother, too. Willigo was at best a feckless youth, and thanks to his grandmother Sarah—who ensured his financial independence—a rich and idle one with a drinking problem.

Dy'd at *Harrow on the Hill*, after a long Indiſpoſition, her Grace *Henrietta* Dutcheſs of *Marlborough*, Marchioneſs of *Blandford* and Baroneſs of *Sandridge*, as Succeſſor to her Father, *John* late Duke of *Marlborough*; and Counteſs of *Godolphin*, as Wife to the Right Hon. *Francis* Earl of *Godolphin*, Groom of the Stole, and Firſt Lord of the Bedchamber to the King. Her Grace bore his Lordſhip one Son and two Daughters, the Marqueſs of *Blandford*, who dy'd about two Years ago without Iſſue, her Grace the Dutcheſs of *Newcaſtle*, and the Lady *Mary* about nine Years old. Her Grace's Titles deſcend, according to the Limitation of Parliament, to the Right Hon. the Earl of *Sunderland*, Son to the Lady *Anne*, 2d Daughter of the late Duke of *Marlborough*, who is marry'd to the only Daughter of the Lord *Trevor*.

A lengthy death notice from The Times *explaining how the title came to Henrietta and where it went after her death.*

THE WAY OF THE WORLD

Congreve, a married man, was the love of Henrietta's life and the father of her second daughter. He is best known for his brilliant comedies, *The Old Bachelor, The Double Dealer, Love for Love* and *The Way of the World*. Tellingly, his last play, *The Way of the World,* revolves around a pair of lovers established in an unconventional marriage arrangement in a world inhabited by schemers, fops and fools. Congreve's wit and his characters' sexual licence upset not only his mistress's mother, but also the leading moralists of the day. He died in a carriage accident in 1729, leaving Henrietta his fortune, to the bitter chagrin of his wife.

Henrietta was inconsolable. It was rumoured that she had a mannequin made which was dressed in his clothes, sat at her table and at night was in her bedchamber—but people say the oddest things. She did commission a monument for Congreve's tomb in Westminster Abbey, with the inscription courageously in her own name:

> *'This monument is set up by Henrietta, Duchess of Marlborough, as a mark how deeply she remembers the happiness and honour she enjoyed in the sincere friendship of so worthy and honest a man, whose virtue, candour and wit gained him the love and esteem of the present age, and whose writing will be the admiration of the future.'*

Willigo married on impulse, but died of drink before he could give his young Dutch bride a baby. Sarah was with him at the end. She commented sadly: *'I would have given half my estate to have saved him. I hope the Devil is picking that man's bones who taught him to drink.'* Henrietta died two years later, in 1733. Sarah wrote the following to her granddaughter Lady Di:

> *'I…feel much more than I imagined formerly I would. I am convinced that there is such a thing as natural affection, though I have heard many people laugh at that notion. I have made several attempts to be reconciled to that unfortunate woman… But nothing I said or did had the least good effect…As to this last shock, it would have been much greater had she lived with me and loved me as she once did.'*

Family affairs

Sarah's favourite daughter, Anne, born in 1684, was married to Charles Spencer, third Earl of Sunderland, a remarkable and gifted man of letters in pole position in the government of George I. Anne died in 1716 and Charles in 1722, the same year as Marlborough. Their eldest son, Robert, had reached his majority, but the younger children, including Charles and John, were left in Sarah's care. Needless to say, Sarah kept meticulous accounts of how much she was spending, especially on Charles and John, who were off to the Continent on the obligatory Grand Tour. The boys had lessons in fencing and dancing, and they needed expensive clothes, including eight pairs of shoes every three months. Sarah grumbled:

> *'For my own part I never thought travelling was much use but to teach them perfectly the language and to keep them out of harm's way while they are so young that they can't keep the best company in England, and to make them see that nothing is so agreeable as England.'*

DRINKING AND GAMBLING

What Charles did learn during his five years of travel was to gamble. When he finally came home, Sarah was shocked, both at the state of her grandson's finances and at his French, which he apparently pronounced like an Englishman—in the way of his illustrious descendant, Sir Winston.

At that time, Henrietta had the title, and although her son Willigo was still drinking his way around London, there was no reason to doubt that he would succeed to the dukedom and the line of descent would pass down the Godolphin side of the family. The eldest Spencer boy, Robert, had inherited his father's estates. While his brothers Charles and John had been on their travels, Sarah had busied herself finding safe seats for them in Parliament, although Charles in particular was never keen and the constituents were even less so.

Within the space of two years, however, Robert had died unmarried, leaving extensive gambling debts, and the unfortunate Willigo had succumbed to a deadly binge-drinking session at Balliol College, Oxford. As a result, the extravagant Charles Spencer was now Marlborough's heir. Being a gambler, like his late elder brother, he raised his stakes—and lost even more. Sarah set about putting things to rights, moving money around to make the inheritances more balanced and seeing to it that the Spencer estates were passed to her favourite grandson, Charles's younger brother, John.

Charles found his grandmother very difficult to deal with, and avoided her as much as he could. He was intimidated by her financial power as trustee of Marlborough's will and wary of her formidable, demanding spirit, so he was often economical with the truth in his dealings with her. When she found him out, as

I have receiv'd yours of the 14. of feb. N.S. I cannot approve of your way of reasoning about the Ridiculous Expences that the Brothers have made, You say that it is more than it would have been if they had had a greater Spirit of Oeconomy, but 'tis less than if they had been Extravagant, in any thing but pocket money, this is only saying that a man that spends a Thousand pounds a year more than he has, will not be so soon ruin'd as if he spent two, I am not much inform'd or Satisfy'd with that sort of reasoning & the mony they have had return'd since they left England, has been enough to Support Extravagance upon every Article. You say that you have £.2250 to account for. Till I look into the Accounts I can't say what it is, but I am Confident since Charles went out of England to this time, he & his Brother have not had less than £.5000. & with the help of this mony they have lost so much of their time, that if they know any thing more than they did when they left England, it is only what they could hardly avoid, Learning to speak french, but as I beleive they generally kept English Company, I have my doubts even of that, & for writing french I suppose they never try'd at that it being so uneasy to them to write their own Language; you say they have given their money away, & squander'd it, [illegible] & Charles says in his letter that he has not been so carefull of his mony as he should have been, but he has avoided play a good many months, which imply's that he has play'd tho at your first going I so positively forbid it & as to the Article of

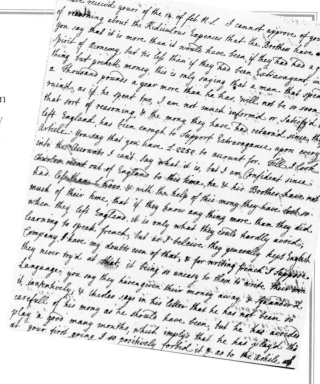

she inevitably did, she would be even more furious than before. One move of Charles's that made Sarah practically incandescent with rage was his almost clandestine marriage to Elizabeth Trevor—the daughter of one of Marlborough's avowed enemies in Parliament. Sarah was angry with Charles, with his sister Anne—who was very close to Queen Caroline, whom Sarah suspected of masterminding the marriage in order to spite her—and with John for attending his brother's wedding. It was a bitter pill for Sarah, made all the more difficult to swallow because it was destined to be the happiest of marriages.

ABOVE: *Sarah railed against the supposed excesses of her grandsons as they toured Europe for their education. In this undated letter, written probably to their tutor during the extensive 'tour', she complains: 'I cannot approve of your way of reasoning about the ridiculous expenses that the brothers have made... the money they have had returned since they left England has been enough to support extravagance upon every article.' She continues gloomily that 'if they know anything more than they did when they left England, it is only what they could hardly avoid'.*
BL, Blenheim, 61445

LEFT: *A portrait by an unknown artist, circa 1720, of Elizabeth, Lady Trevor, whom Charles married behind Sarah's back.*

To
The Memory
of
QUEEN ANN
Under Whose Auspices
JOHN DUKE of MARLBOROUGH
Conquered
And to Whose Munificence
He And His Posterity
with Gratitude
Owe the Possession
of
BLENHEIM
A: D: MDCCXXXX: VI:

FEUDS AND BATTLES

As would be expected of such a restless character, Sarah also found time to meddle in politics. She took a passionate dislike to Sir Robert Walpole, England's first prime minister (1721–42), and he took an equal dislike to her. George I was dead, succeeded by his son George II, who was an altogether different kind of king and who had no history with the Marlboroughs. Sarah barged into a relationship with his wife, the clever and witty Queen Caroline. It started well but finished badly—so badly, in fact, that it prompted Sarah to commission from the sculptor Michael Rysbrack a huge white marble statue of Queen Anne. *'I am at present altering my account of Queen Anne's character,'* she wrote. *'I have begun to love her again since the present lot have become our governors.'* In her attempts to bully the court and the government of the day in the direction of her pleasing, Sarah made more enemies than friends.

She also feuded with her children and grandchildren, threatening to cut them out of her will if they disobeyed her, and used them as pawns in her personal battles. She barely spoke to her eldest daughter, Henrietta, who in the absence of a living male heir had inherited the Marlborough title. She doted on her two favourite grandchildren, Anne's children, Lady Di and John Spencer, to the exclusion of the others. She never had the patience for diplomacy or tact.

The ninth Duke wrote of Sarah:

> *'Hers was a dominating character which, for the last thirty years of her life, lacked scope for action, and therefore asserted itself violently in the narrow field left open to it... No woman not of royal rank has ever held before, or is likely to hold again, such a position as was hers during the critical years of the eighteenth century, when the map of Europe and the constitution of England were in the making.'*

ABOVE: *A portrait, after Kneller, of Caroline, Princess of Wales, in 1716. She became Queen of England in 1727.*

LOYAL COMPANIONS

Sarah found focus in her old age with her love for her granddaughter, Lady Di Spencer, Charles and John's young sister, who could do no wrong in Sarah's eyes and who made a good marriage to the fourth Duke of Bedford. Sadly, she died of consumption at the age of twenty-six, leaving Sarah bereft once more. The Duchess found solace in her dogs:

> *'They have all of them gratitude, wit and good sense: things very rare to be found in this country. They are fond of going out with me; but when I reason with them, and tell them it is not proper, they submit, and watch for my coming home, and meet me with as much joy as if I had never given them good advice.'*

I sense a hint of self-knowledge there.

OPPOSITE: *A flattering marble statue of Queen Anne by Michael Rysbrack commissioned by Sarah to demonstrate her gratitude for their long friendship.*

Nicholas Hawksmoor, whose designs for a column had been turned down, described Lord Herbert's finished column in a letter to a friend: 'The historical pillar is set up in the park. It is 10 feet in diameter and in all above 100 feet high. I must observe to you that the inscription is very long and contains many letters, but though they are very legible, they are but three-quarters of an inch high.'

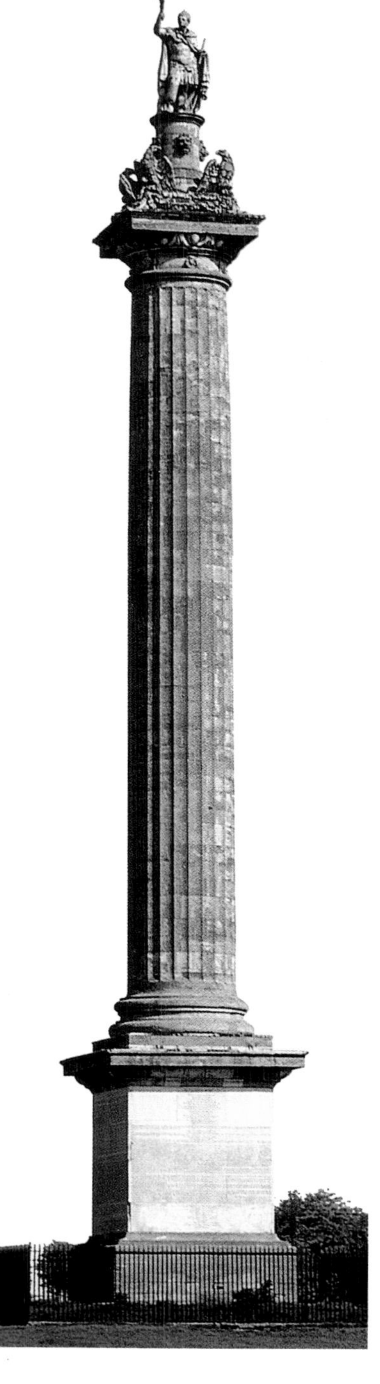

PASSIONS AND PREJUDICES

Sarah was as active in business as in politics. Buying and selling estates, she increased her already considerable fortune and was in a position to lend money to the Crown. She compiled an incredibly detailed inventory of Blenheim (see page 94) while fending off lawsuits and demands for money contingent on the building works, and, undaunted by experience, she built more houses. Having bought a half-finished house in Wimbledon, she pulled it down, had Lord Burlington—who built the elegant Assembly Rooms in York—build her another but didn't like it and so knocked that down and built yet another.

Her passion for houses lay in the architectural detail and the furnishings—a passion I have to admit that I share. *'It is a great pleasure and amusement to be dressing up and making a place pretty,'* she wrote. However, her war with architects was ongoing. Writing of the Wimbledon house, she said:

> *'If I had had only myself and the bricklayers, it would have been the finest place in the world. But I have always had the misfortune to suffer very great mischiefs from the assistance of architects.'*

COLUMNS AND TOMBS

Blenheim was a long time being finished, and Sarah spent as little time in the gout-inducing chill of the place as she could, preferring Marlborough House in London. She spent a lot of time pondering over suitable monuments to the Duke, and, setting aside her vigorous opposition to Vanbrugh's proposal for an obelisk, asked Hawksmoor to design a column for the park and a marble tomb for the chapel. Typically, Sarah kept changing her mind over the designs for years before eventually throwing them out. Then she commissioned the sculptor Michael Rysbrack and the architect William Kent to create a monumental tomb for the chapel, and the 'architect Earl' Lord Herbert to design a triumphal column.

The monuments engaged her, as did Marlborough's reputation. As she grew older and more ill, she spent time dictating her memoirs. Her book—*An Account of the Conduct of the Dowager Duchess of Marlborough, From her first coming to Court to the year 1710*—was a publishing sensation of the time, the British public having finally warmed to this fearless and eccentric old lady. Having tried and failed to get a number of prominent writers and historians interested in the task of writing a biography of the Duke, she left money in her will to that end.

SARAH'S LEGACIES

The end came for Sarah in her eighty-fifth year, in 1744, by which time only one of her daughters was still living. Anne's son Charles Spencer had become the third Duke on Henrietta's death in 1733. Henrietta had never lived at Blenheim and Charles did not do so until after Sarah's death. It was Sarah's domain. Her generous will provided many thoughtful legacies, and the bulk of her personal possessions, lands and estates went to Charles's younger brother, John Spencer, from whom the Earls Spencer are descended. (John's son was made Earl Spencer in 1765.) With Sarah gone, the third Duke was now free to move into the palace. His children and his children's children were well provided for, but there was little or nothing left for the upkeep of Blenheim.

Sarah, that most troublesome, opinionated, fascinating, passionate and charismatic of my ancestors, is buried beside Marlborough in the Blenheim chapel. *'My will and desire,'* she wrote in her will, *'is that I may be buried at Blenheim, near the body of my dear husband John late Duke of Marlborough.'*

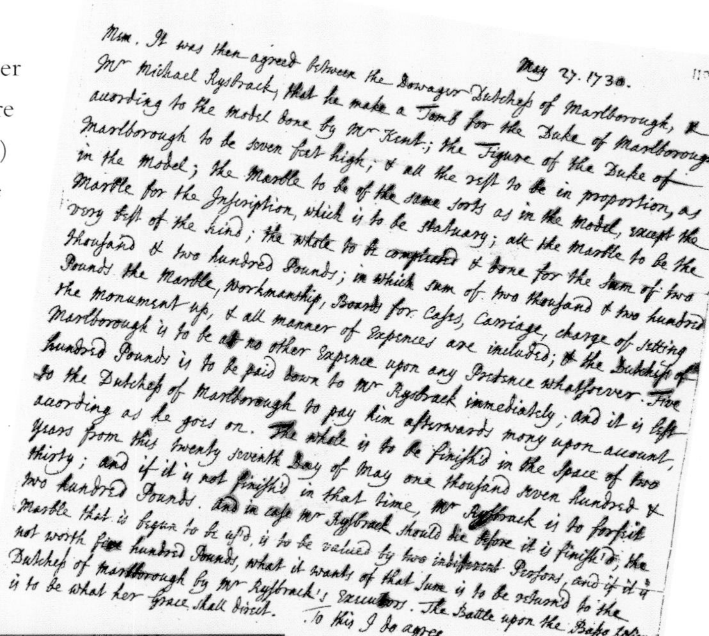

May 27. 1730.

Mem. It was then agreed between the Dowager Dutchess of Marlborough, & Mr Michael Rysbrack, that he make a Tomb for the Duke of Marlborough according to the Model done by Mr Kent; the Figure of the Duke of Marlborough to be seven feet high; & all the rest to be in proportion, as in the Model; the Marble to be of the same sorts as in the Model, except the Marble for the Inscription, which is to be Statuary; all the Marble to be the very best of the kind; the whole to be compleated & done for the Sum of two Thousand & two hundred Pounds; in which sum of two thousand & two hundred Pounds the Marble, Workmanship, Boards for Cases, Carriage, charge of setting the Monument up, & all manner of Expences are included; & the Dutchess of Marlborough is to be at no other Expence upon any Pretence whatsoever. Five hundred Pounds is to be paid down to Mr Rysbrack immediately; and it is left to the Dutchess of Marlborough to pay him afterwards mony upon account, according as he goes on. The whole is to be finish'd in the Space of two Years from this twenty seventh Day of May one thousand seven hundred & thirty; and if it is not finish'd in that time, Mr Rysbrack is to forfeit two hundred Pounds. And in case Mr Rysbrack should die before it is finish'd, the Marble that is begun to be us'd, is to be valued by two indifferent Persons, and if it is not worth five hundred Pounds, what it wants of that Sum is to be return'd to the Dutchess of Marlborough by Mr Rysbrack's Executors. The Battle upon the Basso relievo is to be what her Grace shall direct.

To this I do agree

S. Marlborough

ABOVE: *A letter of agreement from May 1730 clearly setting out the terms of Michael Rysbrack's commission to create Marlborough's tomb. Stipulating a cost of £2,200 'at no other expense upon any pretence whatsoever', it specifies that the figure of the Duke should be seven feet high, and that all marble should 'be the very best of the kind'.*
BL, Blenheim, 61354

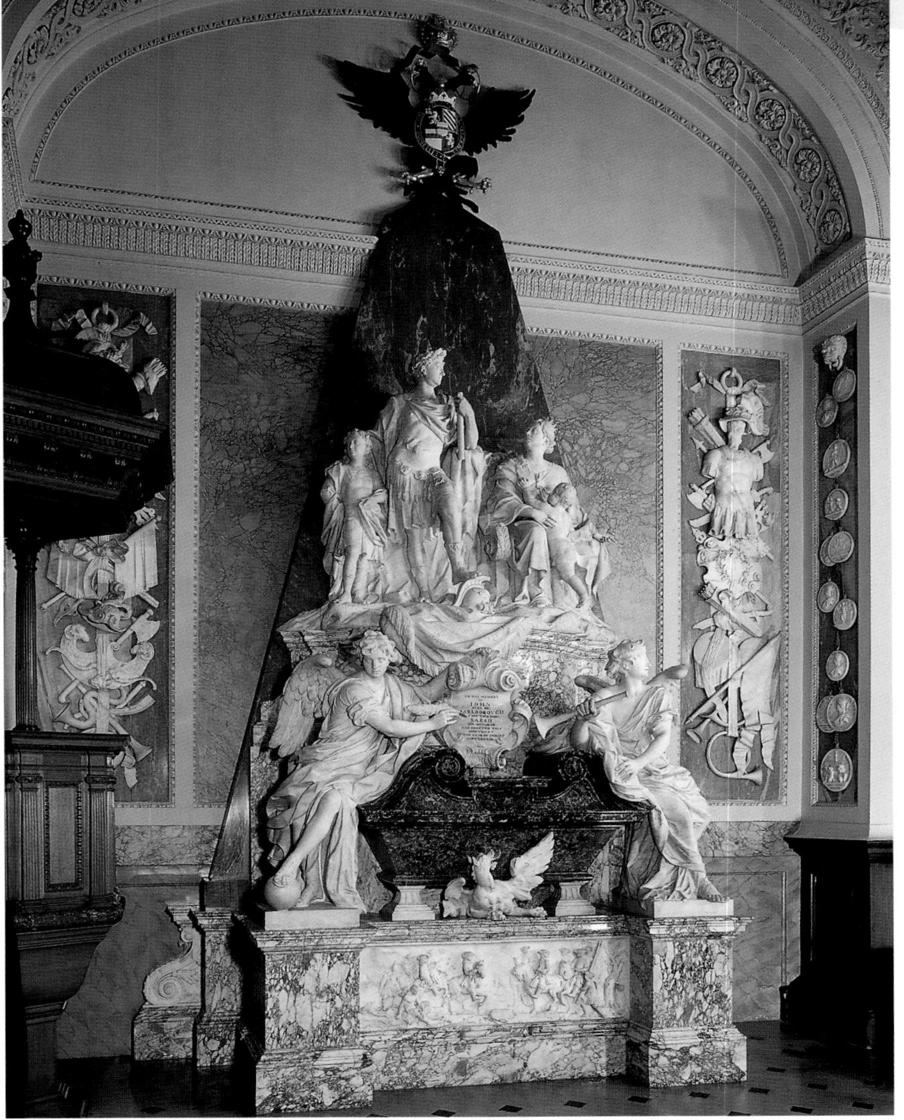

LEFT: *Marlborough's monument, designed by William Kent and sculpted by Michael Rysbrack in 1733, is immense and ornate—very un-Sarah. But she wrote proudly: 'Considering how many wonderful figures and whirligigs I have seen architects finish a chapel withal, that are of no manner of use but to laugh at, I must confess I cannot help thinking that what I have designed for the chapel may as reasonably be called finishing of it as the pews and pulpit.'*

Lady Di and her namesake

By all accounts, Sarah's granddaughter Lady Diana Spencer, nicknamed Lady Di, was a pretty girl with an enchanting, outgoing nature and many suitors. Sarah doted on her. But the strange thing is that Sarah was, at one stage, prepared to sacrifice her granddaughter's happiness in order to score a point off Queen Caroline.

The royal family were beset with family problems. Queen Caroline and her firstborn, Frederick, Prince of Wales, were at loggerheads. Frederick was sly and selfish, but Sarah, being Sarah, took the tack 'the enemy of my enemy is my friend', offering a considerable dowry if the Prince of Wales would marry Lady Di.

Frederick was willing and if it hadn't been for the intervention of Sir Robert Walpole, who envisaged a foreign match for the sleazy Prince, Sarah would have had the double satisfaction of thwarting Queen Caroline and seeing her own descendants upon the throne of England. In the event, Lady Di married John Russell and became the Duchess of Bedford, châtelaine of Woburn Abbey, but died tragically young (see page 101).

Lady Di's collateral descendant, Lady Diana Spencer, daughter of the eighth Earl Spencer, was an equally charming young woman who married our own Prince of Wales in 1981. However, there can, of course, be no parallels between Prince Frederick and Prince Charles, who is a charming, thoughtful man.

ABOVE: *The late Princess Diana with my father, the eleventh Duke.*

RIGHT: *Frederick, Prince of Wales, to whom Sarah tried to marry Lady Di. Because in 1751 Frederick predeceased his father, George II, Frederick's son was to become the next King, George III.*

OPPOSITE: *Portrait of Lady Diana Spencer, attributed to Charles Jervas. Lady Diana nearly married the Prince of Wales, and was to die at a young age.*

Lady Diana Sp
Daughter to
Earl of Su
Lady Ann
his Wife
John Duke of

CHAPTER FIVE

Scandals, Extravagances and Debts

The direct Churchill line got off to a rocky start with the death of John and Sarah's surviving son. The succession via daughters could have seen the Churchill name lost to oblivion, but in 1817, in the patriotic aftermath of Waterloo, the fifth Duke thought it fitting to honour our illustrious ancestor by obtaining permission to bring back the Churchill name, and we have been Spencer-Churchills ever since.

BAD TEETH AND BAD DEBTS

As it happens, the first Spencer duke—Charles Spencer, the son of John and Sarah's daughter Anne—proved to be a bit of a disappointment. By the time he became the third Duke of Marlborough, in 1733, he'd run through half a million pounds in extravagant gestures and gambling debts, and his grandmother was seething. She had never really taken to Charles: *'He is well enough as the world goes and has a civil and modest behaviour. But he has an ill habit of speaking through his teeth, one can't tell whether he says Yes or No; it is disagreeable not to speak distinctly.'*

She also loathed Charles's chosen wife, Elizabeth Trevor, on principle, not only because her father and the first Duke had been old enemies in Parliament, but also because she came with precious little dowry and not much breeding.

ABOVE: *The fifth Duke (left) and the sixth Duke (right), both named George Spencer-Churchill.*

OPPOSITE: *Portrait by George Romney of George Spencer, who became the fourth duke of Marlborough in 1758. The painting hangs over the fireplace in the green drawing room at Blenheim* *(see page 112)*.

Sarah wrote of Charles's wife in unequivocal terms:

> *'The woman herself (as they say, for I have never seen her) has been bred in a very low way and don't know how to behave herself upon any occasion; not at all pretty, and has a mean, ordinary look. As to the behaviour, if she has any sense, that may mend. But they say she has very bad teeth, which I think is an objection alone in a wife, and they will be sure to grow worse with time.'*

'FORFEITING RESPECT'

Charles and Elizabeth were family-oriented and very happy together, but neither of them left much of a mark on Blenheim. Horace Walpole described the third Duke as follows:

> *'He had virtues and sense enough to deserve esteem, but always lost it by forfeiting respect. He was honest and generous, capable of giving the most judicious advice and of following the worst.'*

He was an indifferent statesman, a bad businessman and a mediocre soldier. The first Marquess of Lansdowne said:

> *'[He was] an easy, good-natured gallant man, who took a strange fancy for serving, to get rid of the ennui attending a private life, without any military experience or the common habits of a man of business, or indeed capacity for either, and no force of character whatever.'*

Volumes of leather-bound books in the long library, cataloguing the original volumes of the Sunderland Library, which was sold in 1882 by the seventh Duke *(see page 156). Just imagine how many books that represents.*

THE SUNDERLAND LIBRARY

The third Duke had no love for Blenheim, but he did love his books. His father, the third Earl of Sunderland, who was married to the first Duke of Marlborough's daughter Anne, had collected books from a young age. Making the most of his life as a statesman and courtier, he had used foreign postings to collect rare books from all around Europe. By 1703 his fledgling collection was being described as the finest in Europe. Eventually, the Earl had amassed 24,000 volumes. At one stage, the King of Portugal offered to buy it, and a scholar who had been sent to assess it described it as 'the most curious collection in Europe'. Charles Spencer, the Earl's son, who had become third Duke of Marlborough in 1733, inherited the Sunderland Library. By the middle of the eighteenth century, the collection—which had had its beginnings at Althorp, the seat of the Spencer family—had been moved from Sunderland House in London to Blenheim.

The third Duke installed carved bookcases in Hawksmoor's gallery to house the Sunderland Library. However, the satirist Jonathan Swift noted that the installation of the bookcases had not been entirely successful—the shelves blocking the windows at the north and south suffered from damp, while those on the east wall were exposed to sunlight.

The transition from gallery to library was about the extent of the third Duke's contribution to Blenheim. He lavished his time and talents on Langley Park, near Windsor, a finely proportioned Georgian house in a rolling landscaped park. The irony is that Sarah would have loved it.

This 1778 painting, which hangs in the red drawing room, is by Sir Joshua Reynolds and depicts the fourth Duke and his family. (Two more children were born after the painting was completed.) Reynolds has caught the children delightfully at play and the painting is revealing of their characters. The smallest girl hides bashfully behind her sister's skirts, her sister teases her with a mask, and George, Marquess of Blandford, the young heir, has a prescient fragility about him. The statue (top right) represents the first Duke. The Duchess, who dominates the group, was not pleased with her depiction, and a portrait of her alone was subsequently commissioned from George Romney.

BLENHEIM COMES INTO ITS OWN

In 1758 the third Duke died of dysentery while campaigning in Germany, leaving his eldest son, George, aged nineteen, to inherit the title. George was a highly strung, sensitive young man—he'd hated his time in the army—who had fallen under the spell of Blenheim as a child on the family's infrequent visits there.

George was young, good-looking, shy, indecisive and very, very rich. On his father's death he inherited £500,000 pounds in capital, an annual income of £70,000 from rents and, for his lifetime, all the treasures of Blenheim. Not surprisingly, the young Duke was considered the greatest catch in England after George III, and the matchmaking mamas of England were out in force. In spite of his shyness, the young man did his best to make the most of his opportunities. He had a reputation for being, as one young acquaintance put it, *'excessively wild and given to women'*.

Lady Caroline Russell, a forthright young lady with a notoriously pushy mama, finally caught him. According to contemporary gossip, *'Eight and forty hours after his Grace declared himself a lover,'* George and Caroline were at the altar, in 1762. Henry Fox wrote in his memoirs:

> *'On Monday August 23, the Duke of Marlborough married Lady Caroline Russell. The mean and unbecoming artifices the Duchess of Bedford [her mother] made use of to bring this match on... are not to be described.'*

At any rate, the persistent Duchess's ploys did the trick. And whether or not the pair were forced together, confident, strong-willed Caroline was just what the diffident and indecisive Duke needed, at least in the early days.

Having been brought up at Woburn Abbey, in Bedfordshire, Caroline was not in the least intimidated by Blenheim. (Her mother, the Duchess of Bedford, was the second wife of the fourth Duke of Bedford. His first wife had been Sarah's granddaughter Lady Di, whom he had married after the episode of Sarah's unsuccessful matchmaking between Lady Di and the Prince of Wales.)

Blenheim's time had come. The unloved building site, the massive monument to Glorious Deeds, was now, finally, to become a home. But there was much to be done. The rooms were cold and dusty, the park untended and overgrown. Horace Walpole, who had visited Blenheim in 1760, wrote with characteristic venom:

> *'It looks like the palace of an auctioneer, who has been chosen King of Poland, and furnished his apartments with obsolete trophies, rubbish that nobody bid for, and a dozen pictures that he had stolen from the inventories of different families. The place is as ugly as the house, and the bridge, like the beggars at the old Duchess's gate, begs for a drop of water, and is refused.'*

REFURBISHMENTS INSIDE AND OUT

First of all the interiors were completely refurbished. Caroline called in the upholsterers and out went all the dark damask, to be replaced by sunny silks in yellows and cheerful blues and greens. Dark panelling was painted white, Sarah's heavy furniture was consigned to the attic and in came elegant Chippendale chairs, comfortable, gracefully curved upholstered sofas and intriguing Chinese lacquer cabinets. As was the new fashion of the time, chairs and tables were now grouped companionably about the rooms instead of ranged around the edges like sentinels.

The Duke threw himself into the expensive delights of decorating, purchasing the very best of everything. In 1769 he called in the architect Sir William Chambers to redecorate the palace, to refurbish the east gate, to construct a new bridge and to build the temple of Diana.

The fourth Duke's wife, Caroline, and child. At the age of twelve, Caroline had been described as being 'as beautiful as an angel'.

Next, the fourth Duke turned his attention to Henry Wise's formal gardens. Finding them unsympathetic and unfashionable, he commissioned Lancelot 'Capability' Brown in 1764 to re-landscape the park. The lake that Brown created finally made sense of Vanbrugh's grand bridge—once described as *'a monstrous bridge over a great hollow'*. His work at Blenheim, which took the best part of ten years and cost the Duke £21,500, was much acclaimed. Even Horace Walpole had to admit that the steep sides of the valley had been transformed into *'the bold shores of a noble river'* and the grand bridge had lost its *'extravagance'* and found *'propriety'*. The rector of Woodstock wrote:

> *'In this singularly picturesque landscape, the beautiful and the sublime are most intimately combined: all that can please, elevate or astonish, display themselves at once... The park... is one continued galaxy of charming prospects, agreeably diversified scenes.'*

Sir Sacheverell Sitwell, the twentieth-century English writer and art critic, described Brown's magnificent lake as *'the one great argument of the landscape-gardener. There is nothing finer in Europe.'* I can't help but agree.

OVERLEAF: *The Romney portrait of the fourth Duke has pride of place over the fireplace in the green drawing room.*

The Blenheim spaniel

The first Duke of Marlborough took a special interest in breeding the red-and-white variety of King Charles spaniel that became known as a Blenheim spaniel. The breeding of spaniels at the palace continued into the twentieth century, and the Blenheim spaniel was recognized as a separate breed until 1923.

Legend has it that Sarah, while anxiously waiting for news of her husband, who was away on a campaign, repeatedly pressed her thumb on the forehead of a pregnant bitch sitting on her lap. When the puppies were born shortly after, each had a red thumb-mark on its head. This 'Blenheim spot' became one of the most desirable characteristics of the breed.

The nineteenth-century art critic and writer John Ruskin dashed off this affectionate rhyme about his Blenheim spaniel called Dash: '*I have a dog of Blenheim birth, With fine long ears and full of mirth; And sometimes, running o'er the plain, He tumbles on his nose. But quickly jumping up again, Like lightning on he goes!*'

ABOVE: *Detail from Sir Joshua Reynolds's painting on page 110 of the fourth Duke and his family.*
BELOW: *Gladys Deacon, second wife of the ninth Duke, was besotted with the breed. Here she has photographed a few of them in her car. There were over forty more at home.*

Capability Brown

Lancelot ('Capability') Brown by Nathaniel Dance (Sir Nathaniel Dance-Holland, Bt), oil on canvas, circa 1769.

Lancelot 'Capability' Brown (1715–83), who was brought in by the fourth Duke to revamp the Blenheim gardens, was one of the most celebrated and respected professionals of his day and Britain's most fashionable and influential garden designer. His nickname arose from his habit of telling clients that their gardens had excellent 'capabilities'.

CULTIVATING THE PICTURESQUE

Brown was influenced by the Picturesque movement fashionable in the eighteenth century, when romanticism and the longing to 'return to nature' swept through the arts. Rejecting the regimented, symmetrical geometry, radiating avenues, topiary and artificial ornament of baroque garden design, Brown would invariably sweep away his clients' old formal gardens, replacing them with parkland designed with an artful informality. Nature, assisted by man, was allowed to dominate. Hallmarks of Brown's gardens were flowing lawns, winding lakes, artistically placed clumps of trees and picturesque 'ruins' carefully placed to enhance nature.

Having worked on many properties designed by Vanbrugh, Brown was familiar with the architect's work and understood his aims. Indeed, the two men, though separated by half a century and by fundamentally different approaches to design, had similar attitudes to the landscaping of the park, as the following comment by Vanbrugh proves:

> *'That part of the park which is seen from the north front of the new building has little variety of objects, nor does the country beyond it afford any of value. It therefore stands in need of all the help that can be given, which are only two: buildings and plantations. These rightly disposed will indeed supply all the wants of nature in the place.'*

Brown began work on Blenheim in 1764 and worked there on and off for the next ten years. His biggest achievement was the lake. Until then, the monumental bridge spanned only marshland and the little river Glyme. But by damming the river near Bladon and cutting through two causeways, he forced more water to flow under the bridge, forming the present fine lake on either side of it. Not only did this form a perfect complement to the statuesque bridge, but it was also much more in proportion to the palace itself.

Around the lake Brown strategically positioned clumps of trees, and he also introduced trees extensively through the park, while respecting the trees already planted by Wise. He showed less respect for Wise and Vanbrugh's formal grand parterre, which he grassed over.

Sadly, much of the original documentation for Brown's transformation of the estate no longer exists, but we know he was involved in turning the hunting lodge, High Lodge, into a Gothicized castle, and adding Gothic elements to Park Farm at the north end of the park. Having involved himself in architecture to make existing outbuildings fit better into his grand plan, he became known for his Gothic embellishments, though he never received the same recognition for them.

OVERLEAF: *I am sure that Vanbrugh would have been delighted with the splendid lake Capability Brown created around Vanbrugh's grand bridge.*

A MASSIVE LEGACY

In great demand among landowners, Brown transformed many of England's finest estates into picturesque landscapes, including Petworth House, Chatsworth, Syon House, Alnwick Castle, Longleat, Burghley House, Ragley Hall, Sledmere House, Harewood House, Highclere Castle and Warwick Castle. One can only admire this genius whose client list reads like *Who's Who* and whose talent and energy produced an extraordinary legacy still be seen today all over the country.

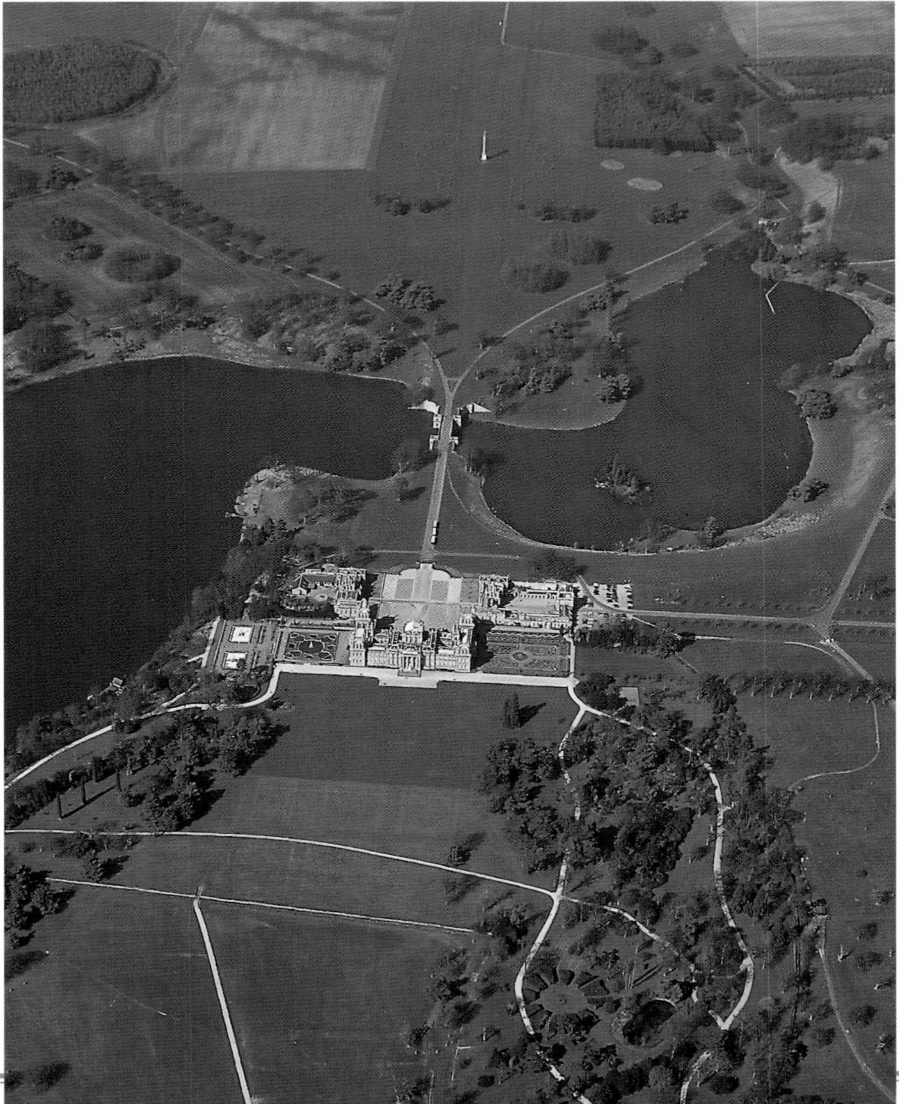

LEFT: *Spinneys and clumps of trees were crucial to Capability Brown's approach to landscape design, which aimed to surround the building with parkland rather than with formal gardens.*

THEATRICAL OF FASHION.

Blenheim Theatre opened on Friday laſt, for two nights only, with the ſame brilliancy of attraction which has long characteriſed this ſeat of real Elegance and genuine Taſte.

General Conway's Comedy of False Appearances, and Mrs. Cowley's Who's the Dupe? had the diſtinguiſhed honour of being repreſented in a ſtile of excellence that muſt have been extremely flattering to their reſpective authors, had they been preſent.

Fewer tickets having been diſtributed on account of the warmth of the ſeaſon, the company was not ſo numerous as uſual; but what it wanted in numbers, it compenſated for in faſhion.

The abilities of the noble Corps of Performers, who tread the Blenheim Stage, have long been aſcertained and admired: Mr. Nares, ſon of the late Judge, was the only new recruit, and a very valuable acquiſition he makes. His *Abbé* could not be ſurpaſſed.

The Dramatis Personæ *were*,

False Appearances.

Men.

Baron,	Mr. Spencer,
Marquis,	Lord Henry Spencer,
Governor,	Lord Charles Spencer,
Abbé,	Mr. Nares,
Robert, *Champaign,* }	Servants.

Women.

Counteſs,	Lady Elizabeth Spencer,
Lucile,	Lady Caroline Spencer,
Cœlia,	Miſs Peſhall,
Liſette,	Mrs. Savage.

Who's the Dupe?

Men.

Doiley,	Lord Henry Spencer,
Sandford,	Lord Charles Spencer,
Granger,	Mr. Spencer,
Gradus,	Mr. Nares

Women.

Elizabeth,	Lady Elizabeth Spencer,
Charlotte,	Miſs Peſhall.

ABOVE: *The cast of the Blenheim amateur theatricals consisted predominantly of the fourth Duke's offspring, as this playbill shows* *(see also paintings on page 120)**.*

THE AGE OF ELEGANCE

By the 1760s, Blenheim resonated with all that was elegant and fashionable. The fourth Duke had replaced the majority of Marlborough's heavy European acquisitions with the best of British craftsmanship and taste. Britain's empire was flowering, and both economically and culturally Georgian Britain was the centre of the world.

Blenheim was its own little universe, a self-contained island of pleasure. The birth of each child—there were eight—was celebrated in great style. Soon the nursery resounded to charades and noisy games. In one of the household books is a debit of five guineas for the services of a 'giant' to entertain at a party.

There were card games and billiards and books and, in the park, shooting, hunting, walks, rides and a menagerie with a tiger, which got through twenty-four pounds of beef every two or three days. There were lavish amateur theatricals in the orangery, hunts and shoots, and glamorous parties with men in velvet and women in silk and lace attended by footmen in livery.

In 1786 King George III and Queen Charlotte came for the day and were suitably impressed. *'We have nothing to equal this!'* the King enthused. And they didn't: the royal residence in London, Buckingham House, was a plainly furnished, unprepossessing building with a few Canalettos on the walls.

It was not just the King who was impressed by Blenheim. Public days, held every Tuesday, drew large crowds to view the state rooms and the park, at nine or ten shillings a head.

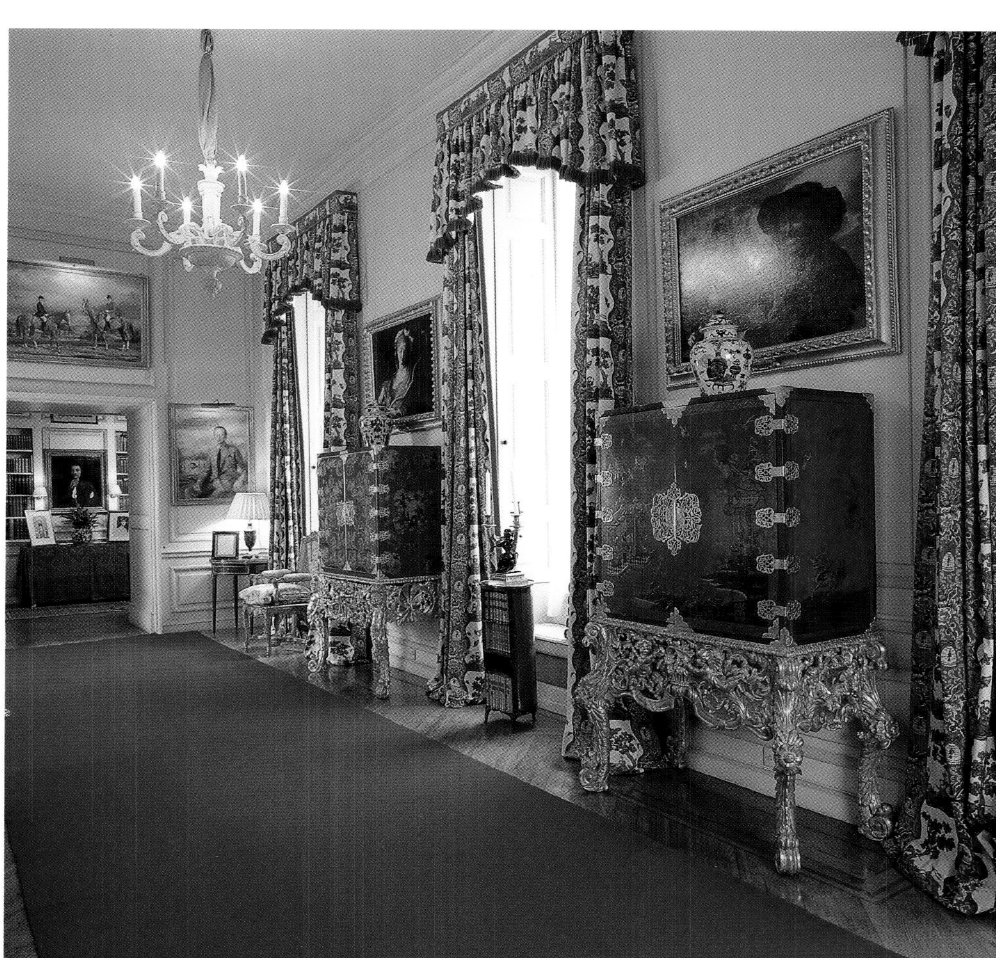

RIGHT: *The corridor leading to the smoking room and sitting room on the private side, showing a stunning pair of eighteenth-century chinoiserie lacquer cabinets on carved gilded stands.*

Private home, public monument

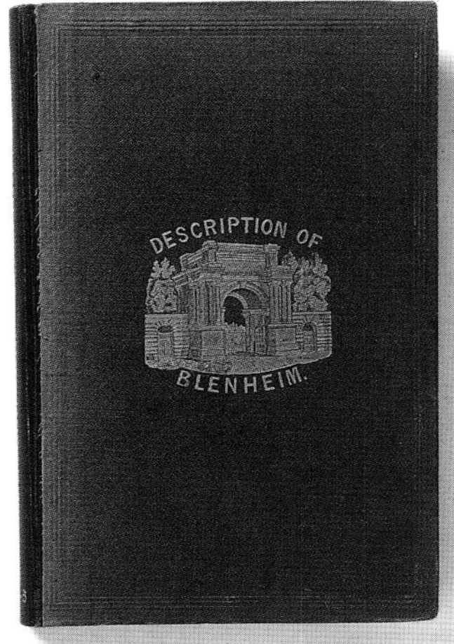

From its very beginnings, Blenheim has been a public monument. Even as a building site it was a popular tourist attraction. Marlborough directed his comptroller of works, Henry Joynes, to show visitors around without charging them a fee, but Sarah later accused Joynes of raking in the tips. Guidebooks to Blenheim first appeared in about 1750, usually as appendices to tour guides of Oxford. Public complaints about the crowds, the price of admission and the rudeness of staff were common. In the latter half of the eighteenth century, the family restricted opening hours to the afternoons, but the park was open most days, all day. Blenheim has always been made available for local public events.

The family would usually receive any distinguished visitors, but Admiral Nelson, accompanied by his mistress Emma Hamilton and her husband, had the misfortune to visit in 1802 during the reign of the taciturn fourth Duke. The Duke skulked indoors and had sandwiches sent out to them (which they returned). The fifth Duke, desperate for revenue, charged by the hour for shooting and fishing, while the sixth Duke caused bad feeling by raising the entrance fee. '*The [sixth] Duke sells tickets admitting six persons for ten shillings,*' grumbled the American writer Nathaniel Hawthorne in the 1850s. *'If only one person enters the gate, he must pay for six; if there are seven in company, two tickets are required to admit them!'*

In 1856 the fee was settled at one shilling per person and the price remained unchanged until the First World War, when all revenues were handed to the Radcliffe Infirmary in Oxford. In the early years of the twentieth century, public access was restricted as the family spent more time at Blenheim, and by 1920 only the grounds were open to the public. The palace reopened in the 1950s, attracting larger and larger crowds, and now, under my father's enlightened stewardship, visitor numbers exceed half a million a year.

ABOVE AND BELOW: *A guidebook to Blenheim annotated by the sixth Duke. Guidebooks to Blenheim first appeared in the mid-eighteenth century.*

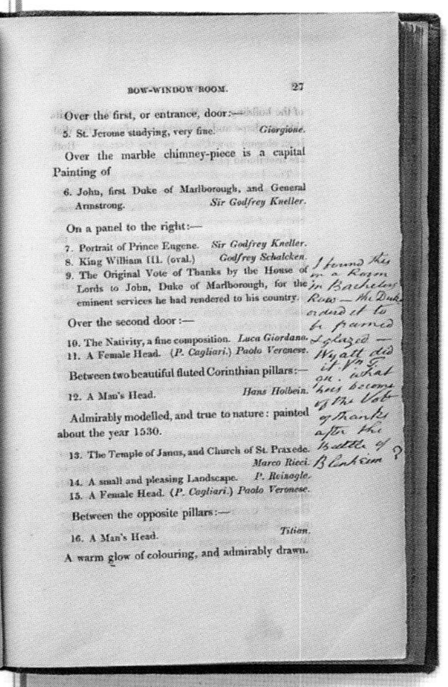

BOW-WINDOW ROOM. 27

Over the first, or entrance, door:—

5. St. Jerome studying, very fine. *Giorgione.*

Over the marble chimney-piece is a capital Painting of

6. John, first Duke of Marlborough, and General Armstrong. *Sir Godfrey Kneller.*

On a panel to the right:—

7. Portrait of Prince Eugene. *Sir Godfrey Kneller.*
8. King William III. (oval.) *Godfrey Schalcken.*
9. The Original Vote of Thanks by the House of Lords to John, Duke of Marlborough, for the eminent services he had rendered to his country.

Over the second door:—

10. The Nativity, a fine composition. *Luca Giordano.*
11. A Female Head. (*P. Cagliari.*) *Paolo Veronese.*

Between two beautiful fluted Corinthian pillars:—

12. A Man's Head. *Hans Holbein.*

Admirably modelled, and true to nature: painted about the year 1530.

13. The Temple of Janus, and Church of St. Praxede. *Marco Ricci.*
14. A small and pleasing Landscape. *P. Reinagle.*
15. A Female Head. (*P. Cagliari.*) *Paolo Veronese.*

Between the opposite pillars:—

16. A Man's Head. *Titian.*

A warm glow of colouring, and admirably drawn.

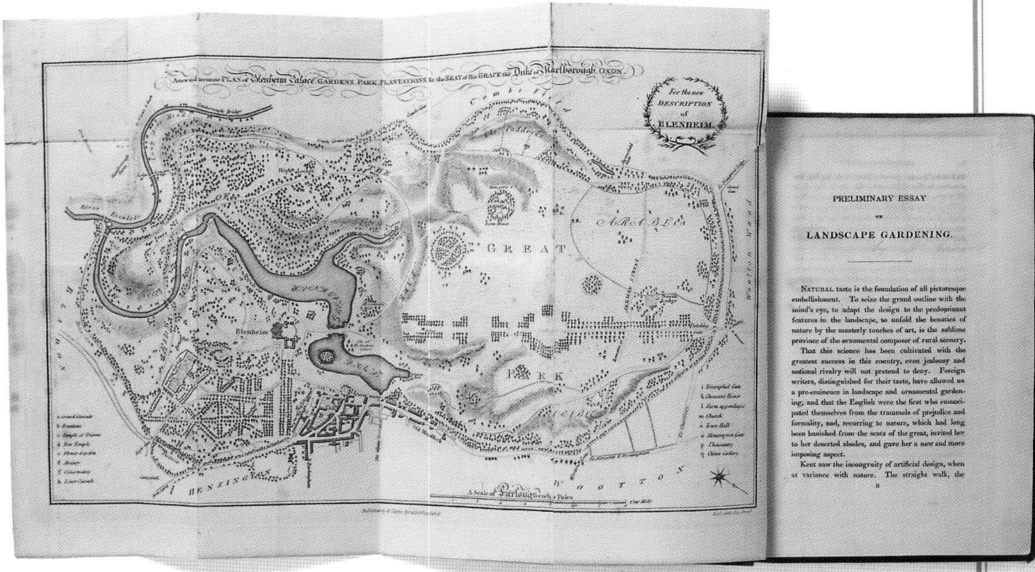

PRELIMINARY ESSAY

ON

LANDSCAPE GARDENING.

NATURAL taste is the foundation of all picturesque embellishment. To seize the grand outline with the mind's eye, to adapt the design to the predominant features in the landscape, to unfold the beauties of nature by the masterly touches of art, is the sublime province of the ornamental composer of rural scenery.

That this science has been cultivated with the greatest success in this country, even jealousy and national rivalry will not pretend to deny. Foreign writers, distinguished for their taste, have allowed us a pre-eminence in landscape and ornamental gardening, and that the English were the first who emancipated themselves from the trammels of prejudice and formality, and, recurring to nature, which had long been banished from the seats of the great, invited her to her deserted abodes, and gave her a new and more imposing aspect.

Kent saw the incongruity of artificial design, when at variance with nature. The straight walk, the

B

SILENT RETREAT

Blenheim under the fourth Duke was like Camelot, and like Camelot it couldn't last for ever. The children were growing up and rattling the bars of their gilded cage, yearning for the stimulation and sophistication of London life. The heir, young George, was learning how to spend money like water, and the Blenheim coffers were suffering.

The Duke was fast running out of money. In 1766 he was worrying about having enough to pay the quarterly bills, and over the next couple of years he made savings. The number of servants was reduced from eighty-eight to seventy-five, and he sold Langley Park, his original family home. Instead of perambulating expensively around the country with their close-knit retinue, the Duke and Duchess—who had always preferred each other's company to the exclusion of others—stayed home.

Over the years, the Duke's natural shyness became pathological, and his way of dealing with people was to avoid speaking to them at all. He would retreat for days at a time to his observatory to look at the stars, or to his study to pore over his gem collection.

His close involvement with political matters ceased, although England was once again at a critical juncture, with the American War of Independence gobbling up resources and ruining reputations and, nearer to home, the Spanish

By the late eighteenth century, many fine homes had private theatres, and in 1787 the fourth Duke converted the orangery into a theatre that held over two hundred people. For two years, his family regularly staged plays before invited audiences, and the productions were relatively lavish, as these contemporary paintings suggest.

fleet moored off Plymouth waiting to invade. The King, in between bouts of madness, was in a parlous position and begging for help to strengthen his hand against an increasingly vociferous government and a country on the edge of revolt. But Marlborough was too far down his own track.

The Duke's reputation as a recluse was growing. After a party attended by the Duchess on a rare solo outing, a society lady wrote to a friend: *'The Duchess is in hopes to bring the Duke into such company next winter in hopes to make him speak.'* Another contemporary gossip recalled:

> *'[The Duke] had been for some time a confirmed hypochondriac and dreaded anything that could in any way ruffle the tranquil monotony of his existence... it is said that he remained for three years without pronouncing a single word.'*

John Moore, the Marlborough tutor, who was eventually to become Archbishop of Canterbury, was the Duke and Duchess's concerned confidante during this time, acting as a go-between for them, the world and their children. In 1778 the Archbishop wrote:

> *'I have seen with pain how much your Graces have both withdrawn yourselves from the world of late. Your children are now growing up apace and they must mix with the world and how much better under your own eyes.'*

THE WILD BUNCH

The children mixed in their own way. George, the eldest son, recklessly borrowed money all over London, estranged from his parents. Daughter Caroline toyed with suitor after suitor, randomly breaking hearts and dashing hopes. Daughter Charlotte eloped with a commoner, was banned from Blenheim and never saw her childhood home again. Young Henry was a brilliant, witty and charming young man who was set to have a remarkable career in government—but in 1795 he died suddenly from fever, aged twenty-five.

The life that had invigorated Blenheim was slipping away. The Duchess died in 1811 but a reconciliation with her eldest son had taken place. The fourth Duke never again left Blenheim or the grounds. He died in his sleep in January 1817, fifty-nine years after succeeding to the title.

The Duchess of Marlborough continues in a very alarming state. Since her Grace's illness, she expressed a desire to see her eldest son, the Marquis of Blandford, whom she had not seen for these 18 years—when a happy reconciliation took place, to the great satisfaction of the family.

A bit of early nineteenth-century tittle-tattle about the lives of the rich and famous from the pages of The Times.

The Marlborough Gems

The fourth Duke started his love affair with carved gems on his honeymoon in Venice when he bought the Zanetti collection. The purchase led to an obsession that defined his character to such a degree that in the renowned family portrait by Reynolds (see page 110) he is depicted holding one of his beloved gems, while his heir is entrusted with one of the red leather boxes that housed them.

In his lifetime, the Duke collected no less than 739 carved emeralds, sapphires, garnets and other gems, some dating back to ancient Egypt. He kept them in red leather cases and took enormous delight in the exquisite intricacy of the carving. The images are either cameos (in which the image is raised and the background cut away) or intaglios (in which the image is cut into the stone). The Duke gave Josiah Wedgwood permission to take a cast of his favourite cameo, 'The Marriage of Cupid and Psyche', for reproduction on Wedgwood ware.

Various images of the Marlborough Gems taken from the original sale catalogue, compiled by the seventh Duke. Sadly, all we have left of the gems are pictures in this catalogue and books of engravings.

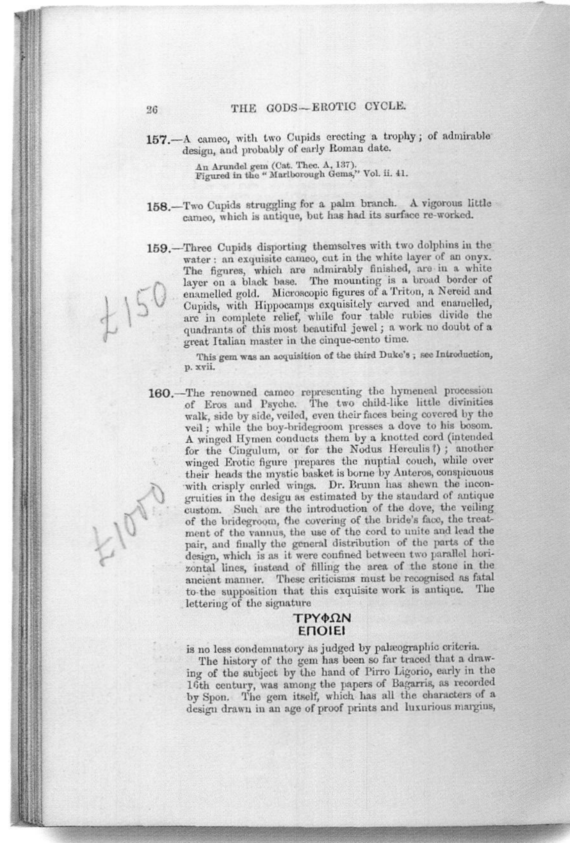

26 THE GODS—EROTIC CYCLE.

157.—A cameo, with two Cupids erecting a trophy; of admirable design, and probably of early Roman date.

An Arundel gem (Cat. Thec. A, 137).
Figured in the "Marlborough Gems," Vol. ii. 41.

158.—Two Cupids struggling for a palm branch. A vigorous little cameo, which is antique, but has had its surface re-worked.

159.—Three Cupids disporting themselves with two dolphins in the water: an exquisite cameo, cut in the white layer of an onyx. The figures, which are admirably finished, are in a white layer on a black base. The mounting is a broad border of enamelled gold. Microscopic figures of a Triton, a Nereid and Cupids, with Hippocamps exquisitely carved and enamelled, are in complete relief, while four table rubies divide the quadrants of this most beautiful jewel; a work no doubt of a great Italian master in the cinque-cento time.

£150

This gem was an acquisition of the third Duke's; see Introduction, p. xvii.

160.—The renowned cameo representing the hymeneal procession of Eros and Psyche. The two child-like little divinities walk, side by side, veiled, even their faces being covered by the veil; while the boy-bridegroom presses a dove to his bosom. A winged Hymen conducts them by a knotted cord (intended for the Cingulum, or for the Nodus Herculis?); another winged Erotic figure prepares the nuptial couch, while over their heads the mystic basket is borne by Anteros, conspicuous with crisply curled wings. Dr. Brunn has shewn the incongruities in the design as estimated by the standard of antique custom. Such are the introduction of the dove, the veiling of the bridegroom, the covering of the bride's face, the treatment of the vannus, the use of the cord to unite and lead the pair, and finally the general distribution of the parts of the design, which is as it were confined between two parallel horizontal lines, instead of filling the area of the stone in the ancient manner. These criticisms must be recognised as fatal to the supposition that this exquisite work is antique. The lettering of the signature

£1000

ΤΡΥΦΩΝ
ΕΠΟΙΕΙ

is no less condemnatory as judged by palæographic criteria.

The history of the gem has been so far traced that a drawing of the subject by the hand of Pirro Ligorio, early in the 16th century, was among the papers of Bagarris, as recorded by Spon. The gem itself, which has all the characters of a design drawn in an age of proof prints and luxurious margins,

ABOVE: *The original gem 'The Marriage of Cupid and Psyche', which was the fourth Duke's favourite piece in the collection.*

ABOVE: *This blue jasper ware cameo was copied from the Duke's original gem by the leading neoclassical sculptor John Flaxman at Wedgwood, circa 1778.*

RIGHT: *Carved from turquoise, this Roman cameo from the Duke's gem collection shows Livia and a bust of Augustus. It dates from Rome's Early Imperial Period.*

Upstairs, downstairs

A regiment of servants was needed to run an eighteenth-century palace with little running water and only the housemaids' roughened hands to wash and clean it. Upstairs, the smooth running of the household was taken for granted, and life for the family and friends of the fourth Duke followed a leisurely routine, thanks to the labours of up to eighty-eight indoor servants.

A DAY IN THE LIFE UPSTAIRS

Breakfast: An informal meal, served from 10 am onwards. People came and went, read the papers and made plans for the day.

Morning, early afternoon: Women read, went for walks, embroidered, gossiped and wrote letters. The men hunted and attended to business.

Dinner: Served at about 5 pm, this formal meal could go on for hours and was expected to include lively conversation and lots of food—up to thirty different dishes in two servings, or removes, dished up on a table laid with perfect napery, crystal glasses, gold forks and Meissen plates. Finger bowls would appear at the end of a meal either to rinse out one's mouth or to dip one's fingers in.

After dinner: The last napkin crumpled onto the table signalled the time for the ladies to withdraw. The gentlemen would linger on for two or more hours over claret and port, often consuming two or even three bottles each (but bottles were a good deal smaller in those days) and relieving themselves in chamber pots kept in the sideboards. Eventually they would stagger in to the ladies, who'd be playing the harpsichord or dealing hands of whist.

Supper: A mercifully light meal was served at around 11 pm.

FROM THE WAGES BOOK

French hairdresser £80 per annum

Head cook James Beckley £73 per annum

Butler Mountenay £45 per annum

Head footman John Wheeler £30 per annum

Running footman (*whose job it was to run, dressed in gold-fringed breeches, in front of the Duke's coach at a steady pace of seven miles an hour)* £20 per annum

Kitchen maid Mary Corner £7 per annum

Confectionery maid Mary Meredith £6 per annum

Postillion James Cowdray £4 per annum

ABOVE AND RIGHT: *The original house bells, which are located on the lower ground floor outside the kitchen. Connected to most of the major rooms in the house, these were used by family and guests alike to summon the servants.*

HOUSEMAID'S HEIGHTS

Life cannot have been easy for any eighteenth-century servant, especially in a house like Blenheim where distances between rooms and between floors were so great. One can only admire their skills in ensuring that the water was hot for washing and the food was hot to eat—no mean feat with the kitchen a few hundred yards from the dining room and the stoves for heating the water at least double that distance.

The staff sleeping accommodation, nicknamed 'Housemaid's Heights', was tucked away in the attic above the main bedroom floor. It was reached via surprisingly substantial staircases and hidden behind grand mahogany doors. Presumably there were separate areas for the male and female servants, as the bath (added in Victorian times) sits proudly in the middle of a large room. However, there is evidence of a freestanding screen having been in place. Most of the rooms had a small fireplace but many had little natural daylight other than a small skylight or floor-level window. I cannot imagine that the servants spent much time in these quarters, as their days would have been long and full.

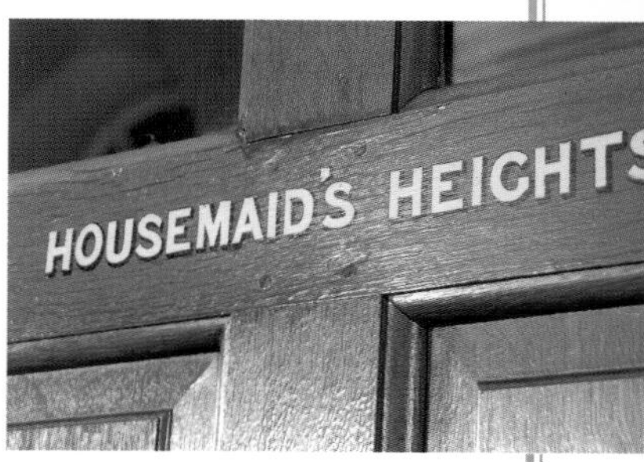

RIGHT: *The landing at the top of the stairs to accommodation (top); one of the staff bedrooms in the attic (centre); the doorway leading to the staff accommodation—'Housemaid's Heights'—in the attic (bottom).*

LEFT: *One of the many staircases that lead to intriguing places. Go up and you'll reach one of the towers; go down and you are in the former servants' rooms between the two main floors.*

The china room

East-facing and flooded with morning light, the china room is set in the private apartments and is the storage place for all the different sets of crockery used for family meals over the generations. Even the pair of 1920s pendant lights are not glass but Wedgwood china. The stone floor is original, having been chosen by the first Duchess, and the arches also remain untouched since Vanbrugh's time. (Blenheim's fine china, including Minton, Sèvres and Wedgwood, is on display elsewhere, in the China Anteroom. Many of the pieces kept there are valuable antiques, such as the Meissen porcelain with sliced-lemon handles on the tureens.) But this china room (right) holds a Blenheim secret; when the palace is closed, the Duke's children play ping-pong in it to while away the long winter evenings.

BELOW AND OPPOSITE: *The china room displays a variety of pieces from various old dinner services that are now retired from family service.*

'Ingenious far beyond the ordinary'

The fourth Duke's sister, Lady Diana (1734–1808), often visited Blenheim. First married to Lord Bolingbroke, she was delivered into what she called *'court slavery'* as an attendant upon the dull and depressing Queen Charlotte. Diana had a real Spencer-Churchill spirit: she was a lively, amusing, artistic woman who embodied all that was best of privileged eighteenth-century womanhood. The historian Edward Gibbon described her as *'handsome and agreeable and ingenious far beyond the ordinary rate'*. She boldly divorced the brutish Bolingbroke, having fallen in love with Topham Beauclerk, whom she married in 1768.

The great-grandson of Charles II and his mistress Nell Gwyn, and a friend of Dr Johnson, Topham was a handsome, devastating charmer with no money at all. A tale is told that at the family Christmas gathering one year, Topham was the unwitting cause of an outbreak of hair lice—very inconvenient for the ladies with their high, powdered wigs. When informed of the lice problem, Beauclerk declared: *'I have enough to stock a parish!'*

Nits aside, Topham proved an exciting but demanding and time-consuming spouse, and it wasn't until he died, in 1780, when his wife was in her forties, that

A self-portrait showing what a talented artist Diana was.

Diana's artistic talents flowered. She owned a small house in Twickenham, Little Marble Hill, and there she painted murals on the walls in her own delightful light and airy style.

CHERUBS AND CHILDREN

The ageing Horace Walpole was enchanted by her work, describing rooms festooned with geraniums, lilac and ivy, and another decorated with cherubs and children wreathed in honeysuckle: *'Such figures! Such dignity! Such simplicity!'* She was also a talented illustrator, illustrating books by Walpole and Dryden, among others.

Diana's work was influenced by her world—carefree, amusing, romantic and mischievous. She was very prolific and we have some of her portraits in the collection at Blenheim. They are delightful.

ABOVE: *Self-portrait of Diana as a young woman.*

LEFT: *Portraits painted by Diana of her two daughters.*

DIMINISHING FORTUNES

Before his death, the fourth Duke had attempted to control his profligate heir, also called George, by keeping him short of money, but George had responded by borrowing vast sums at impossibly high rates of interest. He had established himself at Whiteknights, a residence near Reading in Berkshire, with a huge library and a magnificent garden full of rare plants that required a staff of twenty full-time gardeners.

George thought nothing of spending money he didn't have. In many ways he resembled the Prince Regent, who was racketing around London and Brighton at the same time, lost in a world of his own pleasures. After plants and books, the love of George's life was undoubtedly the married Lady Mary Ann Sturt, with whom he had a child. He wrote to her:

'My wife, my wife, the adored mother of my beloved child, my affection to you is ten millions of times stronger than ever. Suffer this innocent babe to cement our union, so that it may know no end. Love the little Georgiana for the sake of your George.'

ABOVE: *George Spencer-Churchill, the fifth Duke.*
BELOW: *Lady Susan Stewart, who married George. She became Duchess in 1817.*

Lady Mary's husband attempted to sue for damages—he was asking for £20,000—but the case collapsed when it was discovered he'd been living adulterously with a harpist called Madame Krumpholtz by whom he had five children. The jury awarded him £100.

Being the heir to Blenheim, George was naturally in the sights of the new generation of duke-hunting mamas. He became embroiled in a ridiculous farce involving the determined amateur novelist Mrs Gunning, who was so keen to marry her daughter to the Marlborough heir that she forged a slew of love letters, purportedly from George to her daughter, in an attempt to blackmail him. The ruse failed, and George, still reeling from the experience, speedily married Lady Susan Stewart, the daughter of the seventh Earl of Galloway.

SUCCEEDING AND SPENDING

When George succeeded as the fifth Duke in 1817, he adopted the name Spencer-Churchill by royal licence (see page 107). He also threw a massive party—a dinner in the grand saloon for over seventy people, with bands playing, staff bowing and lanterns twinkling. He spent a little money on the house, turning the area beneath the long library into three rooms lavishly decorated in the style of the day. The decoration is described in a contemporary guidebook:

'Waterloo blue puckered drapery, ornamented at intervals with black rosettes... Two other apartments are now added, the one with a withdrawing room fitted up entirely with a Japan wainscoting round a painted representation of a tiger hunt in India... The refectory is in imitation of an Italian dining room of

Verd d'Antique and Sienna marble with corresponding columns and doorcases… The Doors are of polished Blenheim oak and the floors tessellated with oak and with acacia also grown in Blenheim Park.'

The fifth Duke spent a massive amount of money on the gardens, dividing them into planting areas including a flower garden, a Chinese garden, a rock garden and a rose garden, and then added aviaries, fountains, streams, temples, grottoes, an Eskimo hut and a melon house. And he bought books—always more books—including a rare Boccaccio for £2,260.

The famous edition of *Boccacio*, which, at the Duke of ROXBURGH's sale, was bought by the present Duke of MARLBOROUGH for the enormous sum of £2,260, was yesterday purchased by Messrs. LONGMAN at the far inferior price of 875 guineas. Mr. EVANS, of Pall-mall, had in both instances the disposal of it.

ABOVE: *A newspaper cutting reporting the fifth Duke's purchase of a rare book by the fourteenth-century Italian writer and poet Giovanni Boccaccio (spelled incorrectly in the newspaper) for the 'enormous sum of £2,260'.*

'GONE SADLY TO DECAY'

Two years later, the money ran out and the bailiffs moved in. Technically Blenheim and its treasures, being entailed, couldn't be counted as assets and couldn't be sold. Money had to be found from somewhere, so Whiteknights and its gorgeous garden had to go. '*It is impossible to express the beauty of the American plants,*' wrote the Duke of Wellington. '*It is said the gardens have cost the Duke £40,000.*'

The Duke was forced to sell his books for far less than he had paid for them. His Duchess chose to live elsewhere—in a grace-and-favour apartment at Hampton Court—and the Duke retreated to a corner of Blenheim Palace, living off fish and game from the estate and drinking his way mournfully through the cellar of fine wines.

The diarist Mrs Harriet Arbuthnot, who visited Blenheim with the Duke of Wellington in 1824, wrote in her journal:

> *'The family of the great general is… gone sadly to decay and are but a disgrace to the illustrious name of Churchill, which they have chosen this moment to resume. The present Duke is overloaded with debt… and lets everything about Blenheim. People may shoot and fish at so much per hour! And it has required all the authority of a Court of Chancery to prevent his cutting down all the trees in the park. He did melt down and sell the gold plate given the great Duke by the Elector of Bavaria, substituting ormolu ones to deceive the trustees.'*

The account of a Bavarian prince who visited in 1827 is equally bleak:

> *'As we entered… some very dirty shabby servants ran past us to fetch the châtelaine… She required that we should inscribe our names in a large book: unhappily, however, there was no ink in the inkstand.'*

The fifth Duke died a virtual bankrupt in 1840, his only regular income the £5,000 a year from the Post Office that the first Duke had negotiated for himself and his descendants as part of a remuneration package.

BELOW: *A contemporary report of a court injunction to prevent the fifth Duke from selling the gold and silver plate and other Blenheim heirlooms to pay his debts.*

COURT OF CHANCERY, TUESDAY, JUNE 8.
BLENHEIM GOLD PLATE.

THE EARL OF SHAFTESBURY AND LORD ROBERT SPENCER *v.* HIS GRACE THE DUKE OF MARLBOROUGH AND TRIPHOOK.

Mr. SHADWELL moved an injunction to restrain the Duke and the other defendant, from selling, pawning, or disposing of certain gold and silver plate bequeathed by the late Duke to the plaintiffs and a Mr. Blackstone, as trustees for the present Duke. The bill prayed that the defendant, Thos. Triphook, should be ordered to give up such articles of plate as he had, and that he should not be allowed to sell or dispose of any other, till further order; and that the Duke should be also ordered to deliver up such articles as Mr. Triphook had not got in his possession; that if any of the plate was sold or destroyed, the Duke might be ordered to procure plate of an equal value, and deliver the same to the plaintiffs; and that the said articles, when restored, should be lodged in some place of safety, but that the Duke should be meanwhile restrained from removing any articles from Blenheim House. The application now made to the Court was merely *ex-parte*, but he (Mr. Shadwell) had no doubt the Court would accede to it. The will of the late Duke determined, that the gold and silver plate should be for ever considered as heirlooms at Blenheim-house. Inventories of the goods were ordered to be made and delivered to the trustees. By an affidavit, it appeared that Mr. Palmer, of Piccadilly, had been employed to survey the property, and compare it with the inventory, but it was found the plate was gone, on which the deponent applied to his Grace on the subject, and was told the whole was in the hands of a tradesman, except two articles, which had been sent to have the arms engraven on them. The Earl of Shaftesbury could not, however, obtain information about the plate, and though he was told the person was gone to Wales, he could not learn what his name was. A Mr. Pennigar said, that he had got 12 or 1,300*l.* on the plate, by order of the Duke, and that it could not be recovered without that sum being repaid. A letter was sent by Mr. Alderman Cox, of Little Britain, saying that the Marlborough plate was sent to him for sale, but as the arms were covered over with wax, he refused to purchase it; and when he added, that a Mr. John Hone had declared that the said plate was offered in pledge to a Mr. Parker, of Berner's-street, Oxford-road, and that the arms were concealed under wax, these facts spoke for themselves. The learned counsel then entered into a long detail of the subsequent proceedings which had taken place relative to the plate, particularly as to a pledge given on it by a Mr. Guest, of Fleet-market.

The LORD CHANCELLOR, without hesitation, granted the Injunction.

The botanists

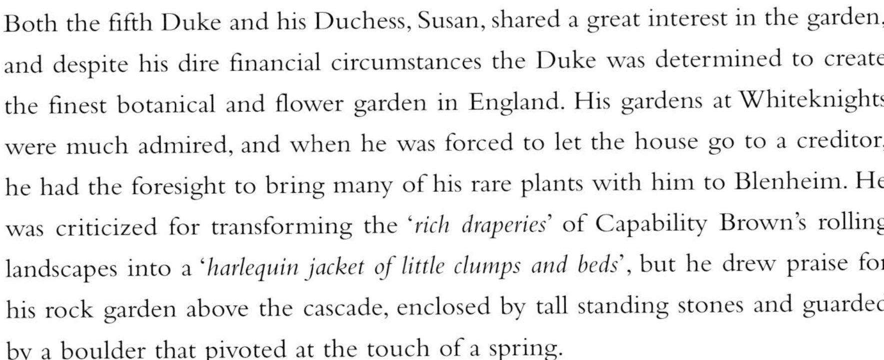

Both the fifth Duke and his Duchess, Susan, shared a great interest in the garden, and despite his dire financial circumstances the Duke was determined to create the finest botanical and flower garden in England. His gardens at Whiteknights were much admired, and when he was forced to let the house go to a creditor, he had the foresight to bring many of his rare plants with him to Blenheim. He was criticized for transforming the '*rich draperies*' of Capability Brown's rolling landscapes into a '*harlequin jacket of little clumps and beds*', but he drew praise for his rock garden above the cascade, enclosed by tall standing stones and guarded by a boulder that pivoted at the touch of a spring.

The Duke closed the western gardens to the public in order to lay out a Chinese garden, an Australian 'Botany Bay' garden, and rose and dahlia gardens '*all surrounded with borders of seedling oaks, kept constantly cut*'.

THE DUCHESS'S DELICATE WATERCOLOURS

While the fifth Duke was busy landscaping parts of the gardens, his wife Susan was showing her skills as an artist and painting scores of floral watercolours, more than a hundred of which are in a leather-bound book housed at Blenheim. Whether she was taught or just had a natural flair for painting is not known, but she was undoubtedly talented, and I was inspired by her paintings to produce a range of fabrics.

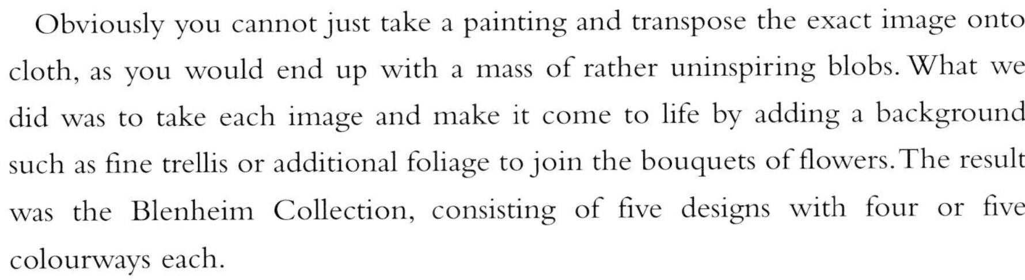

Obviously you cannot just take a painting and transpose the exact image onto cloth, as you would end up with a mass of rather uninspiring blobs. What we did was to take each image and make it come to life by adding a background such as fine trellis or additional foliage to join the bouquets of flowers. The result was the Blenheim Collection, consisting of five designs with four or five colourways each.

Although the line is no longer in production, I still own some of the original screens used for printing the fabric, so who knows? One day they may be re-established in a range of bold new colours.

LEFT: *Various prints taken from one of the many beautiful flower studies that Susan Blandford, wife of the fifth Duke, painted in the late eighteenth century.*

OPPOSITE: *One of the guest bedrooms at Blenheim, which I redecorated in the 1980s using fabrics from a collection I created inspired by the Duchess's floral paintings.*

ABOVE: *Geoerge Spencer-Churchill, who was to become the sixth Duke.*

MULTIPLE MARRIAGES

Lord Blandford, the fifth Duke's heir, distinguished himself at Eton by leading a revolt against a fearsome headmaster. As a handsome youth, he fell for a Miss Susanna Law, an innocent sixteen-year-old with stars in her eyes who insisted on marriage before pleasure. How Blandford responded to this was, of course, inexcusable and came to light only some years later, as the result of a libel case. He persuaded Susanna and her respectable mama that his intentions were honourable and that he had a clergyman brother who would marry them in secret. The 'ceremony' was performed in 1817 at Susanna's family home. She then lived as his wife in private, but not in public. For example, when he went to Scotland for some grouse-shooting, he rode in his fine carriage, while 'Mrs Lawson' and her child travelled on the mail coach. Not much is known about the daughter this mock marriage produced, but we do know that Susanna was given £400 a year by Blandford's mother to keep her peace.

Blandford then married, for real, his cousin Lady Jane Stewart, and after she died in 1844, he married Charlotte Flower. After Charlotte died in 1850, he married another Stewart cousin, also called Jane, who was to outlive him by

RIGHT: *The sixth Duke's first wife, Jane, daughter of the eighth Earl of Galloway.*
FAR RIGHT: *The sixth Duke's second wife, Charlotte, daughter of Viscount Ashbrook.*

some forty years. The sixth Duke legitimately produced five sons and two daughters. He was voted in as Member of Parliament for Woodstock and proceeded to speak up in the House of Commons on country matters and parliamentary reform. A political opponent wrote:

> *'Our opponents are just such as we might have chosen for ourselves: Lord Blandford, who is said to have lost £26,000 at Doncaster Races and not to have paid the debt... These are the careful guardians of the public purse and the persons who are to din economy into our ears.'*

CHOPPING INTO THE ASSETS

When in 1840 the sixth Duke took over the shabby Blenheim his father had left him, he changed the conditions of the Trust so that he could raise some money on mortgages and on timber sales. Engaging the architect Thomas Allason (who created the gardens at Alton Towers in Staffordshire for the Earl of Shrewsbury), he reputedly spent around £80,000 on repairs and renovations, including the elaborate fountain to keep the milk and butter cool in the dairy (now the gift shop).

Public rooms were rearranged—the state bedchamber became the crimson drawing room; and a billiard room and breakfast room replaced the Duke's study in the private apartments. The theatre was turned into offices as the estate administration was moved permanently to Blenheim. New kitchens were created in the basement of the main block, with a staircase sensibly giving access to the dining room above. It is probable that the sixth Duke installed in the main corridors under-floor gas heating powered by Blenheim's own gasworks built outside the stable court.

The sixth Duke wearing his ducal robes.

To find out exactly what he did, we have to rely on the piecemeal memories of others, as the Duke stipulated in his will that all his papers be burned, which left a big gap in the archives. After several years of illness that confined him to a wheelchair, he died in 1857, aged sixty-three, leaving a young family. We do know that when the family were resident in the palace, there were thirty servants and a governess—less than half the number employed by the fourth Duke. We also know that he stipulated that only £100 be spent on his funeral.

CHAPTER SIX

Keeping Up Appearances

ABOVE: *Frances (Fanny) Vane, wife of the seventh Duke and dutiful daughter of the Marquess of Londonderry, looking very much the Victorian matron.*

John Winston, the seventh Duke, was as different from his father and grandfather as it is possible to be. While they frolicked and partied, immersing themselves in debt and dubious relationships, John Winston pursued a life of high-minded, god-fearing rectitude. He was, in the words of the historian A L Rowse, *'a complete full-blown Victorian prig'*.

As Marquess of Blandford, John Winston followed family tradition and entered the House of Commons as the Tory Member for Woodstock. Creating no waves, but plodding dutifully along party lines, he threw his energies into campaigning for an Act of Parliament, known then as the Blandford Act, designed to strengthen the established Church. He was consistent in his views, pushing forward legislation to ban Sunday trading and attempting to stop military bands from playing in parks on the Sabbath, as it afforded *'amusement to the public of a Sunday'*.

VICTORIAN VALUES

On his father's death in 1857, the seventh Duke took his place in the House of Lords where he continued to worry about the *'degraded moral state of the people'*. His opinions were fiercely Victorian and anti-Catholic, probably as a result of an education guided by an excessively devout Protestant clergyman. The prime minister, Benjamin Disraeli, commented: *'He has culture, intellectual grasp and moral energy—great qualities, though in him they may have been developed, perhaps, in too contracted a sphere.'*

In 1843 John had married Frances (Fanny) Vane. A well-meaning, dutiful woman, she produced eleven children, eight of whom survived childhood. Family life was once again the order of day, and Blenheim was rearranged to accommodate the large brood. The children took up most of the private bedrooms, and as a result the whole of the east front came off the public circuit and was reserved for private apartments. In addition, the drawing room west of the grand cabinet became a billiard room and the saloon was refurbished as a drawing room.

As well as family, there were numerous guests to be accommodated, entertained and fed. In spite of their straitened circumstances, Fanny managed this well (although the Lord Chief Justice did complain, via the guestbook, that while he was happy to share almost everything in life, even his wife, he drew the line at half a snipe for dinner).

OPPOSITE: *John Winston Spencer-Churchill, the seventh Duke of Marlborough.*

Gaslight, clutter and a high moral tone

The sixth Duke had already installed a rudimentary system of gas heating, but under the seventh Duke new-fangled gilt gasoliers sprouted from the walls. They cast a bluish-white glare, far less flattering to complexions and furnishings than candlelight, but it was deemed to be progress. Blenheim's beautifully proportioned spaces were divided and subdivided with screens to make the place 'cosy'. Pale Georgian colours were painted over with harsh, unnatural shades of plum and puce and dark green.

The elegant Chippendale furniture acquired by the fourth Duke was relegated to the attics and replaced with overstuffed sofas and chairs, all buttoned and padded and plumped. Every tabletop and shelf was cluttered with a confusion of knick-knacks, every surface smothered with fringed throws and rugs. The dead hand of Victorian fuss and ornament laid waste the faded Regency elegance.

ABOVE AND RIGHT:
Photographs of the smoking room, on the private side of the house at the south-east corner, showing how it was decorated and furnished in Victorian times (above) and how it looks today (right). Hanging on the wall of the smoking room today is the tapestry Alexander's Triumphal Entry into Babylon.

LEFT AND BELOW: *The Duchess's sitting room in Victorian times (left) and today (below).*

OUTLINES
FROM THE
TITIAN PAINTINGS,
IN THE POSSESSION OF
His Grace the Duke of Marlborough.

Drawn and Engraved by W. Mathews,
OXFORD.
1852.

Pages from a book of engravings housed in the long library showing Titian's supposedly risqué drawings of the Loves of the Gods. Sadly, the original oils were destroyed in a fire in 1861.

AN INCENDIARY EFFECT

In keeping with the prudery of the times, nine paintings by Titian, given to the first Duke by the Duke of Savoy, were banished from the great hall. The paintings, depicting the *Loves of the Gods*, dazzled the critic William Hazlitt when he saw them in the 1820s, with their *'purple light of love, crimsoned blushes, looks bathed in rapture, kisses with immortal sweetness'*. They were obviously too much for Victorian sensitivities, however, as was a Rubens painting, *Rape of Prosperine*. These magnificent, priceless works of art were whisked away and hidden from view in a locked room above the bakehouse.

The inevitable happened. In February 1861 fire broke out in the night and the Rubens and Titians—the last vestiges of sensuality at the Blenheim of the seventh Duke—were consumed by flames. At family prayers in the chapel the following morning, the household reportedly sang *'God moves in a mysterious way His wonders to perform'*.

'Not much conversation'

Blenheim's regular schedule of entertainments and dinner parties drew many comments from the invited guests. Of one dinner thrown on a cold November night, Margaret Jeune, the wife of the Oxford vice-chancellor, wrote: *'Furs and hot water bottles kept us warm and prevented any evil results.'* And it seems the atmosphere at these dinners was as icy as the temperature:

> *'The Duchess sat evidently racking her brains for some subject for conversation, but was unsuccessful in finding any sufficiently interesting to excite more than a sentence or two from either of her two supporters. She seems a kind-hearted, motherly sort of person—neither clever nor at all handsome. The Duke is also a "plain" man in all its meanings, but it is in itself an immense merit to be a religious Duke of Marlborough, and this his Grace has.'*

Duchess Fanny in her middle years—a model of rectitude but not exactly sparkling company.

A description of a grand dinner and ball thrown in honour of the Prince of Wales is to be found in Margaret Jeune's diary. Invited for 6.30 pm, guests were ushered into the grand cabinet to meet the Prince and the house guests, *'but there did not seem to be many recognitions or much conversation'*. This awkward moment was followed at 7.00 by confusion over the pairings for the procession into dinner. The assembled company of thirty-six finally sorted themselves out and filed into the grand saloon. During dinner—lobster soufflé, stuffed quail, truffles in champagne—a band in the gallery above the saloon played *'pretty airs'*. But the conversation did not sparkle. *'I suppose state dinners cannot well avoid being formal and rather dull,'* commented Margaret.

At 8.15, at a nod from the Duchess, the ladies swished through to the red drawing room in their huge hooped crinolines, one at a time to avoid collision. The gentlemen joined them half an hour later. The company was *'a little dull'*, commented Margaret, but provided *'time and opportunity... for admiring the toilettes... and the jewels. The ambassadress had superb shoulder knots of rubies and diamonds and the tiara of Lady Macclesfield and the necklace of the Duchess were well worth notice.'*

The evening guests, three hundred of them, were invited for 10.00. There was more champagne and more lobster set out buffet-style in the saloon, and then the company moved through to the first and second state rooms, where the band played waltzes and polkas and the Prince danced energetically until 5 am. Only then could anyone leave. But in spite of the meticulous planning, the attention to detail, the superb food and the pretty airs, the party was not an unqualified success, as Margaret recounted:

> *'If the Duchess had [made] more introductions, nothing would have been wanting, but she has not very agreeable manners herself and is very deaf, which gives her an appearance of awkwardness unfortunate in her position... Some of the Oxford people certainly roamed about looking somewhat disconsolate.'*

The seventh Duke and Duchess and members of the family.

A RIGOROUS REGIMEN

In the overstuffed, buttoned-up drawing rooms of Queen Victoria's England, life for the aristocracy mirrored the royal pattern—one circumscribed by duty and religious observance.

At Blenheim, the seventh Duke, John Winston, and his Duchess, Fanny, set up a fairly rigorous regimen. Servants, children and family all had their own quarters and their own routines and the only time they breathed the same air was in the chapel, every day at 9 am.

The Duke was such a paragon of correctness that Queen Victoria invited him to take up the post of Viceroy to Ireland—but he declined the honour. Keeping up appearances in Ireland as well as Blenheim would have cost him too much, and he was barely getting by on a yearly income of £40,000 from rents. The Marlborough fortune, so assiduously built up by the first Duke and Duchess, had been dissipated on gardens, gambling and books.

REBELS IN THE RANKS

The girls were educated at home, and the boys—George (Marquess of Blandford and the heir) and Randolph, the Duchess's favourite—were sent, according to family tradition, to Eton. Boarding school proved such a release from the constraints of home and from the *'overbearing manner and assumptions of superiority'* displayed by their father, that both boys went wild. George was expelled, and Randolph developed a reputation for being bumptious, headstrong and bad-mannered, though he was also clever and could be charming. Randolph's bad-boy charisma meant he was able to recruit a large number of personal 'fags', younger boys who could be summoned to do his every bidding and ease his way through school. His rebellious streak marked him out at Merton College, Oxford, where he narrowly missed a First-class degree and was fined for breaking windows and for drunk and disorderly behaviour.

Lady Albertha ('Goosie') Hamilton, who married the Marquess of Blandford (later the eighth Duke).

TAKING THE BIT BETWEEN THE TEETH

Randolph's mother adored him, however, writing of her younger son:

'Alas! Had I been a clever woman, I must have had more ability to curb and control his impulses, and I should have taught him patience and moderation. Yet at times he had extraordinary good judgement, and it was only on rare occasions that he took the bit between his teeth, and then there was no stopping him.'

THE TIRESOME 'GOOSIE'

Meanwhile, George was enjoying life as a serving army officer and heir to a dukedom. He was restless, like his brother, Randolph, and unhappy. George had his successes with women but he lacked the easy charm that won people over and influenced them.

George fell briefly in love with Lady Albertha Hamilton, daughter of the Duke of Abercorn, marrying her in 1869. Albertha was beautiful, pious and innocent but stupid, and George soon tired of her. Known as 'Goosie', Albertha amused herself with childish practical jokes. At a dinner party, she slipped small pieces of soap onto the cheeseboard; a guest, too polite to spit out the soap, became ill. She would balance ink-pots on the tops of doors, as well as making 'apple-pie beds' (with the sheets folded to prevent occupants of the beds from stretching out their legs), putting knots in pyjamas and hiding tiny baby dolls in the breakfast dishes. Her behaviour drove George to distraction and, inevitably, into the arms of another woman.

A BREATH OF FRESH AIR

Randolph, the charmer, had more luck in love. In 1873, at a ball given aboard *HMS Ariadne* during regatta week at Cowes, he met the stunningly beautiful nineteen-year-old Miss Jennie Jerome of New York. They met on the Tuesday, were instantly smitten and by the Friday had decided to marry. Randolph's father, the Duke, made enquiries into the Jerome family and was not impressed. He thought Leonard Jerome *'a vulgar kind of man'*, and the rumour (never proved) that the grandmother of Leonard's wife Clara had been impregnated by an Iroquois brave was too much to bear. *'Under any circumstances,'* fulminated the Duke, *'an American connection is not one that we would like. You must allow it is a slight coming down in pride for us to contemplate the connection.'*

Lord Randolph Churchill.

The Duke refused permission for the marriage and Randolph resorted to blackmail, threatening not to take up the parliamentary seat of Woodstock kept warm by family tradition. While the lovely, lively Jennie waited impatiently in Paris, Randolph wore his father down and permission was finally granted for a provisional engagement. In April 1874, eight months after they first met, Jennie and Randolph were married in a simple ceremony at the British Embassy in Paris. The Duke and Duchess did not attend the wedding.

Jennie Jerome

Jennie's father, Leonard Jerome, was a flamboyantly extravagant New York stockbroker, whose three beautiful daughters were brought up in New York and Paris. A dashing and handsome speculator, who made and lost millions, he loved music, horses, yachts and pretty women. He was having an affair with the singer Jenny Lind at the time of his second daughter's birth, in 1854, hence her name, Jennie. Like all glamorous fathers, Leonard was to be Jennie's ideal—almost all the men she loved had something of Leonard in them, in particular his zest for living.

Jennie's mother, Clara, who was more given to shopping than to her husband's adrenalin-pumping passions, grew tired of his flagrant affairs. When Jennie was thirteen, Clara decamped permanently with the girls to Paris. Leonard soon followed—a misjudgement on the demand for railway stock had left his fortune badly dented, so he rented out their Madison Square house and moved to Europe.

Jennie was a glamorous and alluring teenager, with grey-blue eyes, her mother's black hair, a fantastic complexion and a perfect hourglass figure. Men buzzed around her: older men, married men and, inevitably, the Prince of Wales.

In her memoirs, *The Reminiscences of Lady Randolph Churchill*, Jennie says little about the momentous moment at the ball in Cowes, other than that she made Randolph's acquaintance that evening. However, private papers and her letters to her sisters and her parents paint a picture of a young woman intrigued by Randolph's wit, his lively mind, his passion for history and the law—in fact, his difference from the average aristocratic suitor.

'I LOVE HER BETTER THAN LIFE ITSELF'

Randolph had to get the Duke's permission for the marriage as his livelihood depended upon it—Leonard Jerome could afford to settle only £2,000 a year on his daughter. Randolph wrote of his feeling for Jennie in a letter to his father: *'I do not think that if I were to write pages I could give you any idea of the strength of my feelings and affection and love for her; all I can say is that I love her better than life itself.'* Nor was the Jerome family particularly pleased about Jennie and Randolph's engagement. Clara had her sights fixed on a prince, not the second son of a duke. But opposition only fuelled their romance. The couple wrote to one another daily while Randolph contested the Woodstock seat, Jennie socialized in Paris and the fathers-in-law-to-be wrangled over the marriage contract.

The newlyweds settled in London's Curzon Street, and enjoyed a whirl of *'gaieties and excitement'* in the company of some of the most brilliant and important people of the time. If they were poorer than their peers, they didn't let it show.

This, then, was the couple destined to become the parents of arguably the greatest Briton of them all, Winston Churchill.

OPPOSITE: *Lady Randolph Churchill, the former Jennie Jerome.*

Jennie at Blenheim

Blenheim
My dear Mamma
I got your letter
to day & I am
so glad to hear
dear Papa is
better Grandmama
has just come

daisies so much
we went down
to see Grandpapa
at breakfast
this morning
with many
kisses & love
from Winston

I have been out
riding Robroy
to day in the
Park he was
very fresh so
Chapman had
to ride him first
20 times round

the school and
led me in the
Park there
are a great
many violets
in the gardens
Jack does like
gathering the

ABOVE: *A letter from Winston as a child to his mother, Jennie.* OPPOSITE: *At Blenheim, Jenny marvelled at the 'immense' long library 'with its white, carved bookcases and vaulted ceiling'.* BELOW: *Jennie gave this signed copy of her book to the Blenheim library. She wrote it after Randolph's death, when married to her second husband, George Cornwallis-West.*

Jennie had her first sight of Blenheim on a beautiful spring day, in May 1874. A crowd of tenants and local townsfolk met them at the station and, as was the custom, untethered the horses and drew the carriage to the house. *'The place could not have looked more glorious,'* remembered Jennie, *'and as we passed through the entrance archway, Randolph said with pardonable pride, "This is the finest view in England."'* Jennie, used to the very best that New York could offer, was overawed. The lake, the bridge, the park, the grandiose palace were awe-inspiring. But she kept her awe to herself—her American pride constrained her to hide her feelings.

DAILY LIFE

'How strange life in a big country-house seemed to me, who until then had been accustomed only to towns!' she observed. The formal style that John Winston and Duchess Fanny adhered to was totally unfamiliar to her. She recalls luncheon tables groaning with rows of entrée dishes and joints of meat beneath massive silver covers. *'Before leaving the dining room,'* she adds, *'the children filled with food small baskets kept for the purpose for poor cottagers or any who might be sick or sorry in Woodstock. These they distributed in the course of their afternoon walks.'*

The Duchess ruled Blenheim with a firm hand. *'At the rustle of her silk dress,'* recalls Jennie in her memoirs, *'the household trembled.'* The Duchess set the pace and the routine ran like clockwork. For a woman with a lively mind and an independent spirit, it must have been stultifying. In the morning, the women of the house painted their watercolours, stitched at their embroidery, practised the piano and read the papers so they would be up to speed for political discussions over dinner. The afternoons held the dizzy promise of a walk or a visit to a neighbour, then after a lengthy, solemn, formal dinner the ladies retreated to play whist or read. *'Many a glance would be cast at the clock,'* recalled Jennie, as *'no one dared suggest bed until the sacred hour of eleven had struck.'*

Some fun, however, was to be had from eavesdropping, incognito, on the visitors who crowded through the palace on certain days of the week. Jennie recalls overhearing an American visitor, pausing in front of a family picture, remarking: *'My, what poppy eyes these Churchills have got!'*

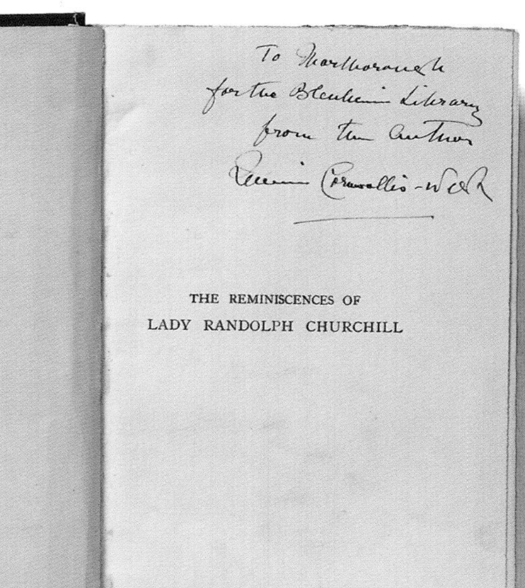

To Marlborough
for the Blenheim Library
from the Author
Jennie Cornwallis-West

THE REMINISCENCES OF
LADY RANDOLPH CHURCHILL

'THE BOY IS WONDERFULLY PRETTY'

A story often told, but not quite in accord with Randolph's own account, is that one Saturday in November, 1874, Jennie, who was over seven months pregnant, went out in a pony-trap to follow the guns at a shooting party. At the ball that evening, Jennie danced happily until suddenly seized by labour pains. A ground-floor room was quickly prepared for her. The room had been converted into a ladies' cloakroom for the evening and so had to be hastily cleared.

The following Monday, November 30, Randolph wrote to his mother-in-law:

Dear Mrs Jerome, I have just time to write a line... to tell you that all has up to now, thank God, gone off very well with my darling Jennie. She had a fall on Tuesday walking with the shooters and a rather imprudent and rough drive in a pony carriage brought on the pains on Saturday night... They went on all Sunday... The country doctor is a clever man and the baby was safely born at 1.30 this morning after about 8 hours' labour. She suffered a good deal poor darling, but was very plucky and had no chloroform. The boy is wonderfully pretty so everybody says dark eyes and hair and very healthy considering its prematureness. My mother and Clementine have been everything to Jennie, and she could not be more comfortable. We have just got a most excellent nurse and wet nurse coming down this afternoon... PS I hope the baby things will come with all speed. We have to borrow some from the Woodstock solicitor's wife.

The room in which Winston Churchill was born on November 30, 1874. It was originally occupied by Dean Jones, the resident chaplain. On this particular night, it had been used as a cloakroom for the party, and the bed was piled high with furs, feather boas and velvet capes, which had to be quickly removed.

The next morning a peal of bells at Woodstock church announced the birth. The young family remained at Blenheim, spending Christmas there, and baby Winston Leonard Spencer-Churchill was baptized in the chapel.

MOTHERHOOD AND MARRIAGE TROUBLES

Many commentators claim that Jennie was an uninterested mother, leaving the upbringing of her sons to nurses and a nanny until they grew old enough to be interesting. But I feel her behaviour has to be seen in context. Jennie was more involved with her children than were most women of her social set at that time. As Winston, in particular, grew to early manhood, he and his mother became very close, with Winston treating Jennie more like a sister. Randolph was not a loving father. A chronic illness, originally believed to be syphilis but now thought possibly to have been a brain tumour, may have had something to do with this.

Jennie and her sister, Clara, who was staying with her, threw themselves into London's social whirl. A growing tension between Jennie and Randolph was kept private, and the dashing young couple put on a brave public face.

TROUBLES AT THE PALACE

The Duke and Duchess did their best to keep up appearances at Blenheim but it was getting increasingly difficult. The seventh Duke's heir, the Marquess of Blandford, was a disappointment; no one had any expectations of him and his marriage was in deep trouble. Randolph seemed to have lost interest in his political career, and the Duchess had fallen out with the delightful and vivacious Jennie over an alleged flirtation between her and Blandford. Basically, it was a typical mother-in-law-type rift exacerbated by Jennie's *joie de vivre* and modern thinking, which irked the Duchess. *'I can't tell you how jealous Randolph says the Duchess is of Jennie,'* wrote Jennie's sister Clara to their mother after a visit to Blenheim. Jennie, who spent a lot of time at Blenheim, wrote to her mother:

> 'I loathe *living here. It is not on account of dullness,* that *I don't mind, but it is gall and wormwood to me to accept anything or to be living on anyone I hate. It is no use disguising it, the Duchess hates me simply for what I am—perhaps a little prettier and more attractive than her daughters. Everything I do or say or wear is found fault with. We are always studiously polite to each other, but it is rather like a volcano, ready to burst out at any moment.'*

Lord Randolph Churchill in Parliament.

BLACKMAIL AND BANISHMENT

Meanwhile, following a scandal involving Blandford, Randolph and the royal family (see pages 150–52), the Spencer-Churchills were ostracized by society. Randolph, Jennie and young Winston were bundled off to America to visit the in-laws. Disraeli came to Marlborough's rescue by renewing the offer of the viceregal position in Ireland. He suggested the Duke take the troublesome Randolph with him as his private secretary, in hopes that while they were away rifts would heal. Marlborough was less than pleased to discover that he would have to pay for Randolph himself, as no salary would be forthcoming. In her book, Jennie characteristically airbrushes her account:

> *'On our arrival in London, we found that the Duke of Marlborough had been appointed Viceroy of Ireland. This post [Disraeli] had pressed him to accept, thinking it might distract his thoughts from certain family worries which at that time were weighing rather heavily upon him. Hating to be parted from Randolph, his father and mother persuaded him to go with them to Ireland. Not being in favour with the court, from which London society took its lead, we were nothing loath to go.'*

The Marlborough clan set off for Ireland in December 1876, leaving Blandford in London, and Blenheim in the care of agents and a skeleton staff. Jennie loved Ireland. She rode and hunted and wrote dutiful letters to Randolph as he pursued his parliamentary career, mostly back in London. She found the people (especially the men) warm and witty and more interested in substance than Victorian rectitude: *'During the three years we lived there, I cannot remember meeting one really dull man. From the Lord Chief Justice to the familiar car man, all were entertaining.'*

The Aylesford Affair

At his wits' end with Goosie, Blandford was on the lookout for trouble. Rather like a character in an Oscar Wilde play, Blandford's aim in life was to seek temptation. He found it in Edith, Lady Aylesford, the young, spoiled wife of Joseph Finch, seventh Earl of Aylesford, a hard-drinking womanizer known to his friends as 'Sporting Joe'. In the autumn of 1875, the Prince of Wales (later Edward VII), or Bertie to his friends, took his cronies—including his boon companion 'Sporting Joe'—on a tiger hunt in India. Blandford promptly seized the opportunity and moved from his home into an inn near the Aylesford estate. According to the dictates of the times, extramarital affairs were tolerated if they were kept secret from the children, the servants and especially the press. In this case, the servants were left in no doubt about Blandford's nightly visits to Edith's bedchamber, thanks to footprints left in the snow, and the affair soon became common knowledge. Blandford then announced to his startled parents that he wished to divorce Goosie and marry Edith. News of the affair filtered through to the jungles of India. The enraged Aylesford—supported by the Prince, who declared Blandford to be *'the greatest rabble alive'*—threatened to divorce his wife, citing Blandford.

'I think that any steps that you may take to influence Blandford to give up Lady Aylesford would be for the present at any rate entirely thrown away... Any suggestion of the possibility of parting them only serves to increase his obstinate determination.'

Letter from Edward Marjoribanks to the Duke of Marlborough

A chalk portrait of a young Edward, Prince of Wales, by G F Watts, circa 1874.

AN ILL-CONSIDERED INTERVENTION

A tawdry divorce would have heaped shame and scandal on the Marlborough name, so Randolph decided to intervene. Randolph, who knew the Aylesfords well, remembered that the Prince had innocently flirted with Edith some years before and had written some foolishly compromising letters to her. The idea came to Randolph to head off the divorce by getting the Prince to influence Aylesford to drop the matter. So, armed with the letters, Randolph and Edith proceeded to visit Alexandra, Princess of Wales, threatening that if the divorce went through, the Prince would be called to account for the letters he'd written to Edith. He also insinuated that the Prince had deliberately lured Aylesford to the tiger hunt so that Edith could pursue her affair with Blandford.

The Prince was sailing homewards when he heard all this, and was so enraged that he challenged Randolph to a duel. Luckily, he had cooled off by the time the ship docked. By April 1876 the news of the scandal had spread all around London.

When Aylesford finally arrived home, he dropped the idea of a divorce and extracted a promise from Edith that she'd never see Blandford again. Randolph sent the Prince a brief note of apology, which the Prince promptly rejected, declaring that he and the Princess would never set foot again in the house of anyone who offered hospitality to Lord Randolph or his wife. In the end, the dispute lasted eight years. Finally, after much diplomatic to'ing and fro'ing, the following announcement appeared in *Vanity Fair* on March 15, 1884:

> *'A full and formal reconciliation has been effected between HRH the Prince of Wales and Lord Randolph Churchill, MP, who have for some time been strangers, on account of differences arising though the attitude respectively taken by them in relation to private matters. The reconciliation was effected last week at a dinner given for the purpose by Sir Henry James, MP. It is understood, however, that while Lord Randolph feels much satisfaction at being again on friendly terms with the Heir-Apparent, he does not propose to become intimate with all the Prince's friends.'*

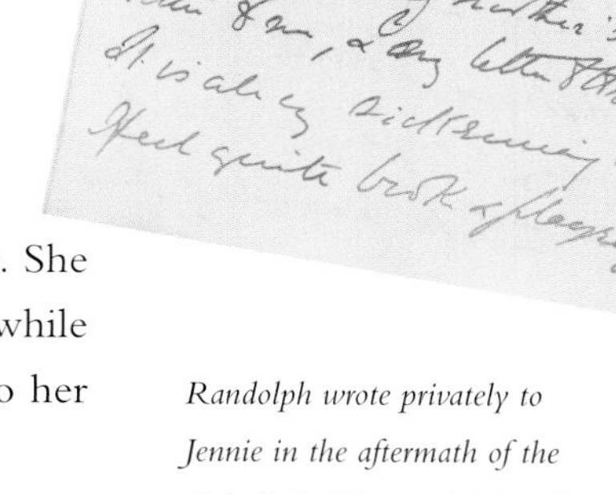
Broxmouth Park,
Dunbar.

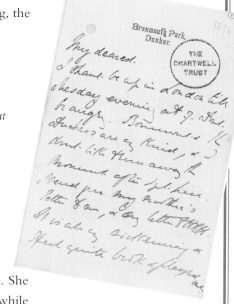

My dearest.

Randolph wrote privately to Jennie in the aftermath of the Aylesford crisis complaining that the affair was 'very sickening'.

THE AFTERMATH: BLANDFORD AND EDITH

The Aylesford marriage was too far gone for Edith to keep her promise. She and Blandford fled to Paris, staying at a hotel as Mr and Mrs Spencer, while Aylesford filed for divorce and left the country. A distraught Edith wrote to her mother-in-law:

> *'By the time this letter reaches you I shall have left my home for ever... I do not attempt to say a word in self-defence, but you can imagine I must have suffered much before I could have taken such a step; how much it would be impossible to tell you... but [Aylesford] will now have the opportunity of getting rid of one who he had long ceased to care for. You do not know, you never can know, how hard I have tried to win his love, and without success, and I cannot live uncared for... For God's sake be kind to the children, and do not teach them to hate their wretched mother, let them think I am dead, it will be the best.'*

In Paris in 1881, Edith gave birth to Blandford's child, a boy they named Guy Bertrand. Legal wrangles with the House of Lords over the child's paternity put an intolerable strain on this pressurized love affair, and Blandford abandoned Edith to a life of comparative poverty (although he claimed to love little Guy more than the four children he had left at home). Goosie forgave her errant husband, momentarily, and Blandford dutifully returned to London. Edith died in 1897, forgotten by Blandford but not by the Prince and Princess of Wales, who sent a wreath to the funeral. Of Guy, tragically, nothing is known. He was seen once by a member of the family some time after the Second World War.

A contemporary photograph of Viceregal Lodge, Dublin, where the Churchills escaped to after the affair. The Duke was hastily appointed Irish Viceroy and took Randolph as his secretary.

THE AFTERMATH: BLANDFORD AND GOOSIE

All might have gone well with the newly reconciled Blandford and Goosie had the susceptible Blandford not bumped into a London neighbour, the talented, creative and brilliant Lady Colin Campbell. The Campbells' sensational divorce, in which Lady Colin accused her syphilitic husband of cruelty and he accused her of affairs with a duke (Blandford), a general, a surgeon and London's fire chief, made headlines.

Because Blandford's reputation as a rake had already been established in the Aylesford case, his name was pre-eminent. When he was asked during cross-examination why he had so often sought Lady Colin's company, the jury could hardly suppress its mirth when Blandford answered: *'Her conversation.'*

Blandford escaped the vengeance of the court, but not that of his wife. By 1883 he was in court again, this time being sued for divorce.

Giovanni Boldini's oil painting of Lady Colin (Gertrude) Campbell, circa 1897.

THE AFTERMATH: SPORTING JOE

Lord Aylesford drifted off to Big Spring, Texas, to find a new life for himself. There he is remembered as a barrel-chested giant of a man who loved horses, dogs, hunting and legendary quantities of whiskey. He died in Texas in 1885. When the doctor removed the Earl's innards in preparation for embalming the body for shipment to England, he found Aylesford's liver to be '*as hard as a rock*'.

'I DID GOOD IN MY DAY'

Marlborough acquitted himself well enough in the difficult Irish situation, and Duchess Fanny threw herself into charitable works. On their return from Ireland in the summer of 1880, she would proudly show the letter she had received from Queen Victoria commending her work for famine relief. Before her death she gave the letter to the Blenheim Archives: *'I may seem a useless old woman now,'* she wrote, *'but this letter will show you I was once of some importance and did good in my day.'*

THE PRICE OF SOCIAL POSITION

The Marlboroughs' social standing was restored after their extremely expensive Irish exile and the neglected palace was brought back to life, but the house and estates had suffered from the absence, as indeed had Marlborough's pockets. Financially, the family's prospects were grim. Compared with other peers of the realm, the seventh Duke was relatively impoverished. He had seven acres of palace to maintain, a large staff, endless social obligations and only £40,000 a year. The Earl of Derby, on the other hand, had an income of £150,000, the Duke of Northumberland over £160,000 and the Duke of Norfolk a comfortable £231,000. As Marlborough gazed out ruefully over the gardens that had cost the fourth Duke £100,000, pondering the upkeep of six expensive daughters and two free-spending sons, he realized that no cavalry would come galloping to the rescue. He had to do something himself.

The Duke's solution was to have a word with his friend Earl Cairns, the Lord Chancellor, who pushed through Parliament the Blenheim Settled Estates Act of 1880, effectively undoing the entail that had protected the Marlborough heirlooms since 1722. The Duke started with the books, the gemstones and a few pictures. It was obviously not too painful for him to part with these treasures. Jennie remarks in her book: *'If familiarity breeds contempt, it also engenders indifference; [no members of the family] seemed to notice these pictures.'*

The seventh Duke resumed his seat in the House of Lords, but the stresses and strains of maintaining his position soon told. He died of a massive heart attack in 1883, aged only sixty-one.

Fanny commissioned for the chapel a white marble standing figure of her husband, the seventh Duke, from Sir Joseph Boehm. He stands very stiff and upright—in striking contrast to the voluptuous curves of the Rysbrack monument to the first Duke *(see page 103).*

THE EIGHTH DUKE

The Marquess of Blandford succeeded as the eighth Duke in 1883 with no wife by his side. He had been a restless youth and even in his maturity he was never to find peace of mind. His father had been impossible to please, not that either Blandford or Randolph had tried very hard. Blandford, as he continued to be known even after his succession, had interests incomprehensible to his stern papa. His passions were for science, mathematics and mechanics, and to pursue them he needed money. Profiting from the broken entail organized by his father, Blandford quickly set about selling the rest of the paintings. Then someone suggested that if he went to America, he might find himself a wife with money.

LILIAN'S MILLIONS

The good-natured Leonard Jerome was only too happy to help. He engineered a meeting between Blandford and Lilian Hammersley, a rich and charming widow, known for her extravagant habit of filling her box at the theatre with orchids. She insisted on being called Lily rather than Lilian (which rhymed with million), thereby denying headline writers a bit of fun at her expense. Leonard reported:

> *'I rather think he will marry the Hammersley. Don't you fear any responsibility on my part. Mrs H is quite capable of deciding for herself. Besides I have never laid eyes on the lady but once. At the same time I hope the marriage will come off as there is no doubt she has lots of tin.'*

Oil painting of Lilian (Lily) Hammersley, a wealthy widowed American who became the eighth Duke's second wife.

Leonard was a witness at the wedding in City Hall, New York City, a few weeks later, and he saw them off on the liner *Aurania* the following morning, having helpfully cabled Dowager Duchess Fanny to smooth the waters.

Luckily, Duchess Lily was happy to spend some of her 'tin' on making Blenheim livelier and more comfortable. In 1888, the year of Lily's marriage to the eighth Duke, a boathouse with Gothic mullions and a half-timbered upper floor was built on the lakeshore. A Willis organ was installed at one end of the long library so that there could be music and singing after dinner instead of yawning and whist.

On a more practical note, the palace roof was re-leaded; central heating and electricity were put in, so there was no more shivering under fur rugs and no more popping gaslight. This new-fangled technology was in addition to Blenheim's new internal telephone system, the installation of which the Duke had himself overseen. All these refinements came to pass, but there was still only one bathroom in the whole palace. I shudder to think how they coped.

LEFT: *The Willis organ installed by the eighth Duke and Lily in the long library in 1891. The inscription on the organ reads: 'In memory of happy days and as a tribute to this glorious home we leave thy voice to speak within these walls for years to come when ours are still.'*

BELOW LEFT: *The organ book is a beautiful parchment-bound volume. In it are recorded details of the performances and guests who attended the recitals. As with all record books, it starts out meticulously kept but then peters out.*

1914

Among the many changes wrought by the Great War of 1914 – 1918 few were more striking than the conversion of the Library into a Convalescent Hospital. All carpets & furniture were removed and fifty beds brought in.
The Organ played an active part in amusing and entertaining the wounded men and many were the expressions of their gratitude to the Duke and of their appreciation of his kindness and hospitality.
The delights of the Blenheim gardens and the charm of the general surroundings (so much pleasanter than anything the poor fellows had hitherto been accustomed to) had a great influence in restoring them to health.
Anyone desirous of fuller information regarding this portion of the history of Blenheim will find ample records in the volume entitled "Blenheim Convalescent Home.

The big sell-off

The Blenheim Settled Estates Act, passed in 1880, allowed the seventh Duke to overrule the entail set up to protect the Marlborough Treasures. He put the Sunderland Library up for sale, using the excuse that *'through age and other circumstances'* the books were deteriorating. *The Times* urged that the library should be bought for the nation at a price of £40,000, but there wasn't enough enthusiasm for the fine collection of classics, the priceless Renaissance works and early books printed on vellum. In the end, the Library was sold off in two portions, each sale taking ten days; the total realized was £56,581. Under the Act, the money had to be ploughed back into the Estate, but the Duke set aside £2,000 to rip out the beautiful early Georgian shelving and convert the library into an art gallery.

THE SUNDERLAND LIBRARY SALE.

This important sale commenced yesterday at the rooms of Messrs. Puttick and Simpson, according to announcement, and by 1 o'clock the large room was crowded with a large audience interested either as spectators or purchasers in the dispersion of the famous collection of Lord Sunderland, so long deposited in the palace of the Dukes of Marlborough. Much speculation has been heard as to the sum likely to be realized in the sale of a library which is said to have cost in its formation at least £30,000. It is known that some large offers have been made for it *en bloc* by the agents employed for American libraries, and it is said that as much as £25,000 has been offered and declined, while one of the largest dealers of London came somewhere near this sum, also to meet with a disappointment.

Every day of the sale of the Sunderland Library, The Times *listed the items sold, charting the destruction of one of the finest libraries in Europe.*

The Marlborough Gems went in one lot at Christie's for £10,000, bought by David Bromilow of Bitteswell Hall, Leicestershire; his family subsequently sold the collection at auction in London. The Museum of Fine Arts, Boston, purchased twenty-one of the Marlborough Gems at this auction (including the prize specimen 'The Marriage of Cupid and Psyche'), and they remain there today. Next to go were over eighty Limoges enamels, which raised £8,226, though some of the pieces never reached their reserve and were withdrawn from the sale.

register and last leaf wanting ; and Epistle of Politian, mounted.—£19. Albertus. Architecture. Translated by Leoni. Fol., Lond., 1726. Plates by Picart.—£2 10s. Alciatus, Livret des Emblemes, &c., Gothic letter, cuts, small 8vo., Paris, C. Weckel, 1536, a tall copy about 8in. by 5in., margins uncut, 112 cuts, old calf, with Sunderland arms and motto, "Dieu defende le droit"—£40; Alciatus, Emblemata, cuts, 12mo., 5in. by 3in., Lugd.,1598—£1 18s.; Alciatus, De Ponderibus et Mensuris, plates,1530-1, 12mo., and other tracts—£4 ; Alcyonius (Pet.), Venetus.De Exilio, 8vo., Venet., Ald., 1522—£1 14s.; Alexander Aphrodisiensis, Aristotelis Commentaria Græce, ed. prima Aldina, Venet., 1520, with another Aldine edition, 1513, and one of 1520, three rare editions, all in good condition, 1 vol. fol., 12in. by 6in., old red morocco, gilt—£8 ; Aleman (Mateo), Vida del Picaro Guzman de Alfarache, and Sec. Parte, 2 vols., vellum, 12mo., 1603—£7 15s. ; Alexander Gallus, Doctrinale seu Grammatica Lat., Metricè, absque ulla nota, circa 1470 in Italia, 4to., 10½in. by 7¼in., calf, 45 leaves printed in Roman letters, 30 lines to a page, with initials painted—a spirited contest for this arose between Mr. Quaritch and M. Techener, in which, however, the French dealer was victorious with his bid of £41; Allard, Discours historique des Familles, 12mo., Grenoble, 1671—£4 10s. ; Allegre, Vies des Empereurs, first edition, small 4to., Paris, 1556—£2 13s. ; Allegre, Vies des Empereurs, second edition, cuts, with index, small 8vo., Paris, 1567—£7 10s. ; Almeyda, (P. Man. de.), Historia Geral de Ethiopia, &c., folio, 1660, with folding map and one of the sources of the Nile—£20 ; Alsatia—La veritable Origine des illustres Maisons d'Alsace, &c., folio, vellum, Paris, 1649—£1 16s. ; Alphanus, Collectanea Juris Civilis, small 8vo., Venet., 1570, old stamped pigskin with designs—18s. ; Alvarez (Fr.), Ho Preste Joam des Indias, Gothic letter, woodcut title, limp vellum with

EVERYTHING MUST GO!

What the seventh Duke started, the eighth Duke finished. As soon as he succeeded to the dukedom, he let it be known that he wanted to disperse the entire Blenheim collection of paintings. The art world spent two years flexing their chequebooks in anticipation. As a taster, the nation got Raphael's *Ansidei Madonna* for £70,000 and Van Dyck's equestrian portrait of Charles I for £17,500. One hundred and twenty small copies of great masters by Teniers, which had once hung in the billiard room, were sold one at a time for a total of £2,031.

The first sale of paintings, including eighteen works by Rubens, a number of Van Dycks and a Bruegel, fetched £34,834. Most went to private collectors. The second sale, mainly of historical portraits, included eight Van Dycks, a Reynolds, a Gainsborough, a Poussin, a Stubbs, and a group of Reynolds studies lovingly collected by the fourth Duke. The third portion consisted of mainly Italian seventeenth-

and eighteenth-century pictures, which were not fashionable then and fetched only £11,411 in total. Carlo Dolci's *Madonna of the Stars*, for which the seventh Duke had turned down an offer of 20,000 guineas, was sold to Agnew for 6,600 guineas.

Huge collections of china and porcelain went next. Part of the Spalding Collection of Chinese and Japanese porcelain was bought by the dealers Duveen for £2,326. A collection of English china fetched £3,646. The Duke wasn't finished yet. Rubens's *The Three Graces* went to Baron Rothschild for 25,000 guineas, while *Lot and his Daughters*, which had hung in the dining room, ignored by the family, went to a Paris dealer for 20,000 guineas.

At this stage the total sales added up to £350,000. Sad to say, most of this incomparable collection went overseas. Randolph loved the paintings and was horrified by his brother's philistine approach. Much to his chagrin, he kept coming across former treasures from his home as he travelled around Europe—a Raphael in a Berlin gallery, a cabinet in St Petersburg—which caused him much pain.

The walls and cabinets at Blenheim were practically bare. The treasures were gone and the eighth Duke now had plenty of money to spend on things much more to his taste: farm buildings, hothouses for orchids and laboratories for scientific experiments.

Where the money went. An old photograph showing the original orchid greenhouses where the eighth Duke nurtured his expensive hobby.

'A YOUTH OF GREAT PROMISE MARRED BY FATE'

The newly remarried eighth Duke threw himself into his scientific experiments, but happiness and fulfilment still eluded him. In 1892, four years after his New York wedding, he died suddenly, aged forty-eight, leaving a bewildered young heir, Charles, who was twenty. In his will the eighth Duke left his personal estate to his wife and £20,000 to Lady Colin Campbell *'as proof of my friendship and esteem'*—no mention of Edith Aylesford or their son—plus £5,000 in trust for roof repairs to Blenheim, and generous bequests to the servants. In what I think was a final gesture of defiance against the father to whom appearances had meant everything, he specified that he did not wish to be buried in the vault in the chapel: *'I dislike particularly the exclusiveness of family pride and I wish... to be buried... in any suitable place that may be convenient in which others of my own generation and surroundings are equally able with myself to find a resting place together.'* However, his brother, Randolph, overrode this request, and the eighth Duke is buried in the chapel vault.

George is referred to as 'the wicked duke', but we have recently uncovered a stash of his papers that reveal him not to be the complete philistine he is made out to be. Many who knew him recognized his talents. Morton Frewen, who was married to one of Jennie's sisters, wrote: *'I have known one or two first-class minds whose achievements have been nil. Take George, eighth Duke of Marlborough—an almost incomparable mind, indeed in receptivity, range and versatility, hardly to be matched.'*

Lord Redesdale, grandfather of the talented and opinionated Mitford sisters, wrote that George was a *'youth of great promise marred by fate, shining in many branches of human endeavour, clever, capable of great industry, and within measurable distance of reaching conspicuous success in science, mathematics and mechanics'*.

The American press couldn't get used to the English hereditary system whereby the new heir takes over the house with the title and the widow is consigned to the dower house.

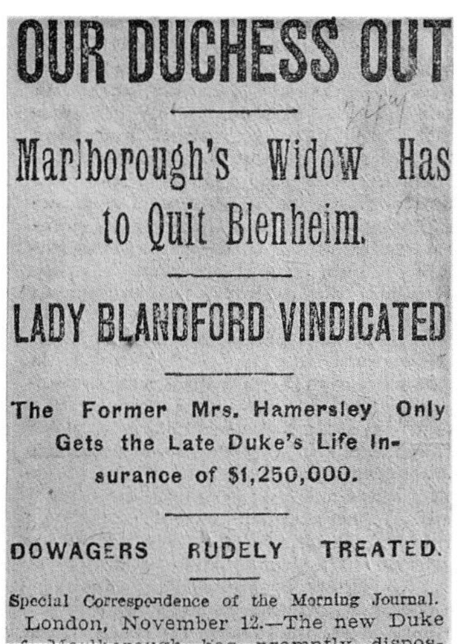

OUR DUCHESS OUT

Marlborough's Widow Has to Quit Blenheim.

LADY BLANDFORD VINDICATED

The Former Mrs. Hamersley Only Gets the Late Duke's Life Insurance of $1,250,000.

DOWAGERS RUDELY TREATED.

Special Correspondence of the Morning Journal.
London, November 12.—The new Duke

'SO MAD AND ODD...'

After the Irish sojourn, Randolph returned to his parliamentary career. In 1880, he became leader of a radical group of Tories known as the Fourth Party. By 1884 he was reconciled with the Prince of Wales and in 1886, at the age of only thirty-seven, he became Chancellor of the Exchequer and Leader of the House of Commons. His mother was delighted, his son Winston was proud and Jennie was very much looking forward to being the wife of the next prime minister.

Unfortunately, Randolph's illness was beginning to affect not only his health but also his moods. Queen Victoria expressed her concern. *'He is so mad and odd,'* she wrote in her journal in July 1886, *'and also in bad health.'* Randolph was rude and bad-tempered to guests, and arrogant and belligerent with colleagues. He strongly disagreed with his prime minister and the Cabinet on many issues. When, as the darling of the party, he offered his resignation over budget cuts, he was taken at his word and it was accepted. *'[Randolph] has thrown himself from the top of the ladder and will never reach it again,'* complained a colleague. He was right.

The growing distance between Jennie and Randolph was evident. Jennie had her own social life and many admirers, in particular Count Charles Kinsky, who was her big romantic melodrama. Newspapers slyly remarked on her affairs, but she did her duty by the dying Randolph. As the illness took its final hold, Randolph's mood swings verged on the violent, while his attacks of paralysis and slurred speech became more acute. Winston, who was now twenty years old, insisted on knowing the cause of his father's illness. The belief that it was syphilis only served to strengthen the deep bond with his mother. Then, two weeks before Randolph died, Count Kinsky married someone else. Jenny wrote to her sister:

> *'I am really in a much better frame of mind that you can possibly imagine as regards this wedding. The bitterness, if there was any, has absolutely left me. He and I have parted the best of friends and in a truly* fin de siècle *manner... He has not behaved particularly well and I can't find much to admire in him but I care for him as some people like opium or drink... Randolph's condition and my precarious future worries me much more. Physically he is better but mentally he is 1,000 times worse... What is going to happen I can't think... Up to now the general public and even society does not know the real truth and after all my sacrifices and the misery of these six months, it would be hard if it got out. It would do incalculable harm to his political reputation and memory and is a dreadful thing for all of us.'*

Jennie's grave at Bladon churchyard, where she is buried next to Randolph.

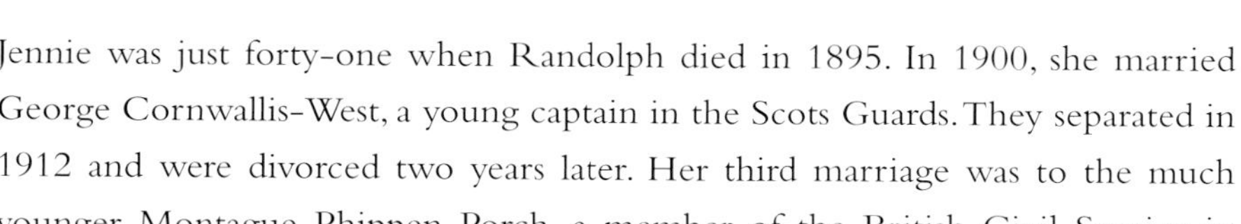

Jennie was just forty-one when Randolph died in 1895. In 1900, she married George Cornwallis-West, a young captain in the Scots Guards. They separated in 1912 and were divorced two years later. Her third marriage was to the much younger Montague Phippen Porch, a member of the British Civil Service in Nigeria. Jennie died in 1921 after surgery to remove a gangrenous leg and is buried next to Randolph in the family plot at Bladon churchyard.

Jennie in her later years.

'I OWE EVERYTHING TO MY MOTHER'

Frank Harris recorded a conversation with Winston about his father that tells us a great deal about Winston's relationship with his parents:

> *'Did you ever talk politics with him?'*
>
> *'I tried, but he only looked with contempt on me and would not answer.'*
>
> *'But didn't he see you had something in you?'*
>
> *'He thought of no one but himself. No one else seemed to him worth thinking about.'*
>
> *'You didn't like him?'*
>
> *'How could I? I was ready enough as a boy, but he wouldn't let me. He treated me as if I had been a fool; barked at me whenever I questioned him. I owe everything to my mother; to my father, nothing.'*

Charles Spencer-Churchill, Duke of Marlborough, Consuelo, Duchess of Marlborough, John, Marquess of Blandford, Lord Ivor Spencer-Churchill.

CHAPTER SEVEN

A Stiff Upper Lip

With the sudden death of the eighth Duke in 1892, his son Charles (my great-grandfather) succeeded to the dukedom and the depleted treasures of Blenheim while still a student at Trinity College, Cambridge. Known as Sunny (because he was Earl of Sunderland), the ninth Duke was a clever, serious young man with innate good taste and an artistic imagination. He cared passionately for his inheritance, writing: *'Blenheim is the most splendid relic of the age of Anne, and there is no building in Europe except Versailles, which so perfectly preserves its original atmosphere.'*

The nickname notwithstanding, Sunny was also exceedingly melancholy and dour. I suspect that the young Duke's introspection was caused partly by his parents' acrimonious divorce in the wake of the Aylesford affair, and was probably also the effect of witnessing his father's gloomy disappointment with life—a gloom that had led the eighth Duke to inscribe a fire surround (appropriately) with the message, '*Dust. Ashes. Nothing.*'

ABOVE: *Sunny, the ninth Duke, as a boy, in the uniform of the Oxfordshire Hussars, with whom he later served.*

OPPOSITE: *One of my favourite portraits at Blenheim. Painted in 1905 by John Singer Sargent, it shows the ninth Duke and his wife, Consuelo, with their two sons, Bert, my grandfather (standing between his parents), and Ivor, my great-uncle (far right).*

FAMILY PRESSURES

THE DUKE OF MARLBOROUGH'S MAJORITY.

BALL AT BLENHEIM.

Blenheim has during the week been the scene of rejoicing connected with the coming of age of the Duke of Marlborough, culminating on Friday night in a county ball at the Palace, for which about 500 invitations were issued. The guests were received by the Duke and the Marchioness of Blandford, in the grand saloon, passing thence through the state rooms, decorated with the famous tapestry representing the scenes of the memorable battles of the great John, first Duke of Marlborough, to the library, where dancing took place. The house party included the Duke of Abercorn, the Dowager Duchess of Abercorn, the Duke and Duchess of Buccleuch, the Marquis of Bath and Lady Beatrice Thynne, the Earl of March and Lady Gordon Lennox, the Countess of Galloway, Viscount Brackley, the Marquis of Camden, Sir Robert and Lady Gresley, Lord Frederick Hamilton, Lord and Lady William Neville, Lady Florence and Mr. Astley, Mr. J. B. Leigh and Lady Rose Leigh, Mr. Launcelot Smith, Miss Ashley, Miss Chichester, and Mr. Fitzroy Stewart. The following, amongst others, accepted invitations to the ball:—Captain and Mrs. Aspenwall, Bicester; Hon. Mrs. and Colonel Holmes A'Court; Sir William and Lady

ABOVE AND BELOW: *Press cuttings reporting Sunny's coming-of-age ball at Blenheim.*

RIGHT: *A ball held in the long library.*

Family life for Sunny in his role as the ninth Duke was far from conducive to personal happiness. Much was expected of him, but little affection or encouragement was given. His American stepmother, Lily, stayed on in Britain after the eighth Duke's death, finding happiness in a second marriage. His mother, Goosie, whom the Churchill family had always thought slightly ridiculous, was sidelined by his redoubtable paternal grandmother, Fanny, the Dowager Duchess. Fanny stepped in and took charge. Once Sunny's coming-of-age celebrations were out of the way, she busied herself with prompting him to find a wife who had plenty of money to put Blenheim to rights, and who would produce a son and heir. As she put it: *'It would be intolerable to have that little upstart Winston become Duke!'*

ll the ladies wore ball-gowns and tiaras, and many men were n "pink"—a truly brilliant and memorable scene. The bill f fare may be of interest to up-to-date hostesses at the present ime :—

POTAGE.
Tortue claire à la Windsor.
POISSONS.
Filets de merluches à la Morny. *Cabillaud, sauce hûitres.*
ENTRÉE.
ôtelettes d'Agneau au Pointes d'Asperges. *Chaudfroid de Volaille.*
RELEVÉ.
Bœuf roti a l'Anglaise. *Faisans braise, sauce Céleris.*
RÔT.
Cailles sur croûte. *Choux fleurs au Gratin.*
ENTREMETS.
Poudings à la Marie Louise. *Soufflé au Maresquin Glacé.*
Canapés du Caviare.

ancing was in the great library, at the door of which Lady landford and the Duke of Marlborough received the guests who ad entered by the north-east door of the palace, and from thence ad traversed the whole suite of splendid apartments.

DOLLARS FOR DUKES

This was the moment that Alva Vanderbilt, daughter-in-law of the American railway tycoon, had been waiting for. She wanted a real English duke for her only daughter, and the fact that seventeen-year-old Consuelo was in love with someone else was merely a minor annoyance. Alva put intolerable pressure on the young girl and heartlessly brokered what could only be called an arranged marriage.

Sunny and Consuelo were introduced during the London season of 1893, and they eventually married in November of 1895, when Consuelo was eighteen. Unsuited though they were, they were each remarkable people. Consuelo was beautiful, spirited and warm-hearted, while Sunny was an intelligent, restless perfectionist with the strong aesthetic streak of his Spencer ancestors. And he was ready to sacrifice everything, including his personal happiness, to restore the glories of Blenheim. '*There was no need for sentiment,*' he remarked about the marriage.

The young American bride had a whole new culture to absorb in those early months, but she was a quick learner. In *The Glitter and the Gold*, the book she wrote many years after the inevitable divorce from Blenheim, she remembered:

> *'My husband spoke of some two hundred families whose lineage and whose ramifications, whose patronymics and whose titles I should have to learn. Then Blenheim and its tenants, its employees and its household servants would claim my attention. It was only later that I found that my personal reactions towards what to me appeared absurd distinctions must be repressed and that I must not expect even a servant who stood high in the hierarchy to perform a task he considered beneath his dignity. On ringing the bell one day I was answered by the butler, but when I asked him to set a match to an already prepared fire he made me a dignified bow and, leaving the room, observed, "I will send the footman, your Grace," to which I hastily replied, "Oh don't trouble, I will do it myself."'*

Photograph of Consuelo looking rather forlorn, which of course she was while married to Charles.

The marriage, though lacking in love, had its consolations. Consuelo was a natural duchess. Elegant, beautiful and sensitive, she moved through British society with such finesse that her mother-in-law was prompted to exclaim: *'No one would take you for an American!'* She entertained in grand style, oversaw the renaissance of Blenheim, produced two sons (Bert, Marquess of Blandford, in 1897, and Ivor in 1898), whom she adored, and won the hearts of servants, tenants and villagers.

120
Nov 22nd 1901 The Duchess of Marlborough visited the School on Thursday morning, and listened to lessons given in Reading & Mental Arithmetic, to the upper Standards, & heard the Recitation in Stand III. Her Grace asked to see the children Drill, & the Needlework, & heard the little ones sing. In the Infant Department she examined the writing and kindergarten work. Her Grace kindly expressed herself well pleased with all she had seen and heard. After the children were dismissed, she told me she thought of starting a Cookery class at Blenheim Palace under her personal supervision, and authorised me to send 10 of the upper class girls, to the course, which starts on Wednesday Dec 11th.

278
May 8th The Duchess of Marlborough & Lady Lilian Spencer Churchill, visited the Schools, on Wednesday morning. They stayed some time, & heard the children questioned on Mental Arithmetic & Geography, & afterwards went to the Infant School, & heard the little folks sing & recite. They expressed themselves well pleased with the children. The Rev. J.A. Rivington visited on Tuesday & gave religious instruction.

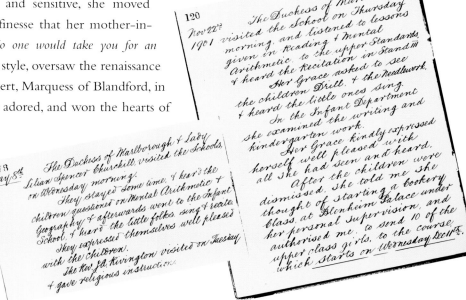

Logbooks from the local school at Bladon, recording Consuelo's great interest in the school and in the local people.

A marriage of convenience

Consuelo's parents were in the midst of a bitter divorce when her mother, Alva Vanderbilt, took it into her head to marry her teenage daughter to a duke. Alva herself had married money. A newly impoverished Southern belle after the American Civil War, she'd set her sights on a New York banker—any New York banker—and captured the prize of William Kissam Vanderbilt. He was the second son of railroad magnate William Henry Vanderbilt, from whom he inherited $60 million. Consuelo grew up in grand houses. Like other members of the wealthy Vanderbilt family, her father built magnificent homes, including mansions on Long Island, in Newport and at 660 Fifth Avenue, Manhattan.

'I was a natural dictator,' Alva wrote of herself. *'I enjoyed nothing so much as tyrannizing over the little slave children on my father's cotton plantation.'* She held much the same sway over her daughter. Consuelo tried to stand up for herself and gain permission to marry Winthrop Rutherfurd, the man she loved, but to no avail. At one stage her mother threatened to kill Winthrop, and when that threat failed she resorted to blackmail, taking to her bed with a 'heart attack' brought on by her daughter's refusal to comply with her wishes.

An etching of Consuelo that appeared in the American press, in the days when photographs could not be instantly reproduced as they can now.

A SENSE OF DUTY

Sunny was the more willing party to the sacrifice. Consuelo was invited to visit Blenheim, and Sunny treated her to a grand tour of the estate, after which Consuelo wrote:

'I don't know what Marlborough thought of me, except that I was quite different from the sophisticated girls who wished to become his Duchess. My remarks appeared to amuse him... It was that afternoon that he must have made up his mind to marry me and to give up the girl he loved, as he told me so tragically soon after our marriage. For to live at Blenheim in the pomp and circumstance he considered essential needed money, and a sense of duty to his family and to his tradition indicated the sacrifice of personal desires.'

On November 6, 1895, a red-eyed Consuelo and a stoic Sunny went through the motions of a 'fairytale wedding' at St Thomas Episcopal Church, New York City.

AN AMERICAN VIEW OF THE DUKE OF MARLBOROUGH'S ENGAGEMENT.
UNCLE SAM: "Wal, I reckon this is gettin' rather serious.

The American press was not misled by the apparent romance of the occasion. 'The roof of the Marlborough Castle will now receive some much needed repairs and the family will be able to go back to three meals a day,' observed the Washington Post.

THE WEDDING DAY

'I spent the morning of my wedding day in tears and alone; no one came near me. A footman had been posted at the door of my apartment and not even my governess was admitted. Like an automaton I donned the lovely lingerie with its real lace and the white silk stockings and shoes. My maid helped me into the beautiful dress, its tiers of Brussels lace cascading over white satin. It had a high collar and long tight sleeves. The court train…fell from my shoulders in folds of billowing whiteness…A bouquet of orchids that was to come from Blenheim did not arrive in time. I felt cold and numb as I went down to meet my father… My mother had decreed that my father should accompany me to the church to give me away. After that he was to disappear. Driving away from my home I looked back. My mother was at the window. She was hiding behind the curtain but I saw that she was in tears. "And yet," I thought, "she has attained the goal she set herself, she has experienced the satisfactions wealth can confer, she has ensconced me in the niche she so early assigned me."'

Not long after Consuelo and Sunny's wedding, the Vanderbilts divorced and both happily remarried. Alva then turned her iron will to the cause of women's suffrage and emancipation.

BACK TO BUSINESS

The honeymoon over, the ninth Duke and his Duchess were welcomed home to Blenheim with huge ceremony. As in the newlywed Randolph and Jennie's welcome two decades earlier, the horses were unhitched from the carriage and a phalanx of employees dragged the carriage up to the house—to start a life that this democratic American would never get used to.

The tenants prepared a wonderful photo album of Blenheim and the park as a welcome to their new Duchess.

The new Duchess was left in no doubt that her first duty was to produce an heir. She was to become, as her husband ungallantly put it, a link in the chain. Consuelo commented:

> *'To one not sufficiently impressed with the importance of ensuring the survival of a particular family, the fact that our happiness as individuals was as nothing in this unbroken chain of succeeding generations was a corroding thought; for although I greatly desired children, I had not reached the stage of total abnegation regarding my personal happiness.'*

An original photograph showing the rapturous reception the newlyweds were given on their return to Blenheim, following their marriage in the United States. 'The whole countryside turned out to greet us,' reported Consuelo.

In the dying days of the nineteenth century, Consuelo produced an heir and a spare, Sunny's cousin Winston took part in the last full cavalry charge in history at Omdurman in the Sudan before dashing off to South Africa as a journalist in the Boer War, and Sunny, too, served in the Boer War.

Back in England, Sunny started spending the Vanderbilt money. He sent for twenty decorators from Paris to prettify the three western state rooms with gilded decorative carving, a move he later regretted. With the French architect and landscape designer Achille Duchêne, he did away with Capability Brown's grassed-over great court and reinstated Vanbrugh's cobbles and gravel. To enclose the courtyard, he installed a parapet, a sunken wall and great iron gates. He dredged the lake and redesigned the gardens on the east and west fronts with paths of crushed brick, topiary and box hedging. He also planted nearly half a million trees, to supplement Capability Brown's plantations.

SACRIFICING COMFORT TO ELEGANCE

In spite of the improvements, Consuelo found living at Blenheim uncongenial:

> *'It is strange that in so great a house there should not be one really liveable room. We slept in small rooms with high ceilings; we dined in dark rooms with high ceilings; we dressed in closets without ventilation; we sat in long galleries or painted saloons. Had they been finely proportioned or beautifully decorated I would not so greatly have minded sacrificing comfort to elegance. But alas Vanbrugh appears to have subscribed more readily to the canons of dramatic art than to those of architecture.'*

CONFLICTING PRIORITIES

The ninth Duke liked to do everything in style, from riding in his crimson state coach, with footmen in satin breeches and powdered wigs, to observing the most arcane points of protocol and precedence. Consuelo's greatest pleasures were galloping across country with the land agent, and meeting the tenant farmers—*'fine men, good farmers and loyal friends'*. She also enjoyed the glitter and glamour of the London season and the opportunities it afforded to get away from Blenheim and meet brilliant men and agreeable women. Meals alone with Marlborough, however, were an ordeal, as Consuelo relates:

> *'How I learned to dread and hate those dinners, how ominous and wearisome they loomed at the end of a long day. They were served with all the accustomed ceremony, but once a course had been passed the servants retired to the hall; the door was closed and only a ring of the bell placed before Marlborough summoned them. He had a way of piling food on his plate; the next move was to push the plate away, together with knives, forks, spoons and glasses—all this in considered gestures which took a long time; then he backed his chair away from the table, crossed one leg over the other and endlessly twirled the ring on his little finger. While accomplishing these gestures he was absorbed in thought and quite oblivious of any reactions I might have... As a rule neither of us spoke a word. I took to knitting in desperation and the butler read detective stories in the hall.'*

ABOVE AND BELOW: *Always immensely stylish, Consuelo dressed at the cutting edge of fashion. She is pictured in these photographs with her two sons.*

When Sunny and Consuelo were not alone, there were weekend parties to organize, a social minefield of protocol that Marlborough left his Duchess to arrange. *'Unfortunately,'* wrote Consuelo, *'he was more inclined to criticize than to instruct and I had to trust to observation to ensure the continuity established by past generations of English women.'* That she managed with such style and grace is a testament to her spirit. The protocol above and below stairs she mastered, but the bathing arrangements at Blenheim were always a point of contention. She felt embarrassed showing guests to their splendid rooms crammed with incomparable artworks, incongruously cluttered with washstands and pitchers, bathtubs and jugs.

> *'The lack of bathrooms troubled my American sense of comfort and awakened stricken feelings towards my housemaids, whose business it was to prepare something like thirty baths a day. But owing to my husband's dislike of innovations, it was not until my son succeeded to the dukedom that sufficient bathrooms were built.'*

A party fit for a prince

The first grand house party that Consuelo and Sunny threw at Blenheim, in November 1896, a year after their marriage, was a real test of Consuelo's ability to adapt, as it was a shooting party to entertain the Prince and Princess of Wales. Consuelo wrote about the preparations in her engaging memoirs, *The Glitter and the Gold*:

> *'The Prince expressed a wish to come to Blenheim, and we at once began the rather onerous preparations such a visit entailed. Our proposed list of guests having been submitted and approved, we became engrossed in plans to make the visit agreeable and memorable. A great amount of staff work was involved and there were endless details to be discussed. I faced this, my first big shooting party, with trepidation, for I had no experience and no precedent to guide me.'*

Throwing a party on this scale was an exercise in logistics—it meant finding room to house and feed a battalion of staff to support the family and their thirty guests. Before the First World War, the usual complement of indoor staff at Blenheim was forty, and the outdoor staff numbered about the same. For such an occasion, every male guest would bring a valet—maybe also a groom and a footman—and every female guest a maid or two.

Pages from the visitors' book for the shooting party of November 1896. This book, which is kept on the private side of the palace, makes a fascinating study. It holds evidence of liaisons and friendships unknown to the public.

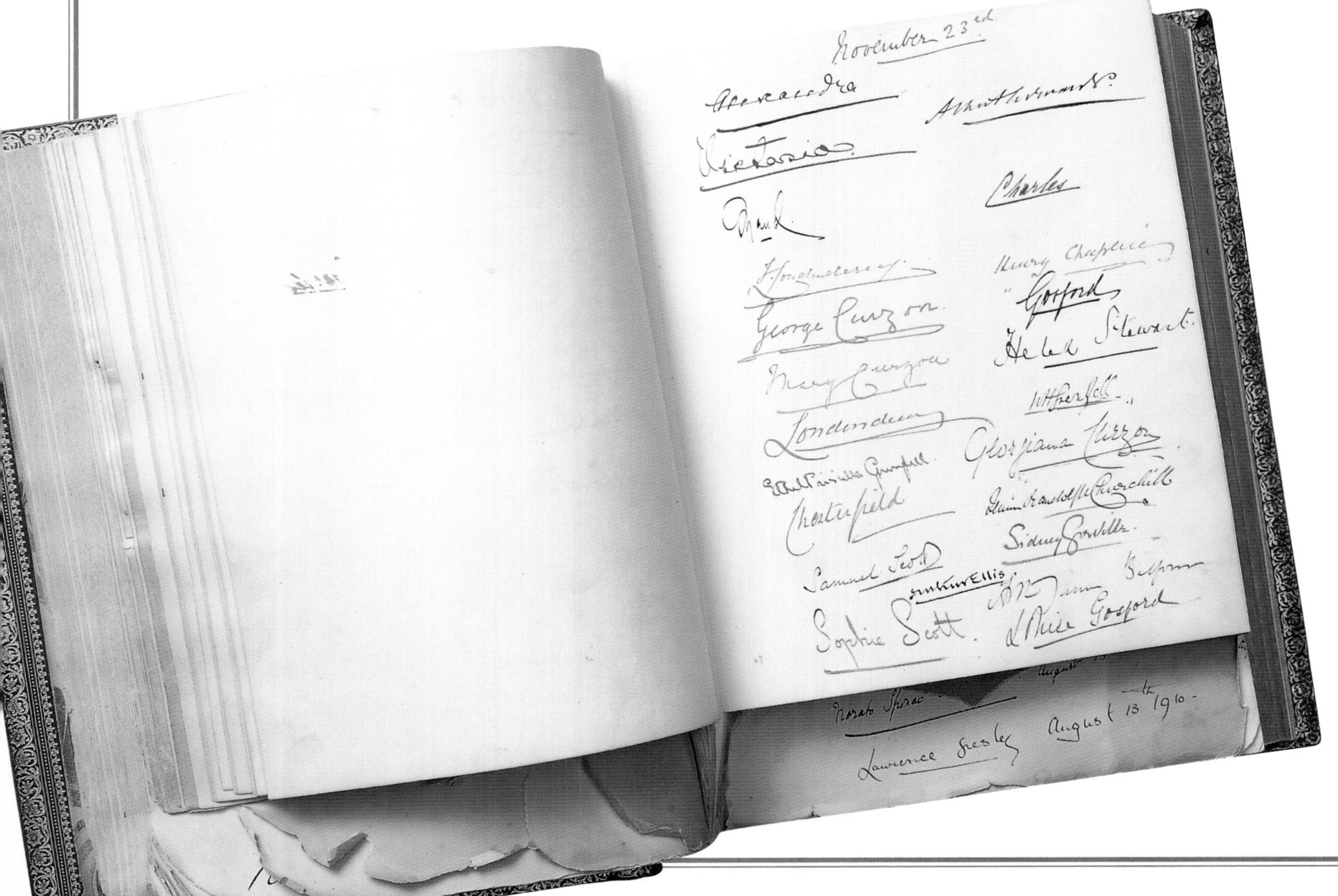

The private apartments were given over to the royal family, and Consuelo and Sunny moved into crowded quarters upstairs. Consuelo didn't much care for the Prince's company, preferring his lively Princess:

> *'Our party lasted from Monday to Saturday and each day I had the Prince as my neighbour for two long meals. This was a terrible ordeal... since he liked to discuss the news and gossip of the latest scandal with all of which I was unfamiliar. The Princess of Wales, gay and animated with an almost childish interest in everything, was easier to cope with. She was full of fun. She made us laugh, telling us how she had to use a ladder in order to get into my bed which was on a dais, and how she kept falling over the white bear skins that were strewn on the floor.'*

Mealtimes were not the only source of stress:

> *'This visit was a tiring and anxious experience for me. The number of changes of costume was in itself a waste of precious time. To begin with, even breakfast, which was served at 9.30 in the dining room, demanded an elegant costume of velvet or silk. Having seen the men off to their sport, the ladies spent the morning round the fire reading the papers and gossiping. We next changed into tweeds to join the guns for luncheon which was served at High Lodge or in a tent. Afterwards we usually joined the guns watching a drive or two before returning home. An elaborate tea gown was donned for tea, after which we*

THE ILLUSTRATED LONDON NEWS

THE PRINCE AND PRINCESS OF WALES AT BLENHEIM: DEPARTURE OF THE ROYAL GUESTS FROM THE PALACE.

A contemporary newspaper feature showing the royal party leaving Blenheim Palace.

played cards or listened to a Viennese band or to the organ until time to dress for dinner, when we adorned ourselves in satin or brocade, with a great display of jewels... one was not supposed to wear the same gown twice. That meant sixteen dresses for four days.'

The guests in their finery made an impression on a young servant, Gerald Horne, a hall boy, who wrote in his diary:

'I went up and looked down and there it all was, all gleaming with wealth. I think the first thing that struck me was the flashing headgear of the ladies. The Blue Hungarian [a band] was playing and there was the Prince himself looking really royal and magnificent in military uniform. The table was laid of course with the silver-gilt service... the royal footmen waiting side by side with our own.'

ABOVE: *Assembled for luncheon outside High Lodge in 1896. Back row (left to right): Earl of Gosford, Lady Emily Kingscote, the Hon. Sidney Greville, George Curzon, General Ellis, the Countess of Gosford, A J Balfour, Mrs Grenfell, Sir Samuel Scott, Lord Londonderry, Lady Helen Stewart, Lady Lilian Spencer-Churchill, Mr Grenfell, Prince Charles of Denmark, Viscount Curzon M.P. Middle row: Earl of Chesterfield, Lady Randolph Churchill, the Duchess of Marlborough, the Princess of Wales, Mr H Chaplin, the Prince of Wales, Mrs George Curzon, the Marchioness of Londonderry, Princess Victoria, Princess Charles of Denmark. Front row: Lady Sophie Scott, Duke of Marlborough, Viscountess Curzon.*

Years later, Consuelo was amused to read an impression formed of this party by one of the guests, Arthur Balfour (then First Lord of the Treasury and later prime minister):

> *'There is here a big party in a big house in a big park beside a big lake... We came down by special train—rather cross most of us—were received with illuminations, guards of honour, cheering and other follies, went through agonies about our luggage but finally settled down placidly enough.*
>
> *Today the men shot and the women dawdled. As I detest both occupations equally I stayed in my room till one o'clock and then went exploring on my bike, joining everybody at luncheon. Then, after the inevitable photograph [see opposite], I again betook myself to my faithful machine... You perceive the duties of society are weighing lightly upon me.'*

GAME BOOK.
Season 1896-97

Date.	Weather.	Name of Beat.	No. of Guns.	Name of Guns.	Game Shot: Pheasants.	Partridges.	Hares.	Rabbits.	Duck.	Snipe.	Woodcock.	Moorhen.	Various.	Total Head Shot.	General Remarks.
1896				Brought forward	73	626	103	2170						2972	
Nov 24	Fine	High Park	8	H.R.H. The Prince of Wales											
				Marquis of Londonderry											
				Earl of Gosford											
				Major Genl Ellis	82		1	1905						1988	
				Hon George Curzon											
				Rt. Hon Henry Chaplin											
				Sir S. Scott. Mr W.H. Grenfell											
25	Fine	North Leigh Coverts	7	H.R.H. The Prince of Wales											
				Earl of Chesterfield											
				Earl of Gosford, Viscount Curzon	881			4						885	
				Rt. Hon George Curzon											
				Major Genl Ellis, Mr W.H. Grenfell											
26	Fine	Monument Park	8	H.R.H. The Prince of Wales											
				Marquis of Londonderry											
				Earl of Gosford Sir S Scott											
				Earl of Chesterfield			1	3328						3329	
				Major Genl Ellis Rt. Hon H. Chaplin											
				Mr W.H. Grenfell											
				Carried forward	1036	626	105	7407						9174	

GAME BOOK
BLENHEIM
Charles Richard John Spencer-Churchill,
DUKE OF MARLBOROUGH.

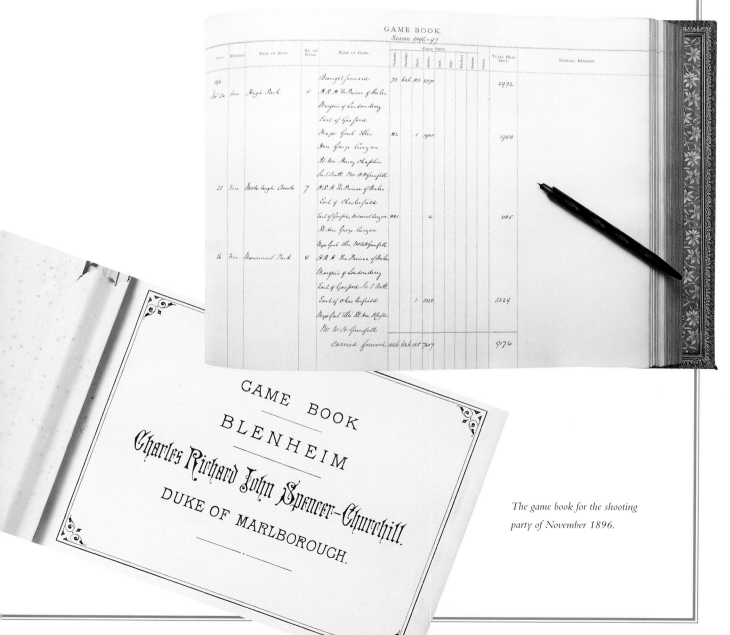

The game book for the shooting party of November 1896.

FRIENDS AND RELATIONS

'Sunny and I were like brothers,' recalled Winston, although their differences in character and ambition could hardly have been more marked. Winston was relatively poor, outgoing and aggressive, building on his reputation as a daredevil soldier and journalist to forge a career in Parliament. Sunny was rich—very rich, thanks to his wife's money—introspective, fastidious and totally fixated on Blenheim. They respected one another: Winston had the fire, brilliance and energy of the first Duke, while Sunny had his ancestor's determination to ensure that Blenheim, and all it stood for, took pride of place.

You've heard of Winston Churchill;
This is all I need to say—
He's the latest and the greatest
Correspondent of the day.

Music hall song inspired by Winston's popular despatches from the Boer War carried in the *Strand Magazine*

'Sunny is still devoutly attentive to Winston's every remark,' Consuelo observed. In fact, Winston's varied interests and talents, as well as his American roots, made him a congenial companion for Consuelo, too. The core of a young and brilliant circle that gathered at Blenheim, Winston spent several days there every month. Consuelo remembered:

> *'His conversation was invariably stimulating, and his views on life were not drawn and quartered, as were Marlborough's, by a sense of self-importance. To me he represented the democratic spirit so foreign to my environment, and which I deeply missed.'*

A photograph of Gladys showing her famous Grecian profile. She subjected herself to an early form of plastic surgery in which paraffin wax was injected into the bridge of her nose.

THE BEGUILING GLADYS

Another friend drawn into this circle was a young American, Gladys (pronounced Glay-dus) Deacon. Gladys had daydreamed about the Duke of Marlborough and Blenheim from afar. Aged fourteen when Sunny and Consuelo got engaged, she wrote despairingly to her mother in 1895: *'Oh dear me. If only I was a little older I might "catch" him yet! But alas! I am too young though mature in the arts of women's witchcraft.'*

Gladys was a beguiling young woman, as well as beautiful. Marlborough was deeply attracted to her, as were many others. She was linked to the art historian Bernard Berenson, the sculptors Auguste Rodin and Jacob Epstein, the painter Edgar Degas, the writer Anatole France and the German Crown Prince. The French novelist Marcel Proust exclaimed that he *'never saw a girl with such beauty, such magnificent intelligence, such goodness and charm'*. She charmed the Duchess, too.

'A beautiful girl endowed with a brilliant intellect' is how Consuelo described her. It is extremely unlikely that Gladys had any part in the eventual separation of Sunny and Consuelo, but she was finally to marry her Duke more than a quarter of a century after her note to her mother.

SEPARATION AND DIVORCE

In the autumn of 1906, Sunny discovered that Consuelo had taken a lover, Reginald Fellowes, grandson of the seventh Duke of Marlborough. (Tellingly, Reginald gets no mention whatsoever in her book.) Divorce in those days was a social nightmare—aristocratic husbands and wives were supposed to manage their affairs discreetly and put on a public front—but the tension between these two had become intolerable. Winston, who was deeply attached to both parties, laboured hard to get them back together, but unsuccessfully. In spite of his interference he remained a lifelong friend of both.

Consuelo finally bid Blenheim goodbye and set up home in Sunderland House, built only a few years earlier with Vanderbilt money as the Marlboroughs' London home. She became involved in philanthropic works and took up political causes, in particular the issues of workers' conditions and trades unions. The Marlboroughs finally divorced in 1920, and Consuelo married the dashing Frenchman Jacques Balsan. They lived happily ever after in France and America.

Marlborough married his mistress of the last ten years, Gladys Deacon. Sadly, their relationship began to deteriorate as Gladys came to realize that Sunny's principal love would always be Blenheim and its fossilized routines and customs that allowed for no real emotions or joy.

Consuelo and Winston at Blenheim in 1907.

Winston and Clementine

Winston (who used Churchill as his surname, treating Spencer as a middle name) had originally joined the Tories but switched to the Liberal party in 1904. By 1910 he was Home Secretary, and the next year First Lord of the Admiralty. Already established as a military history author, Winston's inspired biography of his father, Randolph, left out the Aylesford affair and his illness, and concentrated on setting Randolph's quarrel with the Tory government in context. It was a masterpiece of its genre, and its publication, the preface written from Blenheim in 1906, marked the moment his career really took off.

Clementine and Winston.

In 1904 at a London ball he briefly met Clementine Hozier, an enchanting young woman, tall and green-eyed. They were to meet again, four years later. A smitten Winston invited her to Blenheim that August:

> *'I want so much to show you that beautiful place, and in its gardens we shall find lots of places to talk in, and lots of things to talk about… I think you will be amused by Blenheim. It has many glories in the fullness of summer. Pools of water, gardens of roses, a noble lake shrouded by giant trees; tapestries, pictures and monuments within.'*

BLENHEIM WORKS ITS MAGIC

The young couple went for a walk and it started to rain. They took shelter in the temple of Diana overlooking the lake, and it was here that Winston proposed and Clementine accepted. *'I took the two major decisions of my life at Blenheim,'* wrote Winston, *'to be born and to marry.'*

Clementine's mother wrote of her future son-in-law: *'He is so like Lord Randolph, he has some of his faults, and all his qualities. He is gentle and tender and affectionate to those he loves, much hated by those who have not come under his personal charm.'* Jennie was also delighted, commenting to a friend: *'My Winston is not easy; he is very difficult indeed and she is just right.'* Sunny found the young couple's happiness only served to remind him of his own marital miseries. *'I fear alas!'* he wrote to Winston a week after the engagement was announced, *'that I shall be unable to be present at your wedding. I have had a long and trying year… I hope you will allow me to spare myself the mingled pleasure—and pain—of such a ceremony.'*

The temple of Diana in the grounds of Blenheim, where Winston proposed to Clementine.

Winston was to comment in his autobiography, *My Early Life*, that he married and lived happily ever after—and indeed they were ideally suited. Clementine was no pushover: she focused all her energies on him and became the critic Winston heeded above all others.

Wonderful bronze of Lady Clementine and Sir Winston Churchill by Oscar Nemon.

A CABINET MINISTER'S WEDDING.

Mr. Winston Churchill to Miss Clementine Hozier

At St. Margaret's, Westminster

Saturday Sept. 12, 1908

The Bride Leaving Lady St. Helier's House

Where the reception was given

The Bride

The Crowd Outside St. Margaret's

On Saturday afternoon

The Bridegroom Arriving

Mr. Winston Churchill alighting at St. Margaret's, Westminster

Drawn by Wal Paget

The Marriage Ceremony in St. Margaret's, Westminster

The address to the newly-married couple was delivered by Bishop Welldon, who was formerly Mr. Winston Churchill's master at Harrow School. The honeymoon is being spent at Blenheim and at the Italian lakes

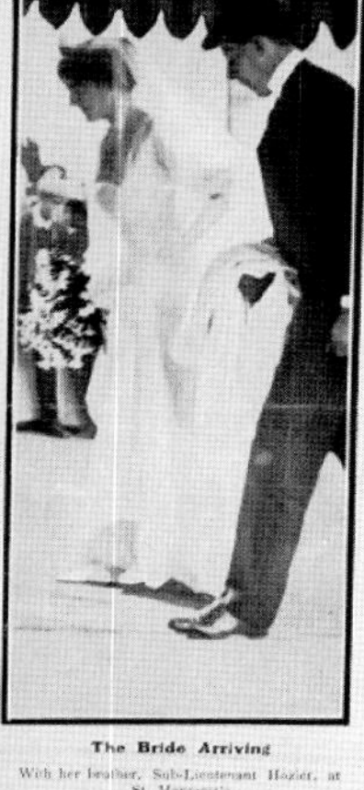

The Bride Arriving

With her brother, Sub-Lieutenant Hozier, at St. Margaret's

Two of the Bridesmaids

Miss Madeline Whyte on the left and Miss Claire Frewen on the right

After the Wedding

The bride and bridegroom

The Bride's Brother

Sub-Lieutenant Hozier

Friends after the Battle

Mr. and Mrs. Joynson-Hicks

A Distinguished Guest

The Duchess of Marlborough at the wedding

THIS PAGE (CLOCKWISE FROM TOP LEFT): *The front page of the* Sphere *newspaper celebrating Winston and Clementine's wedding; the back of an envelope from Clementine to Winston, possibly sent during their engagement; a letter from Clementine to Winston, written during their engagement; an early love letter to Clementine from Winston, who was writing from Blenheim.*

Tacking to the last 2 hours –
Je t'aime passionément – I feel less shy in French
Clementine

Blenheim Palace.

My dearest,
How are you?
I send you my best love to salute you: & I am getting up at once in order if you like to walk to the rose garden after breakfast & pick a bunch before you start. You will have to leave here about 10.30

& I will come with you to Oxford.
Shall I not give you a letter for your mother?
always
W.

My dearest One (13)
I love you with all my heart & trust you absolutely.
Do not analyze but sleep soundly –
I send you all my love –
Clementine

Winston
This is a little Picture of my heart to show what it contains
August 1908

March 5. 1918

My dear Sunny.

During my visit to France last week I made a pilgrimage to a remote village called Jeancourt very near the front line, for the purpose of seeing Blandford. Archie Sinclair & I rode there together, & we found him prowling about halfway up a long valley looking at guns & horses & things. He lives in a weather-proof tin hut on the side of a hill before which runs a road deep in white mud, & just below in the pan of the valley are the lines of the horses & the tents of the men. Just above, towards the enemy, is the village of Le Verguier, & Blandford is in command of a party of about 80 Household Cavalrymen who live at this point & go up each night to dig trenches in or just behind the front line. In the event of an attack they would hold the village of Le Verguier just above them.

The enemy's artillery was firing on the hills just beyond the head of the valley, & Blandford told me they often bombarded the upper part, but not so far the part in which he & his men are living.

He looked very well, & quite happy, & was I think agreeably surprised by the sudden advent of an avuncular relation. We walked about in the mud for some time, & talked, & he came a long way down the road with us as we rode homewards. I expect he finds it rather lonely, as only one other officer in the regiment is with him. He doesn't like whiskey, & he hasn't been able to get any port, so he is for the time being a teetotaler.

He charged me to give you all messages & his best love. I thought you would like to know exactly how I found him.

Yours affly

W.

This 1918 letter from Winston to his cousin was found quite recently where Sunny had left it, tucked into a book in the muniments room.

RSVP

Around 1911, Sunny again took to entertaining on a grand scale. He filled the house at Christmas and New Year with up to thirty guests and their attendant retinues. Winston and Clemmie were regulars, as were F.E. Smith, later Lord Birkenhead, and his family. The Birkenhead children recalled the distinctive smell of Blenheim as *'rather like the weighty smell of locked-in history, with hints of decaying velvet'*. They disliked the clatter of eating from gold plates, and they worried that bits of gold might chip off and get mixed up with the vegetables. Lord Birkenhead and Winston would join them in war games in the great hall, but the children fled, finding the boisterous game of 'French and English' altogether too dangerous. Freddie Birkenhead later recalled his childhood visits to Blenheim:

> *'...the woods white with winter, and on the wooded eyot in the centre of the lake the trees were powdered with rime, and skates rang on the ice. One passed through arch after arch before turning to the left and approaching the building... There was in it an atmosphere and a scent that none of us could forget... Inside the great hall with its painted ceiling, the housekeeper, Mrs Ryman, stood waiting, a bunch of keys at her waist, to take us to rooms with memorable names... some with great four-poster beds and dark tapestries... Every aspect of this house...filled us with excitement and invited exploration... the great hall with its radiators on which we lay on our backs... the dark turreted stairs leading to unexpected places...'*

WAR WORK

Within Blenheim, the ninth Duke held firm to his daunting habits of eating from gold plates and suchlike, but his work on the estate was surprisingly progressive. He expected a lot from his workers, demanding to know every fine detail of production, and also contributed some fairly radical ideas on farming the land.

During the First World War he moved into the east wing, giving over the long library to a fifty-bed military hospital. Still unable to marry Gladys, because he was not yet divorced, the Duke was nevertheless influenced by her, and he pulled strings to enable her friend from her Paris days, the sculptor Jacob Epstein, to be classed as a war artist, thus avoiding the rigours and dangers of the trenches.

As a further contribution to the war effort, Sunny upped his food-production activities, growing cabbages in the flower beds, putting sheep to graze in the palace gardens and patriotically donating five hundred head of cattle to the Food Controller, to help relieve the meat shortage.

In the early days of the war, the Duke served as Lieutenant-Colonel on the General Staff and was later appointed Joint Parliamentary Secretary to the Board of Agriculture. By 1915 he'd been totally re-embraced by the establishment and made Lord Lieutenant of Oxfordshire. But he still wasn't happy.

Major Winston Churchill, in the meantime, had gone off to fight in France, exulting in the adrenalin rush. In 1916 he was promoted to Colonel. Winston described the conditions to Clementine in a letter: '*Filth and rubbish everywhere. Water and muck on all sides. Troops of enormous rats creep and glide to the unceasing accompaniment of rifle and machine guns.*' Yet he also acknowledged: '*I have found happiness and content such as I have not known for many months.*'

ABOVE: *Gladys and Sunny on their wedding day. They married at the British Consulate in Paris.*

WEDDING DAYS

In 1921, Sunny finally married Gladys. She had her Duke at last. Struggling with the new world-order of post-war England, the Duke turned his attention from his new bride to the west side of the palace. Here, he created a formal, Versailles-style water-terrace garden to link Vanbrugh's heroic facade to Capability Brown's free-form lake.

BELOW AND RIGHT: *Gladys on her wedding day in June 1921.*

'The thirteenth Duchess'

Gladys Deacon (1881–1977), when she married the ninth Duke, became the thirteenth woman to hold the title Duchess of Marlborough. In light of what was to become of her, this unfortunate number could not have been more apt.

Gladys's childhood was even less stable than Sunny's had been. She was eleven years old when her father, Edward Deacon, burst into his wife's hotel room in Cannes and pumped three shots into her lover, killing him. Edward went to prison, ending his days in an insane asylum. Gladys reacted by throwing herself into her studies, learning many languages and taking a particular interest in art. She built up a fine collection of Impressionist paintings, including important works by Monet and Cézanne, and enjoyed the society of bohemian Europe's finest characters.

FROM MISTRESS TO DUCHESS

As a young girl Gladys had fantasized about being mistress of Blenheim, inspired by the publicity given to the Marlborough–Vanderbilt marriage in the American press. When she finally met the glamorous couple, they were all three enchanted with one another. After Sunny's separation from Consuelo, she became his mistress. Gladys was enchanting as a mistress, but the obligations of life as a fully paid-up duchess weighed her down. At the time of her marriage in 1921, Gladys was forty (she sliced five years off her age on the official papers) and hoping for babies to fill the long-abandoned nursery.

Gladys Deacon painted by Giovanni Boldini in 1916, while in her mid-thirties.

FROM DUCHESS TO DESPAIR

The disastrous plastic surgery Gladys had had in her early twenties started to affect her life very soon after she moved into Blenheim. An injection of wax to emphasize her classic profile gradually slid down the bridge of her nose to her chin, eventually deforming her features. A series of miscarriages and a husband *'with an ungovernable temper'* also took their toll. A friend from France who came to visit Gladys remarked: *'A battle has been joined between her and Blenheim Palace.'* Two years after the wedding Gladys was writing:

'Most interesting to me is Sunny's rudeness to me. Not very marked in public yet—but that will come. I am glad because I am sick of life here... we will separate perhaps before long and I will then go away for good and ever.'

FROM DESPAIR TO DOGS

In a defiantly destructive gesture, Gladys surrounded herself with dogs, turning them loose in the state rooms and letting them attack the fabric of the palace that she had grown to hate. Randolph, Winston's son, came down one weekend in 1931 with an American cousin, Anita Leslie, who wrote home in graphic detail:

> *'The Duke met us and tea was carried into one of the drawing rooms. The Duchess did not appear for a long time. Finally we heard, not footsteps, but the claw-clatter of many little dogs. "Watch Sunny—he hates her guts—great sport!" whispered Randolph. In came the Duchess, surrounded by a moving carpet of King Charles spaniels. Gladys Marlborough was extraordinary to look at. Absolutely hideous and yet exotic, with golden hair swept back in a bun, and strange blue eyes staring out of the ruin of that stretched face. She advanced in her dirty old clothes, shook hands and waved us graciously to chairs. [At dinner] Marlborough sat looking like a rat caught in a trap, while the Duchess delivered her poisoned shafts.'*

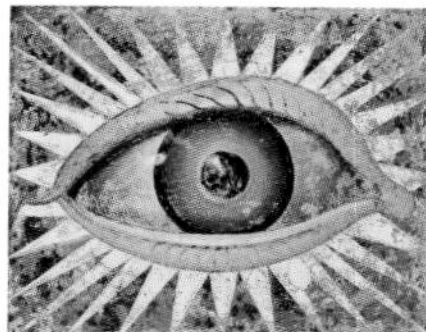

ABOVE: *On the ceiling of the portico above the palace entrance are six panels depicting three blue eyes and three brown eyes, painted by Colin Gill. The blue eyes are Gladys's—she climbed the scaffolding to give the artist a scarf of precisely the right shade of blue for him to match. It is uncertain who the brown eyes represent, since Sunny's eyes were blue, but they might be Consuelo's.*

FROM DOGS TO OBSCURITY

Sunny left Blenheim and everything he'd worked for, just to get away from Gladys—she had become a monster of their own making. He took most of the staff with him to London, leaving her roaming about the palace on her own, dressed in musty old court dresses. Under growing pressure from the Duke to leave Blenheim, Gladys finally in May 1933 hired a removal van, filled it with her Monets, Cézannes and dogs, and drove away.

ABOVE: *A rare picture of Gladys, showing the results of earlier plastic surgery.*

RIGHT: *Departure day. Gladys's camera recorded her leaving Blenheim for ever.*

The water terraces

Blenheim's park and gardens have evolved over the past three hundred years in a similar way to the house, and, like the house, they are a living tribute to the talents of many. Today, with one sweep of the eyes, we can appreciate the vision of Henry Wise, the artful artlessness of Capability Brown and the pleasing architectural structures of Achille Duchêne.

My great-grandfather Sunny employed the French landscape gardener Duchêne to create the Italian garden (see pages 32–3) on the east side, but he then looked at the west side and found it wanting. Judging it to be unbalanced and deserving of a more formal outlook, Sunny threw all his considerable energies—along with his frustrations and disappointments with life—into this formidable task. Between them they created one of my favourite parts of the gardens: the water terraces.

Sunny and Duchêne were not always in agreement. Duchêne favoured running water and fountains, while the Duke wanted to avoid *'a vulgar display of waterworks which can be seen at any exhibition or public park'*. He didn't want to overshadow the natural beauty of the lake, reminding Duchêne: *'Limpidity of water is pleasing and possesses a romance. You have got this effect in the basins and in the... lake. Be careful not to destroy this major emotion which nature has granted you.'*

THIS PAGE AND OPPOSITE: *The Duke faithfully recorded the progress of his vision in a series of albums. (Many of the photographs were taken by Gladys, who was a keen photographer.) It was a huge labour of love, and on the last page of the last album he wrote this moving note—he was too exhausted to do more.*

For various reasons - I have not had the heart or courage to write an account of the six years of labour and study that I devoted in superintending the works on these Terraces - Perhaps I will write one day - But let not the Reader assume that the work was simple - That any architect could have done it - The Result is the combination of Brains, - knowledge of technique, and culture of two men working in harmony - These two men have left the park East and West fronts of Blenheim in perfect architectural design, a worthy frame to the Palace. —
Marlborough 1933.

Constructed in the 1920s but designed in seventeenth-century style, the water terraces took five years to build and involved some complex engineering and landscaping to deal with the sloping ground. Retaining walls faced with local stone were constructed, incorporating steps to and from the upper and lower levels. They were flanked by two lead sphinxes with the facial features of Sunny's second wife, Gladys, in her youth. In spite of the Duke's views, fountains were added in the 1960s. On the lower terrace, the fountain sculpture is by the baroque sculptor Bernini. A copy of his river-gods fountain in Piazza Navona, Rome, it was a gift to the first Duke from the Spanish ambassador to the Vatican.

Sunny died in 1934. Sadly, he had not had much time to enjoy the fruits of his huge efforts. However, his family and visitors alike have had the benefit ever since.

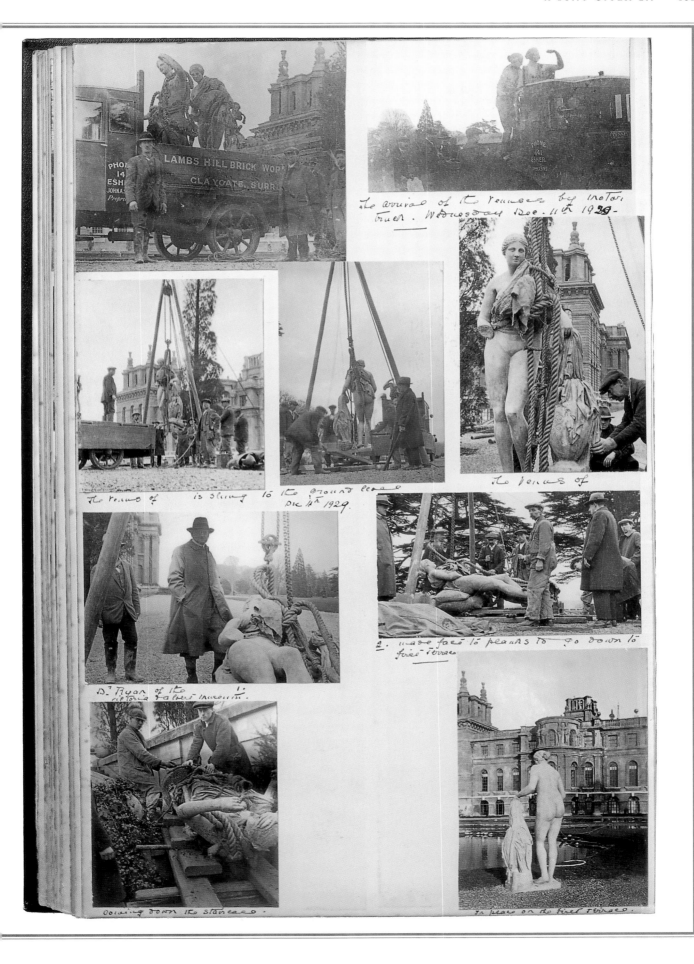

LAMBS HILL BRICK WOR
CLAYGATE, SURR
PHONE
141
ESHER.
The arrival of the venuses by motor truck. Wednesday Dec. 11th 1929.
The venus of is slung to the ground level Dec 14th 1929.
The venus of
Dr. Ryan of the Victoria & Albert Museum.
2. made fast to planks to go down to first terrace
Coming down the staircase.
In place on the first terrace.

Winston paints Blenheim

Winston took up oil painting on his leaves from duty during the First World War—he needed the distraction. With characteristic verve, he swooped into a shop and bought up easels, canvases, brushes, palettes and paints, never having shown any interest in art previously and never having had a lesson. He was later to write that painting a picture was like fighting a battle, *'for both require a good plan and a strong reserve'*.

He described his first campaign versus the canvas thus:

> *'Splash into the turpentine, wallop into the blue and white, frantic flourish on the palette—clean no longer—and then several large, fierce strokes and slashes of blue on the absolutely cowering canvas. Anyone could see that it could not hit back... The canvas grinned in helplessness before me. The spell was broken. The sickly inhibitions rolled away. I seized the largest brush and fell upon my victim with berserk fury. I have never felt any awe of a canvas since.'*

RIGHT: *Winston painting the mill at the Château St-Georges Motel, the home of Consuelo and Jacques Balsan, near Dreux in Normandy, France, in August 1939. He remarked to a fellow guest: 'This is the last picture I shall paint in peacetime for a very long time.'* OPPOSITE: *Oil painting by Winston of the great hall at Blenheim.*

House parties at the palace

Edwardian house parties were notorious for the opportunities they presented for illicit dalliances. It was the task of the mistress of the house to allocate rooms to guests while bearing in mind the ease with which a certain gentleman might gain discreet access to the room of a certain lady.

At Blenheim these nocturnal adventurers, known as corridor creepers, were able to take advantage ofVanbrugh's room layout. On the second floor the rooms are arranged as an *enfilade* so that each room has a connecting door to the next, with a space in between. (The precision ofVanbrugh's design was remarkable. It is rumoured that if you open every keyhole in every door of the *enfilade* on the main floor on the south side of the house, you can see from one end to the other.) Today these spaces between rooms are commonly used as hanging wardrobes, but I would imagine they were originally designed to provide sound insulation. At any rate, the *enfilade* conveniently allows guests to wander from room to room undetected.

When the rooms were occupied by family, the arrangement was useful because nannies and housemaids could slip easily from one charge to another. On the other hand, children could (and did) play havoc, dashing and diving between the rooms at all hours of the night.

As children we were also to be found using these hidden spaces to our advantage by playing a number of practical jokes on poor unsuspecting guests, either by pretending we were ghosts or by removing their clothes just as they were about to change for dinner.

RIGHT: *The spaces between the guest bedrooms now generally serve as wardrobes.*

OPPOSITE: *The* enfilade *of second-floor bedrooms, spanning the entire east and south wings. Most of these are used as guest bedrooms.*

ABOVE: *Entertaining the* literati *at Blenheim—Gladys's portrait of a tea party includes the* enfant terrible *of the Bloomsbury group, Lytton Strachey, standing over the seated Edith Sitwell.*

A PASSION FOR GARDENS

Sunny's obsession with the construction of his water terraces in the 1920s occupied so much of his time that his new Duchess, Gladys, grew restless, and so she looked around to find an outlet for her own creative passions. She was beginning to find the palace stultifying, with its majestic silence and rarefied lifestyle. Inside Blenheim she could do nothing, apart from hanging a few of her Impressionist paintings, but out in the gardens there was a great deal more scope.

Gardening was an interest Gladys and Sunny shared. As well as photographing and recording his progress with the water terraces, she set to work on a rock garden at the foot of Capability Brown's grand cascade. Gladys performed a lot of the work herself, doing battle with grass snakes and often staying there all day with a picnic lunch.

ABOVE: *The ninth Duke with Epstein and his unfinished sculpture of the Duke.* BELOW: *One of three sculptures of the ninth Duke by Jacob Epstein.*

A NEW BREED OF GUESTS

Gladys tried to breathe life into the stuffy palace by inviting to Blenheim the lively group of bohemians whose company she had so enjoyed in her youth. The writer H G Wells invited himself, turning up unannounced, and helping himself to tea.

'But you haven't been invited!' remonstrated Gladys.

'No matter,' replied H G, reaching for another bun, *'you interest me.'*

In 1923 the writer Lytton Strachey wrote to a friend about a weekend he'd spent at Blenheim:

> *'Nobody was particularly interesting (except perhaps the Duchess)—it was the house which was entrancing, and life-enhancing. I wish it were mine. It is enormous, but one would not feel it too big. The grounds are beautiful too, and there is a bridge over a lake which positively gives one an erection. Most of the guests played tennis all day and bridge all night... they might as well have been at Putney.'*

The novelist Arnold Bennett commented: *'Enormous house. Soup and fish off silver plate. The Duchess collects French pictures. She said I was the first person who had* any *interest in them.'* It was true that Sunny cared little for modern art. (He once waved at one of Gladys's Cézannes in the dining room, declaring it to be a Van Gogh. No one argued with him.) And by this time, he cared even less for Gladys.

Jacob Epstein came down to Blenheim to sculpt a bust of Sunny and was apprehended in the park for looking suspicious. Blenheim and Bohemia were not mixing well.

Winston came less often, partly because his attention was more focused on his own country estate of Chartwell, and partly because he didn't get on with Gladys and found the growing tensions between the Marlboroughs hard to take.

Mr. Churchill At Deathbed Of The Duke Of Marlborough

HEIR'S ESTATES AT BILLESDON

HUNTING LINKS WITH COUNTY

NEW DUKE A FARMER

The new Duke

The late Duke

THE Duke of Marlborough died at his London house in Carlton-terrace to-day, after a short illness. Mr. Winston Churchill was among the relatives present at the bedside when death took place.

He was the father of the Marquess of Blandford, of Lowesby Hall, Billesdon, who is the new Duke, and was a prominent figure in the Leicestershire hunting fields a number of years ago.

TWO AMERICAN WIVES

THE Marquess and Marchioness of Blandford were present when the Duke died. The end was very peaceful, a "Leicester Evening Mail" representative was informed.

The Duke was a descendant of the famous Duke of Marlborough, and was the ninth holder of the title, to which he succeeded in 1892.

He held many other titles and distinctions. He was a Knight of the Garter, a Privy Councillor and Lord Lieutenant of Oxfordshire." Mr. Winston Churchill is his first cousin.

The late Duke had one great love, his famous and historic palace of Blenheim, given by a grateful country to his ancestor, John Churchill, the first Duke.

Though maintaining a town house in Carlton House-terrace, the Duke spent

As Colonel Balsan is a Roman Catholic the Duchess wished to regularise her religious position, and applied to the Southwark Diocesan Church for her marriage to the Duke of Marlborough to be annulled by the Roman Catholic Church. The Duchess declared that she had "entered into the marriage through the motive of grave fear, unjustly brought to bear upon her by others, with the idea of driving her into marriage."

The Sacra Romana Rota, the Supreme Court of Justice of the Holy See, confirmed the judgment of the Southwark Diocesan Court, and the marriage was declared null and void. It was not until 1926 that the findings of the Court were made public.

His bride was Miss Gladys Deacon, daughter of Mr. S. P. Deacon, a millionaire of Boston, U.S.A.

The Duke of Marlborough still holds the titles conferred upon his distinguished ancestor. He is a Prince of

This article about the death of the ninth Duke appeared in a contemporary newspaper. It correctly acknowledges that the Duke 'had one great love, his historic palace of Blenheim'.

AN ACRIMONIOUS END

Weakened by miscarriages and increasingly disfigured by the wax slippage, Gladys gave up gardening and any pretence of marital bliss. She sniped constantly at Sunny and surrounded herself with a pack of Blenheim spaniels—about fifty of them—not caring about the mess they made. The housekeeper at the time, Miss James, remembered the Duke spending hours each day examining the silk and velvet curtains and the priceless carpets for stains.

Sunny had had enough. He'd sacrificed everything for Blenheim and yet could find no comfort there. He converted to Roman Catholicism and decamped at the end of 1931 to his London home, leaving Blenheim to the increasingly eccentric Gladys and the dogs. He was on the point of abandoning his poisoned chalice of a heritage, retiring to a Benedictine monastery in Spain and selling off the Blenheim archives to Yale University for £50,000, when he was diagnosed with liver cancer. He died in June 1934, aged sixty-two, and was buried in the Blenheim chapel, surrounded by the smell of incense and the chant of Latin plainsong.

One obituary described Sunny as *'a pathetic figure, like a lonely peacock straggling through deserted gardens'* and '*[a sad man] sowing seed after seed where none can ever grow*'. His cousin Winston, who had grown up with him, loved him and understood him, was able to put the life of the ninth Duke in context:

> *'Always there weighed upon him the size and cost of the great house which was the monument to his ancestor's victories. This he conceived to be almost his first duty in life to preserve and embellish… He sacrificed much to this—too much, but he succeeded; and at his death Blenheim passed from his care in a finer state than ever.'*

Three years after separating from his second wife, Gladys, and moving out of the palace, the ninth Duke was buried in the chapel at Blenheim.

Consuelo, the ninth Duke's first wife, is buried in the unassuming Bladon churchyard in the sight line of Blenheim Palace. Her wish was to be buried near her younger son, Ivor, who had predeceased her.

CHAPTER EIGHT

War and Peace

'Wodehouseian' is the adjective often used to describe my grandfather, the tenth Duke—a bluff old-school aristocrat prone to twinges of gout and with a growling bark that was worse than his bite—a duke straight from the pages of a P G Wodehouse novel. He was an anachronism even way back then, with his '*What? What?*' mumbled speech patterns. He once complained that his toothbrush failed to foam, not realizing that his valet always squeezed out the toothpaste for him.

John Albert Edward William, Marquess of Blandford—or Bert, as he was more familiarly known—was only nine when his parents separated, so he divided his time between boarding school, Blenheim and '*wherever my mother happened to be staying at the time*'. Like most Marlborough men, he went to Eton. After Eton, as war was looming in Europe, he went straight into the army. His concerned mother, Consuelo, sailed back to England on an American steamer three days after the declaration of war. She later analysed her fears:

ABOVE: *Photo of my grandfather Bert at the age of three or four.*
OPPOSITE: *Bert as a young Life Guards officer.*
RIGHT: *Three generations: the ninth Duke with the tenth and eleventh Dukes-to-be.*

> *'To me the future loomed frighteningly, for my sons were at Eton, and Blandford was nearly seventeen. Already I sensed the tragic lot of that doomed generation... Blandford went from Eton to Sandhurst... at eighteen, for the short course of training which was all they could afford to give officers in those hard-pressed days, and then straight into the regiment of the First Life Guards as a second lieutenant. It seemed to me as I went down to spend a day with them that a shadow already obscured the happiness of our times together, for one had to hide one's apprehensions in that young world of high expectancies.'*

In the event, Bert came home safely from the war, bringing with him a lasting affection for the popular songs of the day.

SHOWGIRLS AND HEADLINES

Inevitably, young Bert was a magnet for the mothers trying to marry off their eligible daughters, and Bert happily played the field, telling anyone who would listen that his intentions were always dishonourable. He became entangled with various musical comedy actresses, his 'particular friend' being Betty Barnes, with whom he spent many happy weekends at her cottage on Beachy Head. His separated parents were equally disapproving of the relationship, especially when it made headlines along the lines of *MARQUESS ENGAGED TO ACTRESS*.

WEDDING BELLS.

LORD BLANDFORD AND THE HON. MARY CADOGAN.

KING AND QUEEN PRESENT.

BRILLIANT GATHERING AT ST. MARGARET'S, WESTMINSTER.

ABOVE AND BELOW: *My grandparents Bert and Mary were married at St Margaret's, Westminster, in 1920. Guests at the wedding included King George V and Queen Mary.*

'A TYPICAL ENGLISH ROSE'

Much to the relief of his parents, Bert became engaged to Mary Cadogan, whose family owned vast swathes of Chelsea and whose impeccable lineage had criss-crossed the Marlborough line from the very beginning. Mary, described by a friend as *'a typical English rose even down to the thorns'*, made a perfect wife for blustering Bert. With her steady gaze and her determined jaw, she was born to be a duchess. Consuelo, glossing over her son's past misdemeanours, remembered:

'Early in 1920 my eldest son's marriage to lovely Mary Cadogan, the daughter of Viscount Chelsea, was celebrated in the church of St Margaret's, Westminster, on one of those midwinter days that have the warmth and promise of spring. A fashionable wedding, it was graced by the royal family's presence. It was also my valediction, for steps had already been taken to secure my divorce.'

Bert and Mary settled into married life at Lowesby Hall in Leicestershire where Bert enjoyed his garden, hunted, shot and fished while Mary produced four children. Bert inherited the title in 1934. He remembered:

'I was thoroughly enjoying life when I found myself the owner of Blenheim. It was rather a shock, I'll admit. I'd known it would come to me, but the suddenness was disturbing, to say the least. But one takes these things in one's stride, of course, and I soon began to take my place in local affairs.'

LEFT: *Group photo of my grandparents' wedding.*

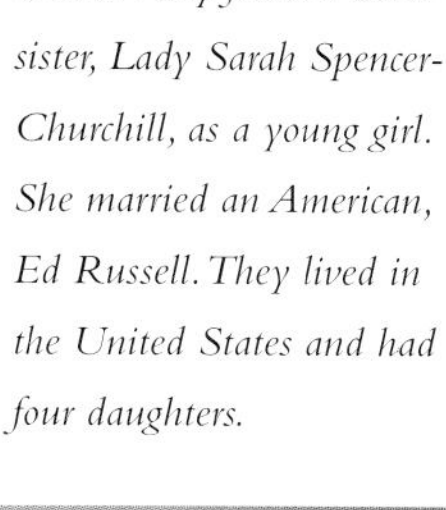

BELOW: *My father's eldest sister, Lady Sarah Spencer-Churchill, as a young girl. She married an American, Ed Russell. They lived in the United States and had four daughters.*

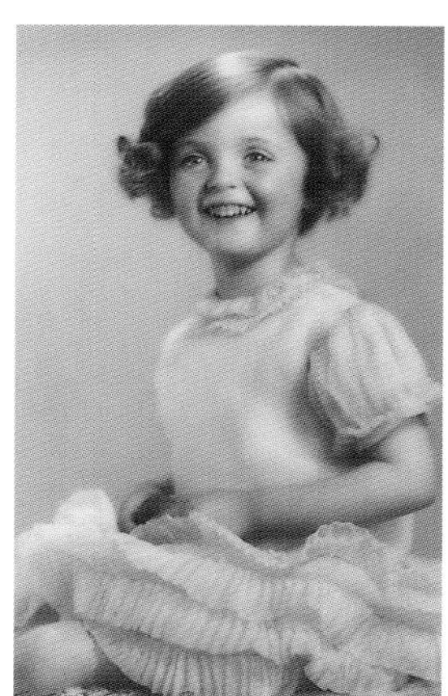

A CHANGE OF REGIME

Bert and Mary moved into the palace, to make it a home once again, dispelling the bad memories of Sunny's despair, Consuelo's unhappiness and the eccentric Gladys's incontinent dogs. The diarist Chips Channon, a family friend, wrote:

> *'Mary Marlborough has improved the house and has enhanced the atmosphere. It is now gay and healthy, and the long corridors echo with childish laughter and screams and huge dogs sprawl about. In the evenings, the fantastic terraces and gardens are floodlighted (I think that all gardens should be floodlit now, it is a wonderful invention and the effect is fantastic, rich and beautiful). On Sunday I was next to Mary Marlborough at luncheon, and got to like her enormously. She is an efficient Duchess, handsome, gay, and serious-minded, very English, very balanced, very conventional and brings up her children in a rather snappy, almost spartan simple way: and they seem to adore her.'*

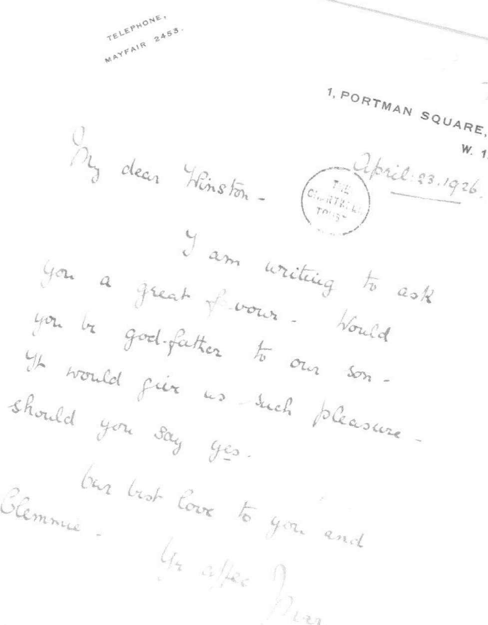

TELEPHONE, MAYFAIR 2453.

1, PORTMAN SQUARE, W. 1.

April 23. 1926.

My dear Winston -

I am writing to ask you a great favour. Would you be god-father to our son - It would give us such pleasure - should you say yes.

Our best love to you and Clemmie -

Yr affec Mary

LEFT: *My grandmother's letter asking Winston Churchill to be my father's godfather. He accepted.*

RIGHT: *My grandmother Mary with her two eldest daughters, Sarah and Caroline. Caroline married Major Hugo Waterhouse and they had three children.*

ABOUT THE HOUSE

Stately Blenheim once more echoed to the sound of children at play. Bicycles whizzed around the cellar passageways, and life was much more relaxed for everyone. At that time, my grandparents Bert and Mary had four children: Sarah, Caroline, John (Sunny, my father, born in 1926) and Rosemary (Rosie). (A fifth child, Charles, was born in 1940.)

Servants enjoyed good accommodation and reasonable wages. The thirty gardeners, instead of scuttling out of the way when a member of the family or a guest came into view, were positively encouraged to be seen doing their jobs. The gardens were open to the public for guided tours at sixpence a head.

The family spilled out from the east wing, making daily use of many of the state rooms. The Duke and Duchess dined formally in the saloon, semi-formally in the bow window room and slightly nearer to casually in the restored Indian room (roughly where the restaurant is now), overlooking the water terraces. Pre-dinner drinks, and coffee and liqueurs after dinner, were laid out in the long library. Guests were entertained on a lavish scale.

Bert and Mary, conscious of the comfort of their illustrious visitors, installed decent plumbing and bathrooms, thus ending the nightmare of emptying commodes and heaving ewers of hot water up the back stairs to fill myriad tin tubs in front of innumerable bedroom fires.

My grandmother Mary with three of her children, Sarah, my father Sunny, and Caroline, about to embark on a fox hunt.

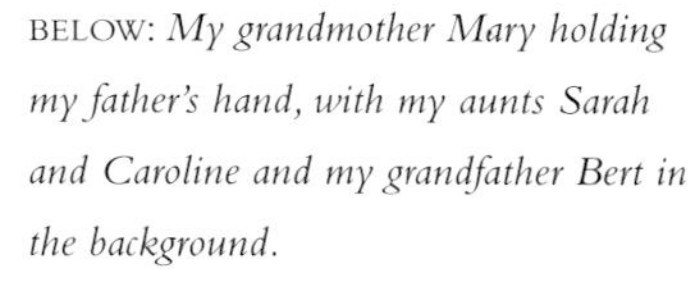

BELOW: *My grandmother Mary holding my father's hand, with my aunts Sarah and Caroline and my grandfather Bert in the background.*

ABOVE: *My aunts Sarah, Caroline and Rosie. They all loved to horse-ride, which was part of the daily routine at Blenheim.*

BELOW: *Family group photograph (from left to right): my aunts Sarah and Caroline, my grandmother Mary, my aunt Rosie and my father, Sunny. My uncle Charles had yet to be born.*

Focus on the garden

At Lowesby, Bert had taken a great interest in his garden. A practical gardener, he had sold produce from his kitchen garden to a shop in London's Belgravia. He brought Tom Page, his gardener from Lowesby, with him to Blenheim, along with a stock of plants.

Tom's first priority was to establish a greenhouse department, employing around six men, to produce the Duke's favourite hothouse fruits and berries. The pleasure grounds employed a further eight, and the kitchen gardens around fifteen. The garden workforce produced flowers for the house (begonias for the shooting season, delphiniums and white peonies for Ascot) and produce for the kitchen—the Duke was particularly partial to peas and spinach.

A NEW LIFE FOR BERT'S GARDEN

In 1954, Bert came into a legacy and he used the money to finance the building of a secret garden. For a man often portrayed as a philistine—he was described by the photographer Cecil Beaton as having an *'arrogant stare and bad manners'*—Bert's secret garden was surprisingly romantic and wild. He created an essentially English version of an early nineteenth-century Italian garden, with pools, a maze of pathways, and rocks transported from Gladys's rock garden.

Work was recently completed on the restoration of the secret garden, which has been open to the public since spring 2004. The layout of the three-acre plot, which is sited opposite the Italian garden, at the south-east of the palace, has been radically altered, but the spirit of the original garden remains intact. The new plan incorporates most of the wonderful mature trees—the cedars, beeches, oaks and chestnuts—and the main water courses that my grandfather installed half a century ago.

BELOW: *View of the newly renovated secret garden opened in 2004 by my aunt, Lady Rosemary Muir. The original garden had been created by my grandfather but had been left neglected for some time.*

A LIFE'S WORK

Bert loved his garden, and worked on it for the rest of life. His assistant in this absorbing venture was gardener Bob Deacon, who recalled that the Duke, on returning from trips to London, would *'leap out of the car and head straight for his garden, arriving there even before his standard could be raised at Flagstaff Lodge to announce his return'*.

OPPOSITE: *View showing the pond and the spring blossom. The garden aims to feature seasonal colour and variation throughout the year.*

OVERLEAF: *The inscription on the boathouse, built in 1888, reads: 'So may thy craft glide gently on as years roll down the stream.'*

The Prince and Mrs Simpson

The Prince of Wales and his 'set' were great party-goers, and they moved in circles guaranteed to be discreet, so the news of who went where with whom was circulated only among the select few and never to the English newspapers. In June 1936 a weekend party at Blenheim included the as-yet uncrowned King Edward VIII, the Duff Coopers, the Winston Churchills, Lady Cunard and Mr and Mrs Ernest Simpson. How Mr Simpson felt about spending time with his wife and her royal lover is not recorded, but a few months later Bert and Mary were guests at Balmoral when the King, having upset the Scots by refusing to open a hospital in Aberdeen, took time out to pick up Wallis Simpson from the railway station.

During the abdication crisis, sides were taken and hostesses who had welcomed Mrs Simpson were suddenly open to criticism. Mary thought that extremely unfair. The diarist Chips Channon wrote of meeting Mary Marlborough at a party given by Lady Cunard:

> *'The Duchess asked me in her frank, breezy way, did I not think that all the while Wallis had been playing a double game? She herself has not yet made up her mind, but she added that it enraged her when people attacked Emerald [Lady Cunard] for entertaining her, as Emerald was only one of many. "We had her to stay at Blenheim, I liked her," was Mary's summing up.'*

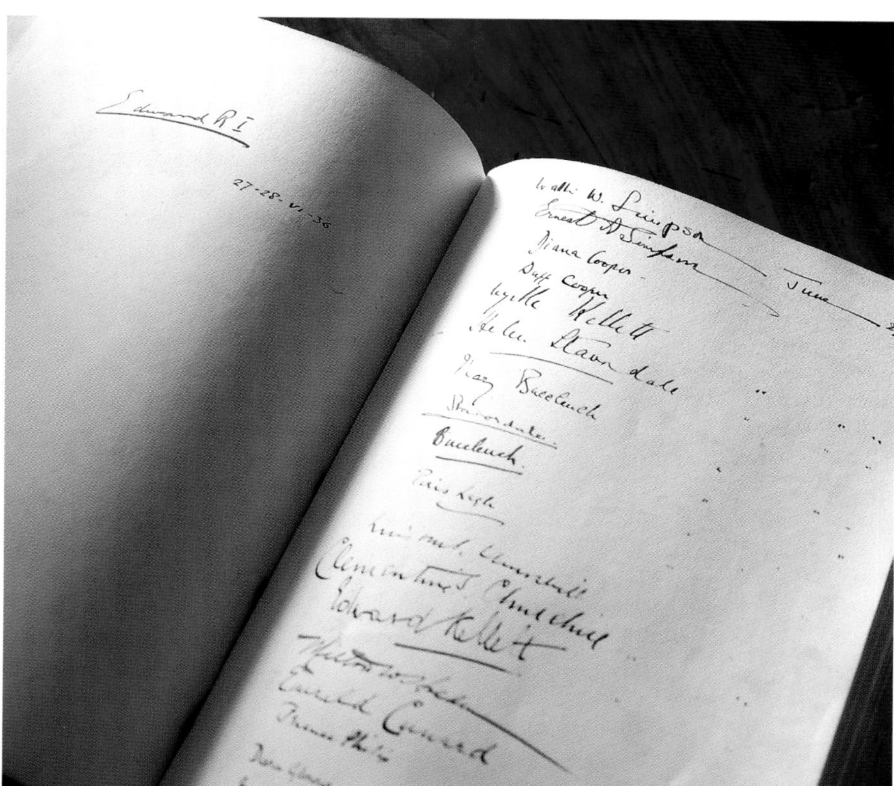

RIGHT: *The visitors' book showing the original signatures of the Prince of Wales and Wallis Simpson.*

'Shall we ever see the like again?'

Probably the most spectacular Blenheim party of all was the coming-out ball that Bert and Mary gave for their eldest daughter, Lady Sarah Spencer-Churchill, in July 1939. It was particularly poignant as it marked the last summer of peace before war once again engulfed the country. Consuelo attended her granddaughter's party:

> *'In 1939 I went to Blenheim with anxious forebodings, for the international horizon was dark... I suffered the same unease that had afflicted me once in Russia when, surrounded by the glittering splendour of the czar's court, I sensed impending disaster. For again, in this brilliant scene at Blenheim, I sensed the end of an era. Only a few months later these rooms were dismantled and the ugly paraphernalia of officialdom installed for the duration of a tragic war.*

My aunt, Lady Sarah, at her glittering coming-out ball at Blenheim on the eve of war in July 1939.

But on that evening the scene was still gay and my pleasure great in meeting so many old friends. I supped with Winston and Anthony Eden and wandered out to the lovely terraces Marlborough had built before his death... How rewarding are my memories of Blenheim in my son's time when his life, with Mary and his children, was all that I wished mine could have been.'

Chips Channon wrote up the event in his diary:

'I have seen much, travelled far and am accustomed to splendour, but there has never been anything like tonight. Tyroleans walked about singing; and although there were seven hundred people or even more, it was not in the least crowded. It was gay, young, brilliant, in short, perfection. I was loath to leave but did so at about 4.30 and took one last look at the baroque terraces with the lake below, and the golden statues and the great palace. Shall we ever see the like again? Is such a function not out of date? Yet it was all of the England that is supposed to be dead and is not. There were literally rivers of champagne.'

The interior was redecorated and refurbished, the palace facades were floodlit, Japanese lanterns and chains of coloured lights festooned the terraces and searchlights played onto the trees.

Guests included Eunice Kennedy, JFK's sister and daughter of Joe and Rose Kennedy, and the writer Sacheverell Sitwell, who was also moved by the splendour of the setting:

'There was a galaxy of light upon this theatrical but heroic building, upon this private monument that is a Roman triumph and a public pantomime; and amid those lights it was possible to admire Vanbrugh's architecture as it may never be seen again.'

After the war, Mary gave an interview to the *Woman's Journal* about that famous party:

'It was the most elaborate party I ever planned. The organization required for coping with a thousand guests was tremendous. Before the ball, we held a private dinner in the saloon, and Sarah had another one for some of the younger guests on the terrace facing the lake. Trees, six feet high, surrounded the dinner table, and lights shining through orange awnings, high up on the terraces, gave an effect like sunlight.'

The next generation: Cecil Beaton's 1950s coming-out portrait of my cousin Serena Balfour (daughter of my aunt Lady Sarah), under the painting of Consuelo, our great-grandmother.

BLENHEIM'S WAR

On September 3, 1939, less than two months after that memorable party, war was declared and Blenheim went into war mode. At the Duke's suggestion, the boys from Malvern College, whose own premises had been commandeered, were evacuated to Blenheim. The family retreated to the east wing, Blenheim's treasures were bundled into storage and within five frantic weeks the palace was transformed to make way for four hundred schoolboys and a hundred members of staff.

The marble floors were hidden under fourteen hundred square feet of linoleum and a thousand square feet of matting. The windows—all one thousand of them—were criss-crossed with anti-shatter tape and hung with blackout curtains. Silk damask curtains were covered with canvas and the mahogany doors padded with protective layers of felt. The three western state rooms and the long library became crowded dormitories, and the great hall became a school dining room. The old laundry became a science lab and the stables a gymnasium. The great court sprouted prefabricated huts containing shower stalls and changing rooms. The magazine *Country Life* patriotically trumpeted: *'If the war will not be won on the fields of Blenheim, they are certainly playing their part in the great business of training the nation, under the shadow of the palace that commemorates the greatest military genius our country has produced.'*

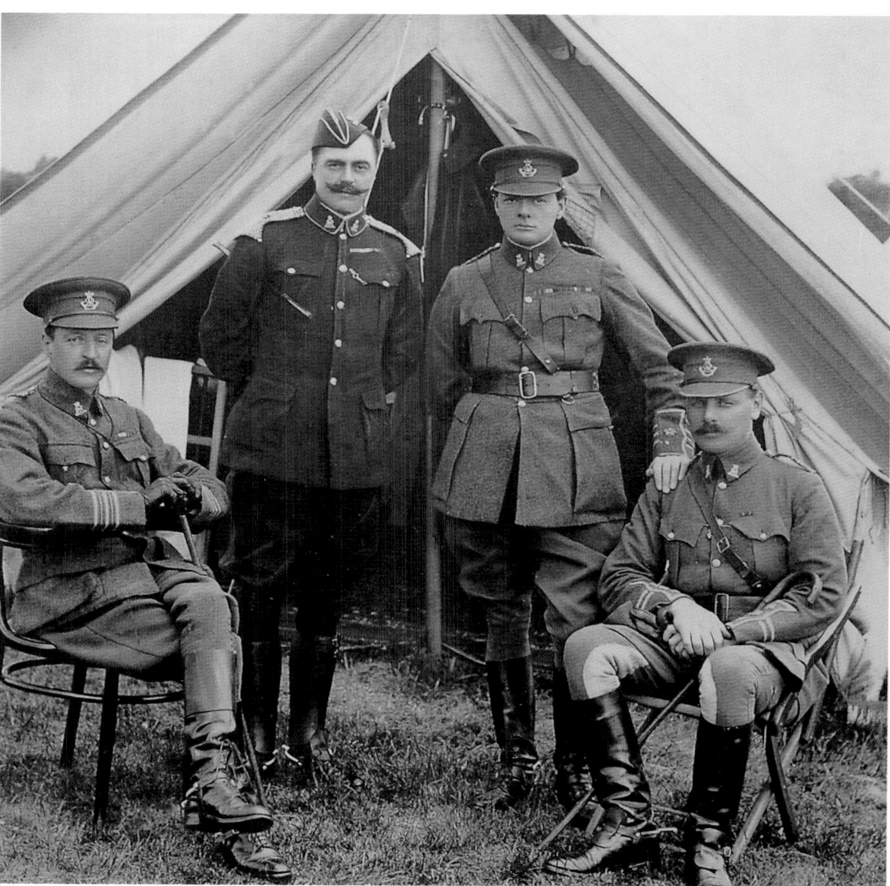

Winston had been an army man for many years. This 1911 picture, a personal favourite of the eleventh Duke's, was taken in camp at Blenheim Park with the Oxfordshire Hussars. Pictured (from left) are the ninth Duke, Viscount Churchill, Winston Churchill and his brother Jack.

OFFICE SPACE FOR SPOOKS

A year later, Malvern College was uprooted once again, this time to Harrow, and an army of diligent spy-masters from MI5 (the British Secret Service), a thousand strong, moved in from Wormwood Scrubs prison (where they had been billeted) with their filing cabinets, their double agents and their plywood partitions. After MI5 came the British Council and the Ministry of Supply.

Meanwhile, out in the park, army training exercises were taking place and the lake was sometimes used for testing landing craft. Fish from the lake were made available to local shops, and the rose beds were dug over and planted with cabbages.

'Altogether it was a very different affair from an historic house,' muttered Bert. And it was, in fact, a turning point for the palace, as never again would the state rooms be used by the family in the course of everyday life: after the war those stately halls had to earn their living.

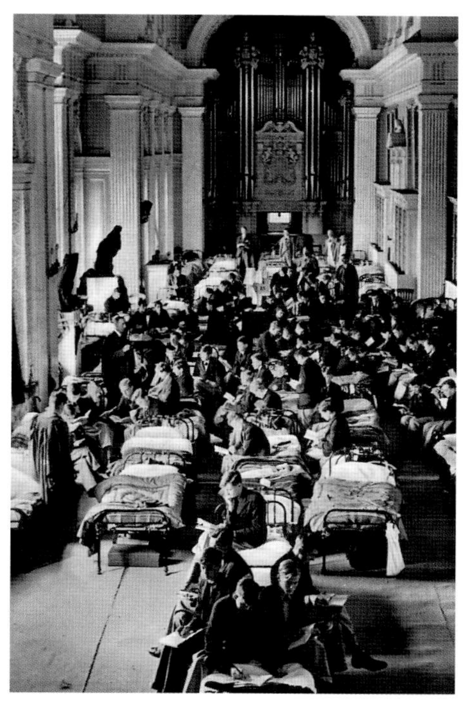

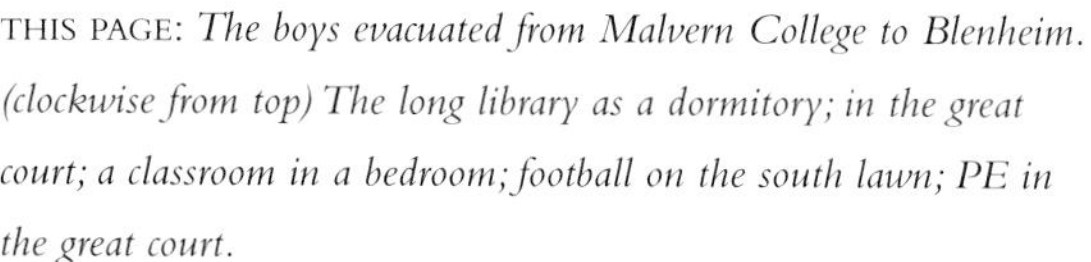

THIS PAGE: *The boys evacuated from Malvern College to Blenheim. (clockwise from top) The long library as a dormitory; in the great court; a classroom in a bedroom; football on the south lawn; PE in the great court.*

THE MARLBOROUGHS' WAR

Bert, long retired from his position as captain in the Life Guards, joined up to become Military Liaison Officer to the Southern Regional Commander. Thanks to his American mother, he also had a position liaising with the American armed forces.

Duchess Mary, with her formidable organizational skills, joined the Auxiliary Territorial Service (ATS), which had been formed in 1938 as a way of recruiting women into the army. Mary was Chief Commandant of the ATS, thus outranking Bert, who referred to her as 'the general'.

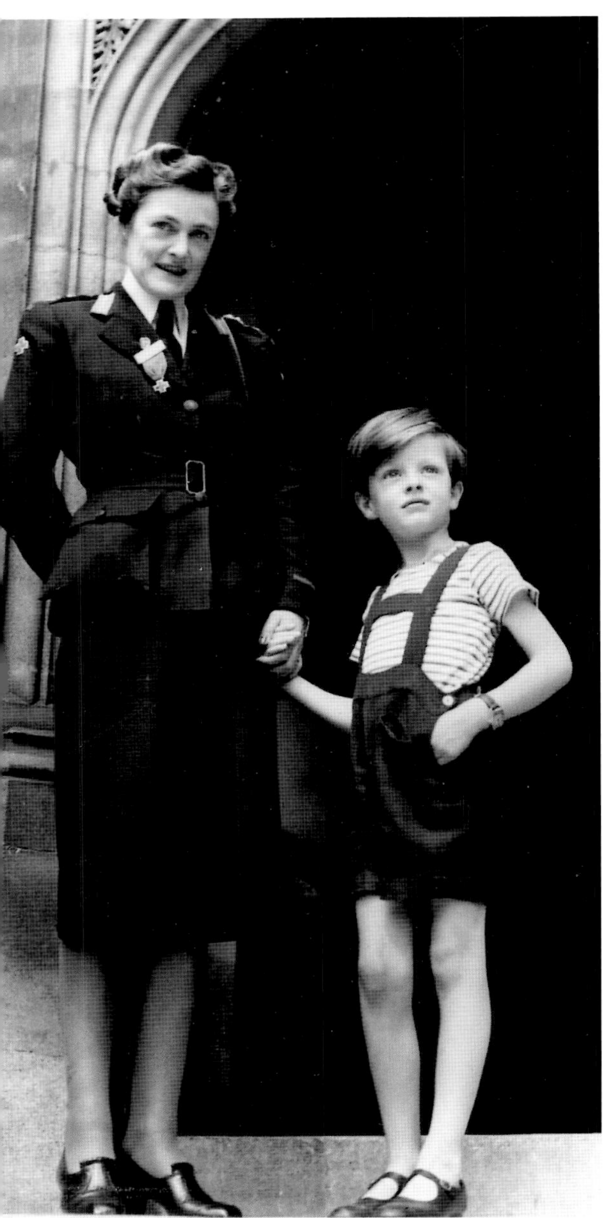

My grandmother Mary in Red Cross uniform, with Lord Charles Spencer-Churchill, her youngest child.

THE NO-NONSENSE DUCHESS

My grandmother had a knack for getting things done—this was, after all, a woman who could organize a spectacular party for a thousand guests and still find time to enjoy it herself. She was happy to rip her way through bureaucracy. On one occasion she was informed that the ATS were short of typewriters, so she jumped in her car, drove straight to the War Office, and refused to leave until the requisite number of machines were loaded into her car.

When her fifth child, Charles, was born in 1940, she relinquished her role in the ATS, but she didn't slow down. She worked tirelessly for the Women's Voluntary Service and took on the role of president of the Oxfordshire Red Cross, which entailed driving miles across the country organizing the 'penny collections' to raise money for many worthwhile wartime causes.

Mary was a formidable woman and, when dressed in her ATS uniform, could look decidedly mannish. (Cecil Beaton once described her as being *'not flattered by the camera'*.) The Countess of Drogheda told a story of a visiting Polish general who found

A
PRESENTATION OF
Monsieur Christian Dior's
PARIS WINTER COLLECTION
IN THE PRESENCE OF
H.R.H.
Princess Margaret
AT
BLENHEIM PALACE
ON
November 3 1954
IN AID OF THE
BRITISH RED CROSS SOCIETY

Mary continued fund-raising for the Red Cross after the war. The programme pictured here is from a Christian Dior fashion show held at Blenheim in aid of the Red Cross.

himself sitting next to a handsome English general talking knowledgeably about wartime strategy, who then paused and took out a powder puff and a lipstick. That was my grandmother.

VICTORY AT ANY COST

Meanwhile Winston, fired by a sense of mission, was focusing his ferocious will on victory at any cost. *'I won't say he's a bad loser,'* Mary confided to a friend, *'but he much prefers to win.'*

Winston at work in the Cabinet Office.

A FAMILY AFFAIR

The whole family joined in the war effort. My aunt Sarah put her ballgowns away and went to work as a machinist at the Morris Motors factory at nearby Cowley—her supervisor there was a former Blenheim servant. In fact, most of the servants who hadn't joined up were assigned to war work, so helping hands at Blenheim were a motley crew. *'I don't suppose I have ever had a stranger-looking staff than the constantly changing odd-job men we had then,'* remembered the Duchess. *'The whole family had to help with the work, and eating was like a continual picnic.'*

'God knows where we should be without him'

The famous 1941 portrait of Winston Churchill, by the great photographer Yousuf Karsh of Ottawa, captures Churchill's steely determination never to surrender.

What was it that made Winston Churchill the right man in the right place at the right time? If one is to believe in the importance of genetic factors, then one would account for his extraordinary character in the following way. The first Duke of Marlborough gifted him courage, a stubborn resolve and political savvy. From the Spencer connection came a love of literature and a strong artistic streak. From his spirited American mother, Jennie Jerome, he inherited wit and social ease. It was to prove a remarkable combination.

Field Marshal Alan Brooke, whose respect for Churchill was total but whose opinion of him as a strategist was less complimentary, wrote:

> *'Winston never had the slightest doubt that he had inherited all the military genius of his great ancestor, Marlborough. His military plans and ideas varied from the most brilliant conceptions at the one end to the wildest and most dangerous ideas at the other.'*

Churchill's instinct was for action. He was impulsive, he was impatient and, like his ancestors before him, he made mistakes, but ultimately, his driving resolve carried the day. *'God knows where we should be without him,'* wrote one of his Chiefs of Staff, *'but God knows where we shall go with him!'*

THE FIGHTING SPIRIT

Churchill's power of rhetoric, his command of the cadences of the English language, was a supreme talent all his own. In 1940 Britain stood alone, defeat looming from the other side of the Channel. Churchill, who became prime minister of a coalition government in that year, had many qualities that made him the ideal person for the job at that critical juncture, but his inspired and dogged determination to rouse the British fighting spirit was perhaps the most important. As he said at the time:

> *'I have nothing to offer but blood, toil, tears and sweat. We have before us an ordeal of the most grievous kind. We have before us many, many long months of struggle and of suffering. You ask, what is our policy? I will say: It is to wage war, by sea, land and air, with all our might and with all the strength that God can give us: to wage war against a monstrous tyranny, never surpassed in the dark, lamentable catalogue of human crime. You ask what is our aim? I can answer in one word: Victory—victory at all costs, victory in spite of all terror, victory however long and hard the road may be; for without victory there is no survival.'*

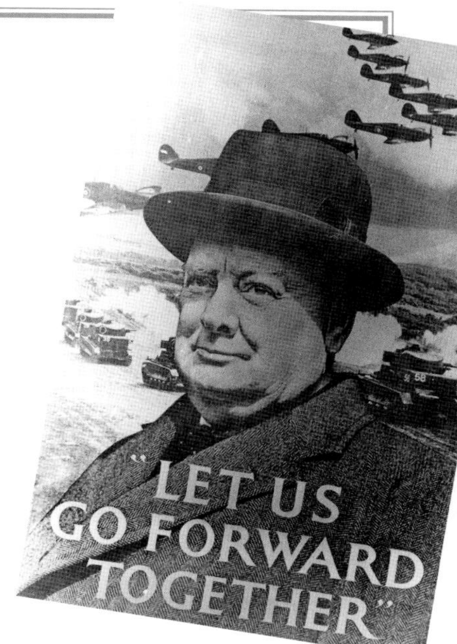

A ROAR OF APPROVAL

Churchill became a familiar figure and an even more familiar voice as a result of his radio broadcasts. His words united government and people, distilling their resolve, while also persuading the American President Roosevelt that Britain was not a lost cause. His famous speech after Dunkirk—not so much a victory as a narrow escape—reverberated strongly with the president and his secretary of state.

> *'We shall defend our island, whatever the cost may be, we shall fight on the beaches, we shall fight on the landing grounds, we shall fight in the fields and in the streets, we shall fight in the hills; we shall never surrender, and even if, which I do not for a moment believe, this island... were subjugated and starving, then our Empire beyond the seas, armed and guarded by the British fleet, would carry on the struggle, until, in God's good time, the New World, with all its power and might, steps forth to the rescue and the liberation of the Old.'*

As President Roosevelt gradually pulled America around to the realization that this war was their war, the relationship between Churchill and Roosevelt became that of intimate friends. Churchill was invited to make a speech to Congress: *'I cannot help reflecting that if my father had been an American and my mother British, instead of the other way round, I might have got here on my own,'* he chuckled. Then, turning the mood to one of angry defiance, he made himself at one with his audience, talking of the Germans and asking defiantly: *'What sort of people do they think we are?'* A roar of approval came back—it was the moment the American people took him to their hearts.

ABOVE: *A wartime poster of Churchill exhorting the Allies to keep the faith. He set great store by air power.*
BELOW: *A wartime photograph showing Churchill and President Roosevelt at one of their frequent meetings. The two men were friends as well as allies.*

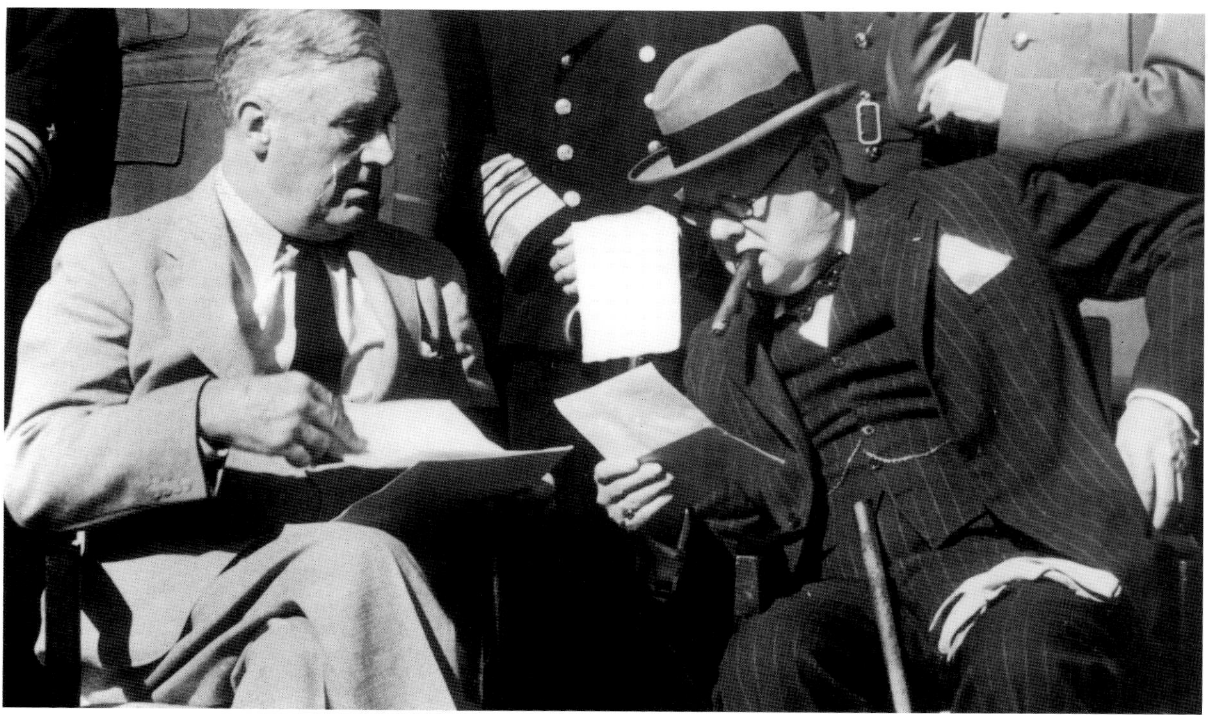

POST-WAR PAINS

At 3 pm on May 8, 1945, Winston Churchill broadcast to the nation the welcome news that the war was over and victory was theirs. He was seventy years old and he had steered the country to victory against huge odds. Later, he wrote:

> *'I have never accepted what many people have kindly said, namely that I inspired the nation. Their will was resolute and remorseless, and, as it proved, unconquerable. It fell to me to express it, and if I found the right words, you must remember that I have always earned my living by my pen and by my tongue. It was the nation and the race dwelling all round the globe that had the lion's heart. I had the luck to be called on to give the roar.'*

Churchill had been, as he put it himself, born for this moment, but at the first post-war elections, the aristocratic descendant of the noble Marlborough line was perceived as belonging to another era, an anachronism in a newly democratized Britain. Churchill was sidelined to the Opposition benches.

POST-WAR PLEASURES

The Ministry of Works lent a hand in putting Blenheim back to rights with a programme of repainting, regilding and reflooring to repair the damage of wartime habitation. Bert and Mary set out to dispel the post-war gloom and the deprivations of rationing with concerts and gatherings. Though never as splendid as before, they were none the less entertaining. Noel Coward came, and Princess Margaret was a frequent visitor. (Her name was romantically linked with my father's for some time.)

My grandfather, Bert, entertaining Princess Margaret at the Blenheim garden party celebrating the coronation of Queen Elizabeth II in 1953.

Noel Coward remembered not the company but the cold caused by the lack of coal, when he came down to Blenheim to give a private piano recital:

> *'[My bedroom at Blenheim was] the coldest room I have ever encountered... Woke frozen. Shaving sheer agony and glacial bathroom with a skylight that would not shut. Loo like an icebox. Breakfast downstairs. Bert Marlborough none too bright—Mary very sweet. Saw Princess Margaret off. Pretended I was going to Oxford... Returned to Blenheim at cocktail time. Small dinner. More piano playing. Back to the Frigidaire.'*

The Duke's shooting parties were not for amateurs. Acknowledged as a fine shot, Bert planned the planting and management of the park with shooting uppermost in his mind. *'He wouldn't have sheep in the park,'* recalled the Duke's land agent at the time. *'He said they made too much bloody mess and ate all his cover.'*

HALF A CROWN A HEAD

While the country struggled towards recovery, Blenheim was losing its roof. Rain started pouring through into the attics, and the south-east tower was badly damaged. These were expenses that Bert simply could not bear, and while he muttered about *'the bloody roof'* the debate was between handing Blenheim over to the National Trust or selling it off to the highest bidder. Neither solution appealed, so Bert found a third way: opening Blenheim to the public as a serious money-making venture. Blenheim was to become a business, not a private house with a few people wandering aimlessly around the park. Consuelo approved of her son's decision:

> *'In the tradition that has kept for England her aristocratic heritage, my son determined to maintain and to hand down the gift a grateful nation had bestowed on his family in perpetuity; so when the Ministry that occupied the house during the war returned to its permanent quarters, he prepared to open Blenheim to tourist traffic on a hitherto unprecedented scale. For in such a way alone could taxation be met and the upkeep of so large a house assured. His efforts have been crowned with success. Well over 100,000 tourists, with a price for adults of two shillings and sixpence, visited Blenheim during the opening year [1950], a record since surpassed and maintained.'*

THE DUKE PACKS THEM IN PALACE—AND MAKES IT A £250 DAY

By NOEL WHITCOMB

JOHN Albert Edward William Spencer-Churchill, tenth Duke of Marlborough, sized in the great doorway of his ancestral home, Blenheim Palace, Oxfordshire, yesterday, and beamed at the approaching army of fathers, mothers and kids.

No Time for a Meal

'A Guide Book . . .?'

The Tall Young Man

Necessary, he says

YVES SITS IN FOR THE PRINCESS . . .

ABOVE: *Excited press coverage marked the opening of Blenheim's doors to the public.*

LEFT: *In 1958 Blenheim hosted a fashion show for the celebrated Yves St Laurent.*

BELOW: *A shooting party during my grandfather the tenth Duke's time.*

A LINGERING END

At the beginning of the 1950s, the British economy was wavering and people wanted change. In 1951, Winston was re-elected as prime minister with a small majority. He was seventy-seven years old and unwell. In May 1953, the coronation of Queen Elizabeth II lifted the spirits of a war-weary nation, and Winston accepted the honour of the Order of the Garter—Mr Churchill became Sir Winston. Later that year he suffered a stroke that paralysed one side of his body, but he made a remarkable recovery, especially considering his advanced age. He returned to public life with this sentiment:

> *'If I stay for the time being, bearing the burden at my age, it is not because of love for power or office. I have had an ample share of both. If I stay it is because I have the feeling that I may, through things that have happened, have an influence on what I care about above all else—the building of a sure and lasting peace.'*

In 1955, after suffering another stroke, Sir Winston resigned; he spent the next ten years, impaired by the successive strokes, brooding at Chartwell or at his house in London's Hyde Park Gate, where he died on January 24, 1965. His last coherent words were: *'I'm so bored with it all.'* Winston had once remarked to a young friend whose father had died in his prime: *'Think of the great Duke of Marlborough, how he lingered on into surly decrepitude. How much better it would have been had he been cut off in his brilliant prime—a cannon-ball at Malplaquet.'* Winston's brilliant prime came later than the first Duke's, and I cannot help but think it was a fate he would have chosen for himself. He had told his wife that when his time came, he wanted to be buried as a soldier but, as always with Winston, he thought on a grand scale. He reminded his son, Randolph: *'When it comes to my funeral, dear boy, your mother may have modest ideas, but I want troops, I want troops!'*

BELOW: *This rare photograph of Winston Churchill relaxing, cigar in hand, was taken in the private apartments at Blenheim, probably after dinner.*
BELOW RIGHT: *The grave of Winston and Clementine at Bladon churchyard.*

A FITTING FAREWELL

'Troops' is what he got—thousands of them. Sir Winston Churchill was accorded a state funeral. His body lay in state in Westminster Hall for three days, during which well over 300,000 people filed past to pay tribute, in queues that were often three miles long. The funeral procession set out to the sound of a ninety-gun salute, one for each year of Winston's life. Then the gun carriage bearing his coffin made its slow, dignified way past huge crowds to St Paul's Cathedral where three thousand mourners were gathered, joined in spirit by over 350 million television viewers.

After the service, the coffin was taken to Tower Bridge and was piped aboard a launch that bore his body to Waterloo station. Here the coffin was loaded onto a specially prepared funeral train for his final trip to Blenheim; only his family went with him. He was buried near his parents at St Martin's Church, Bladon.

Sir Winston's last journey. Thousands of people flocked to London to pay their respects to him and to see his funeral procession.

BERT'S LAST STAND

My grandmother died in 1961, after a long battle with cancer, taking her robust gaiety and her considerable management skills with her. Without her, Blenheim was a gloomy place. The visitors kept coming, but the roof continued to eat up the resources and Bert mooched around feeling lonely and bereft. He formed a friendship with the widowed Laura Charteris and asked her to marry him. Laura had doubts, not so much about Bert as about Blenheim, recording in her memoirs:

> *'I was fond of him but, as I frequently explained, Blenheim was so terribly gloomy. It was built as a monument, not a house to live in. At times, Bert would try to counter this statement by quoting the many thousands of paying tourists who flocked to Blenheim each year. But he did not see that this made it even worse than gloomy by turning him and his friends into exhibits, like freaks or animals to be gazed at. I felt this most acutely when playing croquet in the public eye, surrounded by a chain to keep the not unnaturally inquisitive visitors off the lawn. I thought at any moment they would throw us stale bread or nuts as in the zoo… Secretly, I believe Bert was in agreement with me. His reason for continuing to inhabit Blenheim—or as he came (through me) to call it, "the Dump"—was a real fear of being the first Duke not to reside there.'*

Laura finally relented and she and Bert were married at Caxton Hall in 1972. At the wedding lunch at the Connaught Hotel, a frail Bert stood up and movingly, if somewhat shakily, sang to her an old music-hall song, one of his favourites, 'I Shan't Be Happy Till I Make You Happy Too'. It was as romantic a gesture as you could get. Three months later he was dead.

My grandfather was a legend in his own way, and is still remembered with affection by those who knew him. In some ways he was an irascible man with terrible manners who inhabited a nineteenth-century world that had long ago ceased to exist, but somewhere under all that lay the creator of a wild romantic garden and a singer of love songs. A friend wrote a letter to *The Times* after his death:

> *'Times changed, he did not. The type he personified is easy to criticize, yet to dismiss him easily would be to sacrifice character to mundane convention as he had two rare qualities—wit and an appreciation of wit. These, allied to his conservatism, may have made him appear formidable and to strangers frightening, but behind the mumbling and the muttering, the Malacca cane, the gold watch chain and seals lay a kind heart and he was greatly loved by his children and grandchildren while to his friends he was a source of endless pleasure. But above all he was a personality remaining himself, sometimes to be laughed at, more often to be laughed with, but never to go unnoticed. In these grey days he will be sadly missed.'*

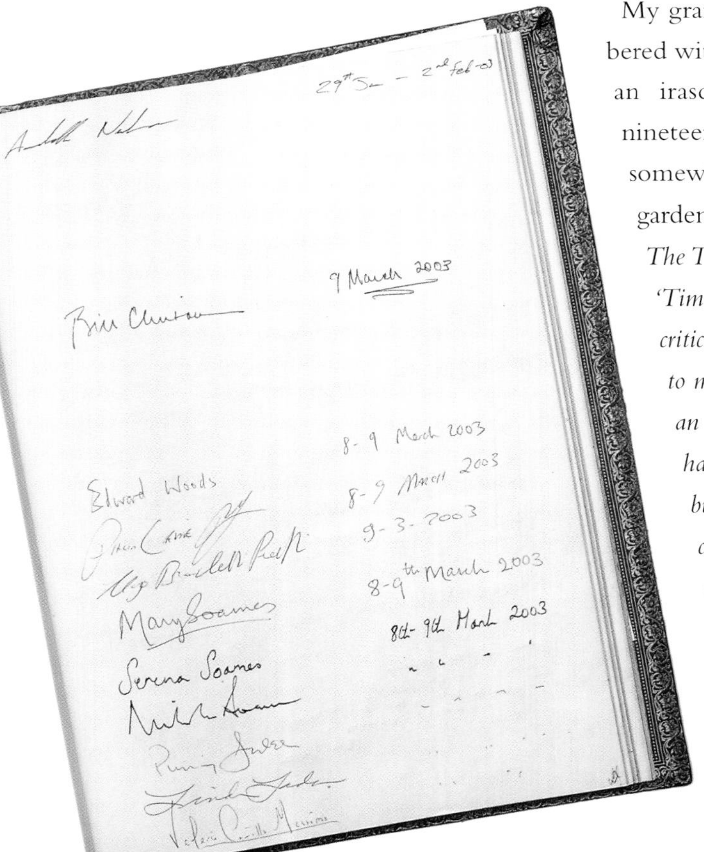

The Blenheim guest book with the signature of the former US president Bill Clinton, who was a guest at the Churchill Memorial Concert in March 2003.

THE ELEVENTH DUKE

My father, John (Sunny), inherited the title of eleventh Duke of Marlborough in 1972, but as he had already taken over the running of much of the estate during my grandfather's time, the burden of inheritance wasn't quite such a shock as it had been to Bert. He was able to meet the inevitable death duty bill by gifting the Blenheim Papers (over 30,000 invaluable documents) to the Treasury. (These are now beautifully cared for at the British Library and have proved a fascinating resource for this book.)

With a lot of hard work my father and his executives have put Blenheim onto a sound financial footing. It is run as a modern business, with professional tour guides, visitor attractions, corporate entertaining facilities, concerts and retail outlets—even the private wing is now open for public tours. The palace is home to events of all kinds, from cheese festivals to jousting tournaments, and boasts an education service that is second to none.

The battle to preserve Blenheim and to keep it in the family, as the first Duke so devoutly wished, can never be decisively won, but my father has gone a long way towards making it a possibility.

My parents' formal wedding photograph in 1951. The wedding, like Bert and Mary's, was held at St Margaret's, Westminster. The group photograph includes the late Queen Mother, Princess Alice and Princess Margaret.

John of the Battles

INNOVATIONS

My stepmother, Rosita, a talented artist with an eye for colour, has made a real difference to Blenheim, updating the decoration of the private side so that it feels like a beautiful home rather than a fossilized stately pile. The state rooms, too, need constant attention and subtle refurbishments to keep the palace alive.

For all its magnificence, for all the highs and lows of its history, Blenheim is a home that has passed through eleven generations of the same family, and they have all, in their way, left their traces. Blenheim has always been a family affair.

LEFT: *A guest bedroom at Blenheim which was formerly used as a pressing room. My stepmother, Rosita, painted the murals on the walls.* BELOW: *The shutters in the room are original, with the panel moulding picked out in gilt.*

THE FUTURE OF BLENHEIM

My brother James will succeed as the twelfth Duke of Marlborough, and his son George, who at present carries the title Earl of Sunderland, will then become the Marquess of Blandford. James, my half-brother Edward and I are trustees of the Blenheim Foundation, which was set up to maintain the house. Along with my half-sister Alexandra, we all do what we can to assist in fund-raising and preserving our heritage. We are acutely aware that we owe it not only to the future generations who will live in the palace, but also to the public who enjoy it as a national monument and World Heritage Site.

As my life and career have developed, I have become increasingly conscious of the importance of my family home. Having resolved to help in any way I can, I am particularly interested in the restoration and development of the various properties, whether for commercial or residential use. Having had my design business for well over twenty years, I can hopefully bring some expertise to the table, to help save some of the much-needed funds.

I enjoy working with local charities and organizing such events as the Churchill Memorial Concert, which was set up in in 1966 as a tribute to Sir Winston's life and as a fund-raiser for music therapy and local Oxfordshire-based charities. Following in the footsteps of my late grandmother Mary, whom I greatly admired, I am also involved with the Red Cross, on both a local and a national basis.

Blenheim, and the history that goes with it, has undoubtedly influenced us all and hopefully will continue to do so in the future.

My sons, David and Maximilian, aged four and one.

My brother James, the Marquis of Blandford, and his son George, the Earl of Sunderland, who are the next heirs of Blenheim.

RIGHT: *My father and myself at a recent fund-raising ball at Blenheim.*

BELOW: *With my sons, Maximilian and David, celebrating my fortieth birthday with a dinner and dancing in the orangery at Blenheim.*

ABOVE *The twelfth generation: my brother James, myself, and my half-brother and half-sister, Edward and Alexandra, at the Churchill Memorial Concert in 2003, when the former US president Bill Clinton gave the tribute to Sir Winston Churchill.*

OVERLEAF: *My father on Branson, and myself on Barney, riding out at Blenheim—a perfect way to see and enjoy the beautiful landscape of the park.*

ACKNOWLEDGMENTS

The author would like to thank many people who have contributed to this book's coming to fruition. In particular my thanks go to my co-author, Alex Parsons, who had a testing challenge unravelling the complexities of my family, and to my photographer, Andreas von Einsiedel, who worked with me on my first book in 1990 and is still a true professional and great fun to work with and to Geoff Dann for his expertise in photographing the archive materials. The team at Cico books have as usual carried out a splendid job, notably Cindy Richards, Georgina Harris, Christine Wood and Alison Wormleighton.

I am extremely grateful to John Forster, our education officer and archivist, whose knowledge about Blenheim and my family is quite remarkable and whose assistance in providing details on individuals and the reference material has been invaluable.

I am also most grateful to Dr Frances Harris at the British Library and Allen Packwood at Churchill College, Cambridge, for their assistance in providing much of the archive material. Thanks also to Jeri Bapasola for her in-depth knowledge on the Tapestries at Blenheim.

In addition, I would like to thank many of the staff at Blenheim, who have been most patient and helpful during various photographic shoots, especially Tim and Stephen and the guides on the public side. My thanks also go to my extended family for providing photographs and permission to use some of the copyright material.

Lastly, I would like to thank my agent, Maggie Pearlstine, for getting this book off the ground after many years of discussion, and my US publishers, Rizzoli, for their continued support, this being my ninth book with them!

The authors would like to thank the writers whose many and varied contributions to the history of Blenheim and the Spencer-Churchill family inspired this work:

The Blenheim Papers courtesy of the British Library.

Balsan, Consuelo Vanderbilt, *The Glitter and the Gold*, George Mann Books, US, 1973.

Cawthorne, Nigel, *The Sex Lives of the Kings and Queens of England*, Prion Books, UK, 2004.

Churchill, Randolph S, *Winston S. Churchill* plus *Companion Volume 1, Part 1 1874–1896* and *Companion Volume 1, Part 2 1896-1900*, Heinemann, London 1967.

Field, Ophelia, *The Favourite: Sarah, Duchess of Marlborough*, Sceptre, UK, 2003.

Fowler, Marian, *Blenheim: Biography of a Palace*, Penguin Books, 1991.

Leslie, Anita, *Jennie: Life of Lady Randolph Churchill*, Hutchinson, UK, 1969.

Martin, Ralph G, *Lady Randolph Churchill*, Cassell, 1969.

Montgomery-Massingberd, Hugh, *Blenheim Revisited*, The Bodley Head, 1985.

Rowse, A L, *The Early Churchills*, Penguin Books, 1969

The publishers would particularly like to express their gratitude to John Forster, archivist at Blenheim Palace, Malcolm Crampton, and Sue Murton of Jarrolds Publishing and Hugo Vickers. Thanks to Allen Packwood and Sandra Marsh of the Churchill Centre, Rory McLeod, Anthea Morton-Saner, Lynn Miller of the Wedgwood Museum, and Neil Fitzgerald. Particular thanks are offered to Jeri Bapasola, author of *Threads of History: The Tapestries of Blenheim Palace* (Lightmoor Press, 2005), whose expertise on the Blenheim Tapestries was invaluable.

ILLUSTRATION CREDITS

The publishers would like to thank the following for their permission to use these illustrations:

Althorp Archives: 39

Blenheim Archives: 1, 49(t), 50–51, 53, 81, 136, 138(t), 139(t), 141–143, 145, 157, 176, 200, 202, 208(l), 209

Blenheim Archives © Cico Books: 20–21, 37, 49(b), 56–57, 62–65, 68, 83, 86(t), 97, 118 (t), 119, 121–122, 130(b), 131, 134(b), 137, 140(t), 146(b), 149, 155(b), 156, 158, 162–170, 171(b), 180, 187, 190, 191(t), 198–199, 207(t), 210

The British Library: 38(t), 42(b), 43, 45, 47, 48, 55, 69–73, 76(b), 86(b), 88–89, 94(r), 99(t), 103(t)

*Estate of Winston Churchill; Broadwater collection:*173, 182. *Churchill Papers,* reproduced with permission of Curtis Brown Ltd on behalf of Winston S Churchill: (CHAR 28/13/11, CHAR 28/97/11-13): 146, 150–151

Churchill College, Baroness Spencer-Churchill Papers (CSCT 5/3/115a, CSCT 1/1/5 and 1/1/6, CSCT 2/1/7): 174(t), 175

Churchill Heritage Collection: 183

Curtis Brown Ltd, on behalf of Mrs Peregrine S Churchill © The Estate of Lord Randolph Churchill (CHAR 28/6/): 151
C&T Publications (CHUR 1/104D/151), The Lady Soames DBE, KG, The Clementine Spencer-Churchill papers (CSCT 1/1/13, CSCT 1/1/5, CSCT 1/1/6), Winston Churchill (CSCT 2/1/7): 175

Andreas von Einsiedel: 12–13, 15, 23–25, 30–33, 40–41, 66–67, 87, 94(t and l), 95, 107–109, 120, 124–129, 130(t), 134(t), 138(b), 153–154, 158(t), 174(b), 179(t), 184–185, 186(br), 191(r), 192–197, 208(r), 212–213, 216–217

Elizabeth Whiting Associates/Andreas von Einsiedel: 26–27, 93, 118(b), 133, 139(b)

Getty Images: 159, 204–205

Hertfordshire County Council: 46

Irish Architectural Archive: 152

Jarrold Publishing: 2, 4–7, 9, 10, 17–19, 28–29, 34–35, 36(t), 38(b), 42(tl), 52, 58, 65(tr), 74(t), 75, 76(t), 78, 84(b), 85, 90–91, 100, 102, 103(b), 111–112, 115–117, 147–148, 155(t), 186(b)

Malvern College: 201

The Duke of Marlborough: 11, 104(l), 206, 211

Museum of Fine Arts, Boston: 123 (l and c)

The National Gallery, London: 74(b), 77

The National Portrait Gallery, London: 60, 82, 84(t), 99(b), 101, 104, 151(b), 152

Queen's Printer and Controller of the HMSO, 2005 UK Government Art Collection: 42(tr), 44

Henrietta Spencer-Churchill: 14, 16, 132, 214–215

Hugo Vickers: 113(b), 161, 171(t), 172, 177–178, 179(b), 186(t), 188–189

The Wedgwood Museum Trust, Barlaston, Staffordshire: 123(r)

Jeremy Whitaker: 54, 96, 105, 106, 110, 113(t), 135, 160

INDEX

Pages in *italics* refer to photos.